Religion, Law, and the Present Water Crisis

AMERICAN UNIVERSITY STUDIES

SERIES VII
THEOLOGY AND RELIGION

VOL. 320

PETER LANG
New York • Washington, D.C./Baltimore • Bern
Frankfurt • Berlin • Brussels • Vienna • Oxford

RICHARD A. HUGHES

Religion, Law, and the Present Water Crisis

PETER LANG
New York • Washington, D.C./Baltimore • Bern
Frankfurt • Berlin • Brussels • Vienna • Oxford

Library of Congress Cataloging-in-Publication Data

Hughes, Richard.
Religion, law, and the present water crisis / Richard A. Hughes.
p. cm. — (American university studies. VII, Theology and religion; v. 320)
Includes bibliographical references (p.   ) and index.
1. Water rights. 2. Human rights—Religious aspects.
3. Economic development—Religious aspects.
4. Water—Religious aspects. I. Title.
K3496.H84   346.04'32—dc23   2011036393
ISBN 978-1-4331-1728-2 (hardcover)
ISBN 978-1-4539-0231-8 (e-book)
ISSN 0740-0446

Bibliographic information published by **Die Deutsche Nationalbibliothek**.
Die Deutsche Nationalbibliothek lists this publication in the "Deutsche
Nationalbibliografie"; detailed bibliographic data is available
on the Internet at http://dnb.d-nb.de/.

The paper in this book meets the guidelines for permanence and durability
of the Committee on Production Guidelines for Book Longevity
of the Council of Library Resources.

© 2013 Peter Lang Publishing, Inc., New York
29 Broadway, 18th floor, New York, NY 10006
www.peterlang.com

Printed in Germany

DEDICATED TO

**The Clean Water Institute
of Lycoming College**

Table of Contents

Chapter Eight: The Right to Water

Conclusion

Preface

When my father died on November 26, 1989, I felt an immediate dislocation with respect to water. He and my mother had been living in a rural home near the shore of Lake Wawasee in northeastern Indiana. That lake was the center of my childhood and adolescence. Lake Wawasee was the site of a church camp I had attended for many years and a place for swimming, boating, and other water-related activities. Since I could not maintain the property, living more than 500 miles away in Pennsylvania, I had to sell it and lose my connection to the lake. On the following March 7, 1990, when the rays of the sun were glistening on the waves of the lake, a young married couple purchased the house. Thereafter, I had to satisfy a deep need to be near a large body of water.

Four years after my father's death I received an invitation to travel to Zürich, Switzerland and deliver a lecture. On June 18, 1993 I spoke on the theme of "The Symbolism of the Bridge" at the University of Zürich. In that lecture I discussed the meanings of the bridge symbol in dreams and in the religions of the world. I suggested that the bridge symbol in dreams signified a transcendent unity of the self in a time of personal change or transition (Hughes 1991: 48).

The existential context for my lecture was the fact that six weeks before my wedding on December 29, 1973 I had a series of bridge dreams with two perspectives. In one a man holding a book and a woman crossed over a bridge spanning a large body of water and reached the distant shore. In the other the same man and woman stepped into a boat at one shore, travelled across a body of water with several islands, maneuvering safely around them, and arrived at the distant shore without mishap. These dreams came to me in a regular nightly succession for six weeks.

The primary meaning of those dreams was that I had made a good marriage choice. If I had fallen off the bridge into the water below or if I had wrecked the boat, then these images would have signified a poor marriage choice. Crossing the water was a successful rite of passage that represented a wholeness at the highest level of selfhood.

My wife and two young children accompanied me to Zürich, and we stayed in the city one week. After the day of my lecture, we took a sight-seeing ride on one of the tourist boats in the city. We stepped into the boat that was docked at a pier on the Limmat River, and we rode to the southern tip of the city which opened out onto Lake Zürich. The boat moved across the lake to the middle, where it stopped unexpectedly and stayed motionless for several minutes. Sitting in the boat in Lake Zürich, which was about the same size as Lake Wawasee in Indiana and gazing at the distant mountains, suddenly I came to terms with my father's death. I felt a profound sense of peace and oneness with the water.

My peace on Lake Zürich was only temporary, however, because a few years later my need to be near water erupted again. On Easter weekend, 1999 my family and I travelled to Virginia Beach, Virginia to visit my sister-in-law. We stayed at an ocean-side hotel, and for most of the weekend I walked back and forth on the boardwalk, intensely contemplating the waves of the sea and watching the ships passing in the distance. At sunrise and sunset I sat on the outside balcony of our seventh-floor room, and I became enchanted by the rays of the sun glistening on the bright morning waves and glowing on the dark evening waves. With twilight at the ocean an acceptance of my father's death came to me again.

Eventually, I realized that I needed to visit large bodies of water every four or five years. Consequently, we returned to Virginia Beach in July, 2003. Once again I walked back and forth on the boardwalk to renew an acceptance of my father's death. During those years, I knew that the ocean embodied two dimensions of meaning. On one level, it was a source of relaxation, as many vacationers enjoyed swimming in the water and walking on the beach. On a more profound level, however, I understood that the ocean provided a regeneration or renewal of life. This deeper meaning has been represented symbolically in the religions of the world, particularly in the creation stories in which life arises from the primordial, oceanic water. In some religions without creation stories the ocean is a nurturing mother to whom we return for a rebirth.

In May, 2006 my wife, son, and I attended commencement at Boston University School of Theology, from where my daughter was graduating. At a weekend seminar I listened to a presentation by John Hart, Professor of Christian Ethics in the School of Theology. He spoke about his forthcoming book *Sacramental Commons* (2006) and explained that he had brought together the sacramental and commons traditions into a synthesis. I became intrigued by the title, and in the fall of 2006 I read the book and was enthralled by its originality and visionary power. The chapter on "Living Water" served as a turning point in my professional life, and it compelled me to initiate a scholarly study of water.

In March, 2009 I responded to a call for papers from Hamline University School of Law, home of the *Journal of Law and Religion*, and decided to prepare a paper on water. Having just published my book *Pro-Justice Ethics* in January of that year, in which I discussed water issues in a preliminary way, I submitted a proposal for an essay entitled "Pro-Justice Ethics, Water Scarcity, Human Rights." I surveyed factors of water scarcity, criticized corporate policies of privatization, argued for a right to water, and contended that all freshwater bodies should be protected under the public trust doctrine. My proposal was accepted, and Marie Failinger, Professor of Law at Hamline and editor of the journal, invited me to present my ideas at the 19th Annual Symposium of the *Journal of Law and Religion* on October 16, 2009 at St. Paul, Minnesota. I presented my paper at the symposium, and in the following spring it was published in the journal (Hughes 2009–2010).

With the acceptance of my essay for publication I decided to expand those ideas into this book. During the years that I was working on the manuscript, a new development took place in northcentral Pennsylvania where I live. A vast underground deposit of natural gas known as Marcellus Shale had been discovered, and by 2008 natural gas drilling had begun. Several gas drilling companies, using a method of hydrofracture, moved into the region and by the spring of 2011 more than 300 natural gas wells were in operation. Through the news media we learned about blowouts of gas wells, spills of fracking water, filled with toxic chemicals such as methane, and contaminating our streams, rivers, and wells.

This book is dedicated to the Clean Water Institute of Lycoming College, ably directed by Melvin Zimmerman, the Frank and Helen Lowry Professor of Biology. With the assistance of students the institute monitors the quality and quantity of water, particularly in the Susquehanna River Basin. Pennsylvania contains 83,000 miles of streams, 4,000 lakes, 120 miles of coastal waters, and 80 trillion gallons of groundwater and aquifers. As of this writing, the institute has completed 43 stream assessments. The institute serves as a valuable resource on water issues as well as a partner with local watershed groups devoted to protecting our most precious natural resource. In the words of the New Testament the institute endeavors to maintain our "rivers of living water" (Jhn. 7:38).

Against the backdrop of natural gas drilling I raise the prospect of a long, twilight struggle to preserve the cleanliness of water. Incidents of blowouts and spills that contaminate surface water and groundwater heighten the concern for the health of our water supplies. Will we continue to enjoy pure running water in support of life and health, or will we suffer the degradation of our streams, rivers, and wells? In my experience water has been a means of coming to terms with death, but the potential perils of contamination pose the possibility of water becoming a means of death.

Acknowledgments

This book was begun in the first week of August, 2009 and completed in the last week of June, 2011. Research for the book was subsidized by the John G. Snowden Library of Lycoming College, Janet Hurlbert director. Library staff members Susan Beidler, Marlene Neece, Susan Nelson, Karla Procopio, and Alysha Russo assisted me with the acquisition of materials. My Lycoming colleagues Thomas Griffiths, Steven Johnson, Robin Knauth, Fred Thayer, and Melvin Zimmerman provided me books, papers, and important internet information.

My departmental colleagues read portions of the manuscript. George Adams reviewed the chapters on the world religions and made helpful comments. Steven Johnson read the biblical materials and suggested some critical changes. John McNassor read the chapters on baptism and natural sacramentality from his unique perspective as a Baptist minister and a member of an Episcopal Church. Melvin Zimmerman reviewed and approved the introductory scientific discussions and clarified a few points.

It was my privilege to work with two distinguished lawyers who specialize in water issues. Rebecca H. Hiers, an Oregon mediation attorney who has worked as a policy analyst for the Umatilla Indian Reservation, supplied court cases, her own papers, and the tribal policy statement on salmon, and she read the chapters on the law. Raya Marina Stephan, a Paris-based international water law specialist and consultant to the United Nations gave me a copy of her paper on Islamic water law. She also read the chapters on international water law and made helpful corrections and comments.

Heather Hughes and James Hughes assisted me in the preparation of the manuscript.

Selections from the Holy Qur'an are taken from Tarif Khalidi. 2008. *The Qur'an*. New York: Viking. Unless otherwise stated, the scriptural passages are from the New Revised Standard Version of the Bible, copyright 1989, by the Division of Christian Education of the National Council of Churches, U.S.A.

Introduction

Water Scarcity

The United Nations (UN) has projected that by 2025 approximately one third of the world's population will be living in regions of absolute water scarcity, and two thirds may have extreme water stress (UNESCO Water Newsletter No.180 2007). Water scarcity means that the volume of water extracted from rivers, lakes, and aquifers is so great that existing water supplies cannot satisfy human and ecosystem requirements. More precisely, water scarcity is present in situations when water availability falls below 1000 cubic meters per person per year (Shiva 2002: 1). Water stress occurs when water consumption surpasses 10% of renewable freshwater sources (Palaniappan and Gleick 2009: 1).

A major factor in water scarcity is population growth. The world's population is expanding by about 80 million people a year and increasing freshwater demands at about 64 billion cubic meters a year (UNESCO Water Newsletter No.249 2011). Water usage has been expanding at twice the rate of population growth in the 20th century, so that already many regions of the world are chronically short of water (UNESCO Water Newsletter No.180 2007). Between 2008 and 2025 the world will need 17% more water to grow food for the larger populations, and by 2025 total water usage will increase by 40% (UNESCO Water Newsletter No.205 2008). Most of the population growth will take place in Southern Asia (30%) and Sub-Sahara Africa (32%). (UNESCO Water Newsletter No. 249 2011). In those regions the urban populations are expected to double between 2000 and 2030, when the cities of the developing world will constitute an estimated 81% of urban humanity (UNESCO Water Newsletter No.249 2011). Although the global population slowed modestly from mid-2009 to mid-2010, increasing only by 1.16%, it was on track to reach seven billion by the end of 2011 (www.worldwatch.org. 2010).

Water scarcity is a basic cause of poverty for about 1.1 billion people (UNESCO Water Newsletter No.159 2006). Problems of poverty are due to a lack of availability of and proximity to water sources, as well as poor quality and limited quantity of freshwater. In many developing countries women and young girls are often the main providers of water for their households (Palaniappan et al. www.pacinst.org 2010). In some countries of the world, such as India and South Africa, women and young girls walk long distances many times a day, carrying pots on their heads, to fetch water for their families.

Water scarcity and lack of basic sanitation are implicated in global health problems. More than 2.5 billion people worldwide have no basic sanitation, and over one billion lack access to safe, affordable drinking water (Palaniappan et al. 2006: 117). These are mainly poor and marginalized indigenous people. Poor water quality is mainly the result of sewage discharge into water sources. Preventable diseases caused by poor water quality and inadequate sanitation kill about 10,000 people every day (International Experts' Meeting UNESCO 2009: 1).

Unclean water is the second leading cause of childhood mortality in the world (UNESCO Water Newsletter No. 183 2007). Each year 1.8 million children die from diarrhea and other water-borne diseases. In water-borne diseases water transmits pathogens in excreta from humans. The World Health Organization (WHO) has reported that contaminated water lurks in 80% of diseases,, and that a child dies every eight seconds from drinking dirty water (Barlow 2007: 2). For every child killed by HIV/AIDS five children perish from preventable diseases caused by unsafe drinking water, poor hygiene, and inadequate sanitation (International Experts' Meeting UNESCO 2009: 1). Lack of clean water for hygiene produces water-scarce infections, such as trachoma which causes blindness (Barry and Hughes 2008: 784–785). Snails and flees breed water-based infections, and mosquitoes, black flies, and tsetse flies carry water-base diseases.

Another category of water-related disease is that caused by pollution of water supplies. As many as 70 million people in Bangladesh are exposed to high levels of arsenic in their drinking water, and a major factor is contamination of at least half of the estimated tube wells in the country (UNESCO Water Newsletter No.215 2009). Arsenic contamination in groundwater is a causal factor in lung, bladder, and skin cancer (Barry and Hughes 2008: 785–786). Three hundred million Chinese lack access to safe drinking water, because water supplies in China are polluted with arsenic, excessive fluoride, and toxins from industrial waste and agricultural chemicals (Gleick 2009: 76, 81).

Cholera, a water-borne disease, is spreading in poverty-stricken Africa. Epidemic cholera indicates contamination of drinking water with human feces (Mintz and Guerrant 2009: 1060). The cholera epidemic persists in Zimbabwe, where the fatality rate remained above 4.7% through February 12, 2009, while at the same time spreading to South Africa and Zambia (Mintz and Guerrant 2009: 1061–1062). In 2005 the reported rate of cholera in Africa was 95 times that in Asia and 16,600 times that in Latin America (Mintz and Guerrant 2009: 1063). Preventable deaths from cholera are the results of inadequate sanitation, inaccessible safe drinking water, and poor health care delivery systems.

During the 20th century, the use of water for irrigation in agriculture increased six times the growth of the population (UNESCO Water Newsletter No.185 2007). Historically, irrigation has taken 70−80% of all water uses, but these percentages will increase with the expected growth of population (UNESCO Water Newsletter No.185 2007). In the American West farmers use about 80% of their respective states' water supplies to grow alfalfa, cotton, wheat, corn, and rice. These are water-intensive crops that could grow more efficiently in other regions of the nation without irrigation (Glennon 2002: 211). In Nevada, the driest state in the country, farmers grow alfalfa to feed cattle.

The older irrigation systems sprayed fine mists of water into the air with high pressure systems, but most of the water evaporated before reaching the ground. Currently, many farmers use center-point irrigation systems that reduce evaporation by low pressure and by unique nozzles that spray large droplets of water into the ground with an efficiency of 90% (Glennon 2002: 149). Center-point irrigation systems produce wide green circles on the ground in sharp contrast to arid landscapes, and farmers employ these systems in the High Plains between Texas and North Dakota.

Generally, extensive irrigation tends to accelerate desertification (Barlow and Clarke 2002: 45). Desertification does not mean the creation of deserts; rather it means the degradation of land in arid, semi-arid, and dry sub-humid climates of the world. It is a process caused by human activities and climate change, both of which are facilitated by population growth. In California irrigation has degraded wetlands, harmed wildlife with chemicals in agricultural drainage waters, and increased toxic levels of selenium (Barlow and Clarke 2002: 68). Over 70% of the world's dry lands are degraded, resulting in dust storms and air pollution, putting one third of the world's population at risk, and reducing annual incomes by US$ 42 billion (UNESCO Water Newsletter No.188 2007). These figures represent, however, only the direct costs.

In California farmers employ irrigation in the more arid and semi-arid regions, where it builds up salt through evaporation (UNESCO Water Newsletter No.185 2007). Salinization diminishes the productivity of 20−30 million hectares of farm land globally, and 35% of this is under irrigation (UNESCO Water Newsletter No.185 2007). As a result of salinizaton, several countries have built desalinization facilities. By 2002 there were

12,500 desalinization plants in 120 countries, mainly in the Middle East, North Africa, California, and parts of Florida (UNESCO Water Newsletter No. 206 2008).

By 2005 the United States had 2,000 desalinization facilities; one half treated brackish water and one fourth river water (Glennon 2009: 153). The two principal problems with desalinization are the enormous amounts of electricity it requires and the question of how to dispose of the salt concentrates (Postel 1997: 45). One method of desalinization is distillation, and the other is running water through filters that block the salt (Glennon 2009: 152). In Southern California water from the Colorado River flowing into the Imperial Irrigation District has an increased salinity rate of 530%, and evaporation from the All-American Canal concentrates the salt (Glennon 2009: 257). Farmers use flood irrigation to leach the salt.

In the 20th century 800,000 small dams and 40,000 large dams were constructed for water delivery management, irrigation, and hydroelectric power; but these dams harnessed 60% of the world's 227 major rives to the detriment of their natural stream flows and ecosystems (Postel and Richter 2003: 2, 13, 16−17). In addition to the dams many dikes, canals, reservoirs, and levees were installed. In the United States the Army Corps of Engineers was founded in 1775 to dam rivers, control flooding, and facilitate navigation. The United States Bureau of Reclamation, founded by Congress in 1902, began building dams in the American West in the 1930s, and currently 75,000 large dams of at least six feet high and 2.5 million smaller dams are in operation (Glennon 2009: 108). Large dams have a reservoir capacity of up to three million cubic meters (Imhof and Lanza 2010: 9). The primary reason for building dams in the West has been the need to control river flows (Glennon 2002: 19−20). In the spring surface flows are abundant due to rainfall and snowmelt, but by mid-to-late summer surface flows tend to diminish. Dams store water in reservoirs, and water is released to stabilize surface flows throughout dry periods.

Half of the world's large dams have been built in China, where since 1950 public policy has ordered transfers of large amounts of water from one region to another (Gleick 2009: 90−91). For example, the Yangtze River, the longest in the country, has an estimated 50,000 dams, including the Three Gorges Dam, the biggest in the world. The dam generates electricity equivalent to that of about 25 coal-fired power plants, but it has been plagued by sky-rocketing costs, corruption, environmental disasters, and human rights violations (Imhof and Lanza 2010: 9−10). The Yellow River, the second longest river in China, has had since 2000 more than 10,000 reservoirs in operation, 23 of these involving large dams for the purpose of hydropower production (UNESCO Water Newsletter No.241 2010). Meanwhile, the general health of the Yellow River has declined, along with the disappearance of wetlands and harm to aquatic life. In mid-January 2007 Chinese officials announced that one third of the fish species in the Yellow had become extinct (Postel 2007: 20–21). Previously, the river had been host to 130 species of fish.

While dam construction may have created immediate benefits, it has led to serious long-range environmental problems. Dams alter natural river flows and increase salt or trap sediment in river basins (Postel and Richter 2003: 131). Normally, sediment nourishes flood plains, deltas, and estuaries. River flow changes are devastating to species, as they eliminate those whose survival correlates with predictable flow patterns. Low flows prevent species from reaching their destinations for feeding or breeding, and they allow non-native species to enter rivers and threaten native species (Postel and Richter 2003: 20–21).

Dams disconnect rivers from flood plains, so that their nutrient loads cannot spread out into river banks normally due to periodic flooding. Reservoirs drown lands and cause mercury-absorbing bacteria to grow and enter the food chain, while releasing carbon dioxide and methane into the environment (Barlow and Clarke 2002: 48–49). Large dams deform the earth's crust and trigger earthquakes. This process is called "reservoir-induced seismicity." In May, 2008 the 7.9 magnitude Sichuan earthquake in China killed about 90,000 people because of the Zipingpu Dam on the Min River. According to one geophysical hazards scientist, the "several hundred million tons of water behind the Zipingpu Dam put just the wrong stresses on the adjacent Beichuan fault" (Imhof and Lanza 2010: 11). There are more than 100 cases of dams causing earthquakes globally.

Dams diminish the capacity of rivers to purify water through watersheds and to carry their pollutants downstream. For example, the Mississippi River drains about 40% of the land on the North American continent, and the fertilizer deposits from upstream farms contribute to algae blooms and the "dead zone" of low oxygen in the Gulf of Mexico (Postel and Richter 2003: 25). This "dead zone" kills fish and other aquatic life in the Gulf. Globally, the most common water quality problem is eutrophication resulting from excessive phosphorus and nitrogen (UNESCO Water Newsletter No.215 2009). Eutrophication constitutes physical, chemical, and biological changes that occur in a lake, estuary, or slow-moving stream after taking in plant nutrients from natural erosion and runoff from adjacent land (Miller 1996: A46).

In the last 60 years dams have displaced 60–80 million people, most of whom have resided in China and India (Barlow and Clarke 2002: 61). Building the Karibu Dam in Africa displaced 57,000 people and destroyed the flood plain (Postel and Richter 2003: 43). By 2010 more than 1.3 million people had been displaced in China to make room for the Three Gorges Dam on the Yangtze River (Imhof and Lanza 2010: 10). Many received only tiny, barren plots of land in compensation, or they were sent to urban slums without adequate housing. The people who relocated in towns around the edge of the Three Gorges reservoir witnessed the collapse of the reservoir in about 91 places, killing many residents or forcing them to flee (Imhof and Lanza 2010: 10). Protests by displaced people triggered repression, imprisonment, and physical assault by government armed forces. Generally, displaced people neither receive a just compensation or resettlement, nor do they retain access to natural resources (Palaniappan et al. 2006: 133). Indigenous people see their ancestral lands desecrated, and ethnic minorities experience discrimination.

Amnesty International has reported human rights violations associated with the construction of the La Parota Dam in Guerrero State in Mexico, a region of high marginalization and low social development (www.amnesty.org. 2007). Begun in 2003, the dam project was intended to produce 1,527 gigawatt hours of electricity a year. The dam wall was supposed to be 162 meters high, flooding an area of approximately 17,000 hectares of land and diverting water from the Papagayo River. This river was the main source of water, transportation, and livelihoods of adjacent communities. The investment for the dam was expected to exceed US$ 850 million.

Local communities were not given adequate information or allowed an informed consent. Questions as to relocation, compensation, and continued access to natural resources were not answered. The people's right to effective legal remedy was violated by death threats, criminalization of opponents of the dam project, and disproportionate use of force against opponents. The right to participate in consultation was denied, and women were largely excluded from any deliberation.

According to international human rights law, Mexico has the obligation to protect local communities from forced evictions. Mexico is a state party to the International Covenant on Economic, Social and Cultural Rights, which recognizes "the right of every one to an adequate standard of living for himself and his family, including adequate food, clothing and housing, and to the continuous improvement of living conditions" (art. 11(1). Forced evictions violate this right, as well as those of informed consent and participation in public affairs. The latter two rights are recognized by the International Covenant on Civil and Political Rights in articles 21 and 25(1), The American Convention on Human Rights in articles 32–33, and the International Labour Organization Indigenous and Tribal Peoples Convention. As a state party to the latter treaty in particular, Mexico is required to secure a free and informed consent of people before they are relocated and to guarantee appropriate legal representation when informed consent cannot be obtained (art. 16(2).

The World Council of Churches has reported on the plan of the Philippines government to construct a 113-meter-high dam across the Laibon River on the island of Luzon. As a public-private venture, the dam was scheduled to be built between 2009 and 2010 in order to divert 2,400 million liters of water daily to Metro Manila (www.wcc-coe.org. 2010). On completion the dam would submerge 28,000 hectares of land and seven villages, displacing 10,000 indigenous people and settlers. Farmers, who had cultivated their ancestral lands for generations, feared the dam would dry up their irrigation supply. Local resistance to the project caused delays and triggered violent opposition against the people.

Historically, water has had only instrumental value in the expansion of industries, agriculture, and cities, but those forces have contaminated freshwater sources with pollutants and wastewater. The latter is water that has been discharged from a point of use after being fouled by various substances, and it still contains liquid waste or solid matter. It is generally understood that one liter of wastewater pollutes eight liters of freshwater, thereby reducing 12,000 cubic kilometers of global water supplies every year (UNESCO Water Newsletter No.184 2007).

In the United States more than 860 billion gallons of sewage are dumped into lakes and rivers every year, and the lower Colorado River, in particular, contains nitrates and fecal coliform bacteria typically present in human and animal wastes (Glennon 2009: 66). In Canada over one trillion liters of untreated sewage are deposited in waterways every year (Barlow and Clarke 2002: 31). Sewage is not only human waste but also mixtures of grease, motor oil, paint thinner, antifreeze, and industrial and household wastes. While water treatment may remove fecal coliform bacteria, it may not eliminate toxic chemicals (Barlow and Clarke 2002: 32). Globally, industrial pollution is expected to increase by 60% before 2025 due to the growth of urban populations (UNESCO Water Newsletter No.215 2009).

In developing countries more than 80% of sewage is discharged in untreated forms, contaminating rivers, lakes, and coastal areas. India's sacred Ganges River flows along a 1,500 mile course, supporting 400 million people, and every day it takes in 1.4 billion liters of untreated wastewater (www.pacinst.org. 2008). Similarly, in China the Yangtze River gets 40 million tons of raw sewage and industrial waste every day (Barlow and Clarke 2002: 30). Untreated industrial sewage dumped into the Yellow River has doubled since the 1980s to 4.2 billion cubic meters every year (UNESCO Water Newsletter No.241 2010). The river has been taking in about 300 different pollutants, and currently only 60% of its watercourse is suitable as a drinking water supply.

Water is a critical component for the energy industry in the production of electrical power, mining, refining, processing coal and gas, and other fuels. In the Canadian province of Alberta about 204 billion liters of water taken mainly from aquifers is pumped into oil wells every year to increase pressure and improve production (Barlow and Clarke 2002: 14). When the oil well is emptied by pumping, the left-over water cannot be recovered, since it contains high concentrations of chemicals used in the extraction process. One Canadian expert estimates that nine barrels of water are needed to produce one barrel of oil (Barlow and Clarke 2002: 15). Within the United States the search for energy sources has turned to corn-based ethanol, but this takes more than four gallons of water to produce one gallon of ethanol (Glennon 2009: 53).

Natural gas is an efficient energy source, but it is also water-intensive. Currently in Pennsylvania, a state containing 86,000 streams and 4000 lakes, the gas drilling industry is extracting natural gas from a deep underground deposit known as the Marcellus Shale. The industry is taking two million gallons of water a day from the Susquehanna River watershed (Thompson 2010 Oct. 17: A6). About 90% of the water extracted from Pennsylvania rivers is used to hydrofracture gas wells. Millions of gallons of pressurized water mixed with sand and chemicals are pumped deeply underground to pulverize the shale and extract the gas trapped within it (Thompson 2010 Oct. 18: A1). The result of this fracking could be the contamination of surface water and groundwater, depending on how the frack water is treated.

The consumption of bottled water is equally troubling. According to the Pacific Institute, American consumption of bottled water in 2006 required more than 17 million barrels of oil to make the bottles, while taking three liters of freshwater to make one liter of bottled water, and altogether discharging 2.5 million tons of carbon dioxide into the environment (www.pacinst.org. 2007). In 2006 Americans spent $11 billion dollars on bottled water, even though testing had demonstrated that tap water was as safe or safer than bottled water (Glennon 2009: 44–45). In 2008 more than 34 billion liters of bottled water were packaged and sold in the United States, and five times this amount were sold around the world, supporting a global system of water bottlers, truckers, and retailers at a cost of over one hundred billion dollars (Gleick 2010: 5). By 2010 Americans purchased 1000 bottles of commercially produced water every day, and they threw away 85 million bottles a day (Gleick 2010: ix).

The total volume of freshwater used to produce goods and services is called the water footprint. The United States has an average water footprint of 2,480 cubic meters per person per year, while the global average is 1,240 cubic meters per person per year (UNESCO Water Newsletter No. 212 2009). Virtual water is the water embedded in the production of foods and commodities. For example, the production of one kilogram of wheat takes 1,350 liters of water and that of beef 16,000 liters of water. Commercially produced water commodities are symptomatic of decaying public water systems, unequal access to water around the world, susceptibility to corporate advertising, and life in societies conditioned to purchase, consume, and dispose products (Gleick 2010: x).

Water Sources

Human life depends on water, and there is no substitute for this precious element. The earth contains about 1.4 billion cubic kilometers of water spread out in rivers, lakes, wetlands, glaciers, and permanent snow cover, but 97% consists of salt water in the ocean (Palaniappan and Gleick 2009: 5–6). The total amount of freshwater reserves is estimated to be approximately 35 million cubic kilometers, but most of this is frozen in glaciers and permanent snow cover and stored in deep underground regions that are inaccessible to humanity (Palaniappan and Gleick 2009: 5). The water supply of the earth is finite because the atmosphere prevents water entering into and escaping from the earth (Glennon 2009: 79).

The renewability of freshwater sources is increasingly threatened by climate change is some regions of the world. Climate change is the result of an imbalance between incoming and outgoing radiation in the atmosphere. When solar radiation enters the atmosphere, some of it is absorbed by the earth's surface and reemitted as infrared radiation, but some of it is trapped by carbon dioxide, methane, and nitrous oxide. These are greenhouse gasses produced by the combustion of fossil fuels, and they cannot be removed from the atmosphere due to deforestation (Shuman 2010: 1061). As greenhouse gasses have reached high levels, global temperatures have risen as well. Consequently, the hydrological cycle has been altered. Some regions of the world get more rainfall and severe storms, other regions endure drought and heat waves. With rising temperatures and shifting rainfall patterns infectious diseases spread by means of insect vectors and contaminated water. Insect vectors are more active in higher temperatures, and periods of drought result in poor sanitation.

In his testimony before the Select Committee on Energy Independence and Global Warming of the U.S. House of Representatives, Peter Gleick stated that climate changes are accelerating faster than expected (www.pacinst.org. 2010 Dec. 1): "Rising concentrations of carbon dioxide are making the oceans more acidic." Elevated sea levels threaten coastal cities and communities. Climate changes also threaten freshwater ecosystems, forests, and high mountain environments due to disappearing glaciers and snowmelt.

Most of the freshwater in the earth is stored underground. Groundwater is 60 times greater in volume than surface water (Barlow and Clarke 2002: 6). Groundwater flows through porous sand gravel or bedrock areas called aquifers. An aquifer is a "geologic formation, containing enough saturated porous and permeable material to transmit water at a rate sufficient to feed a spring or for economic extraction by a well" (Glennon 2002: 237). Many aquifers are like large, slow-moving underground lakes that are replenished as precipitation percolates downward through soil and rock (Miller 1996: 456). Other aquifers are embedded so deeply underground that they are essentially nonrenewable, and they are called fossil aquifers (Miller 1996: 457). Generally, the former flow above rock or clay formations as unconfined aquifers, but the latter are sandwiched between clay, rock, or shale with little permeability, and they are called confined aquifers.

Water flows are interconnected on land, sea, and air, and the flows move through cycles. The sun causes surface water to evaporate, and the wind carries moist air over land where water vapor condenses, and gravity pushes precipitation to fall to the earth. Half of the precipitation returns to the atmosphere by evaporation, but the other half undergoes three processes (Glennon 2009: 79–80). First, trees and plants absorb water and then release it into the environment as water vapor. Second, gravity forces precipitation to flow over the surface of the earth into the lowest points and replenishes bodies of water as surface runoff. Third, water infiltrates the ground and percolates down to aquifers through which the groundwater flows.

Surface water and groundwater are interrelated in the hydrological cycle, but they exhibit different properties. Surface water is visible above the earth, and groundwater is invisible below the earth. Groundwater flows are long-term, as measured in months and years, while surface flows are shorter, as in hours or days (Glennon and Maddock 1997: 7). When rainfall and snowmelt are substantial, the stream flow takes two forms: runoff and base flow. Runoff is the rapid response aspect of a flow, and base flow is the slower response. More precisely, base flow is the regular seepage of water from an aquifer into a stream, and it is important to river ecosystems during periods of scarce precipitation (Glennon 2002: 238). Water that percolates into a river or stream is a discharge. A stream that gets a discharge from an aquifer is a gaining stream, and a stream that recharges an aquifer is a losing stream. Generally, discharge and recharge constitute a natural equilibrium.

Groundwater pumping alters the natural balance between recharge and disharge. The concept of capture means that groundwater pumping reduces the flow in a stream or river and imposes a new discharge on the natural recharge-discharge equilibrium (Glennon and Maddock 1997: 10). Pumping can capture water by increasing the flow out of a losing stream, interrupt groundwater going into a gaining stream, and reduce evapotranspiration (Glennon and Maddock 1997: 12). Evapotranspiration is the combined effect of evaporation and transpiration. Groundwater pumping from a well lowers the surrounding water table, causing it to slope toward the well and form a cone of depression. The cone may be shallow or extensive, depending upon the amount of water it pulls from the surrounding area.

About one quarter of the world's population relies upon groundwater for its drinking water (Barlow and Clarke 2002: 12). One half of the American population extracts groundwater for its drinking water, and two thirds of the withdrawals are in the West where 78% are for agriculture (Glennon 2002: 31). The commercial unit of water use in agriculture, cities, and mines is the acre-foot, that is, the amount of water needed to cover one acre of land with one foot of water, and this volume is that of 325,851 gallons. Extensive groundwater pumping for irrigation and industrialization has contaminated groundwater supplies.

The largest known aquifer in the world is the Ogallala, which extends from Northwest Texas to South Dakota. If the water in the Ogallala were above ground, it would cover the entire lower 48 states with one and one half feet (Miller 1996: 468). In the 20th century farmers on the High Plains have used windmills and steam and gasoline engines to pump water from the Ogallala. Consequently, the Ogallala is losing 50 million liters of water a minute and taking in factory and farm pollutants (Barlow and Clarke 2002: 16, 34). In as much as the region receives so little rainfall, and the pumping is so extensive, the Ogallala is essentially a nonrenewable aquifer. Since 1980, groundwater tables in the High Plains have plummeted to more than 150 feet in some areas, and many wells have gone dry (Glennon 2009: 123−124). In some areas groundwater levels have fallen so low that farmers can no longer operate their pumps economically, and they have shifted to dry land farming (Gleick 2010: 70). Many surface springs have completely disappeared.

After the last Ice Age, the American Southwest became covered with vast freshwater lakes, and the water in these lakes percolated into the ground to form aquifers. Groundwater has several advantages over surface water (Glennon 2002: 28–29). Groundwater is pervasive, as it flows beneath the earth's surface even in dry regions, and unlike surface water in reservoirs it does not evaporate. Groundwater also has a high quality in contrast to surface water which is more saline in the West. Higher saline waters are not conducive to growing such high-value crops as citrus, beans, grains, and legumes.

There are systems on earth that purify and protect freshwater sources, namely forests and wetlands. Metaphorically, forests are the lungs of the hydrological cycle, and wetlands are the kidneys (Barlow 2007: 20). Forests absorb pollution and prevent flooding, while wetlands filter out dirt and toxins before they enter into rivers, lakes, and aquifers. During the 20th century, about one half of the world's wetlands were lost, and in California the loss was 95% (Barlow and Clarke 2002: 38).

In the United States the Great Lakes are the largest freshwater system on earth, containing 20% of the world's freshwater (Barlow and Clarke 2002: 35). Industrial facilities around the lakes are dumping 50–100 million tons of hazardous wastes each year, including chemical and radioactive substances (Barlow and Clarke 2002: 35–36). The Great Lakes are also threatened by groundwater mining and the removal of forests and wetlands along their banks. Thus, water purification and erosion control, formerly done by forests and wetlands, are impeded. Extensive withdrawals of water from the Great Lakes have made them essentially nonrenewable (Glennon 2009: 97). Lowered water levels are especially visible in Lake Superior and Lake Huron, where vast expanses of lake beds are exposed, wetlands destroyed, and swimming areas turned into mud flats.

Globally, it is estimated that lakes contain more than 90% of all freshwater on the surface of the earth (UNESCO Water Newsletter No.244 2011). Unlike flowing rivers lakes have long residence times, which are the average lengths of time water remains in a lake. Lakes with long residence times respond to inputs slowly, such as floodwaters and pollutants, and lakes can absorb those inputs without manifesting sudden changes. Lakes also act as sinks for water and pollutants from their surrounding drainage basins. The mixing of these inputs means that pollutants spread throughout the entire lake and are not confined to portions of the lake. Water-related problems are lake-wide. Thus, lakes function as a kind of barometer that measures the effects of human activities within their surrounding drainage basins.

Commodification of Water

The rapidly increasing crises of water scarcity have led large multinational corporations to advocate the commodification and privatization of water as the most efficient means of delivery and management. The corporations consider problems of water scarcity as symptoms of the inefficiency of governments. The international water industry regards water as a private good to be extracted from the earth and exchanged on free, global markets outside state ownership and government regulation (Shiva 2002: 15,19). The driving forces behind commodification and privatization are (1) the increasing costs and political liabilities of urban water systems for local governments; (2) pressure from the International Monetary Fund (IMF) and World Bank on poor countries to reduce their public sector debt and water subsidies on the condition of privatizing their water systems; and (3) the power of corporations in pursuit of profits from the sale of freshwater (Postel and Wolf 2001: 62).

The interests of water corporations are promoted by the triennial World Water Forum. These forums are organized by the World Water Council (WCC) and supported by the World Bank and the UN. The consistent definition of the forum program is that water is a human need but not a human right. When meeting in Istanbul, Turkey in 2009, the Fifth World Water Forum announced on March 22 the following policy statement: "We recognize that access to safe drinking water and sanitation is a basic human need" (www.worldwaterforum5.org. 2009). To define water as a need and not a right justifies the selling and trading of water for profit in the private sector. Commodification and privatization interests are at the forefront of the global water initiative (Varody et al. 2008: 21–23).

The global water industry is dominated by two French firms, Veolia Environnement and Suez Lyonnais des Eaux. Some of the others are Nestlé, Coca-Cola, Pepsi, Bechtel United-Utilities, and Thames Water. Having built the Suez Canal, Suez Lyonnais des Eaux has a world mission that comprises four basic enterprises: water, energy, communications, and waste management. Veolia Environnement provides water to 100 million people throughout Europe, Asia, Africa, and the Americas, and it actively pursues contracts around the world for water privatization and diversion projects such as dams. Veolia has been seeking contracts in China for wastewater supply plants, desalinization facilities, and wastewater treatment and management systems. Its Chinese market could become 20% of its global initiatives. The privatization of water has aroused intense opposition around the world. One Argentinian opponent of privatization contended that water is "a gift from God," and the president of Veolia responded: "Yes....but he forgot to lay the pipes" (Glennon 2009: 247).

Since the 1990s, the IMF, World Bank, and the African, Asian, and Inter-American Development Banks have pressured poor countries to privatize their water systems. This pressure has imposed a free market economic model in the northern countries, where the water corporations are based, upon the global South. Generally, privatization involves forming public-private partnerships, and these take three principal contractual forms (Barlow 2007: 40). First, concession contracts give a private company a license to manage a water system, charge customers, and make a profit. Second, leases are contracts by which the company operates and repairs the water system, while the local government makes new investments. Third, management contracts hold the company responsible for operating the system but not for making investments.

Typically, public-private partnerships consist of lease and management types, and they usually involve governments deferring to corporations. Whatever form the contracts take, corporations get profits. Profitability comes largely from corporations cutting costs, raising water rates, and laying off employees at public water utilities (Barlow and Clarke 2002: 124). Water corporations normally do not invest in infrastructures, and they damage environments by depositing wastewater. The World Bank, IMF, and World Trade Organization (WTO) provide legal cover and financial support for global water corporations.

Between 1990 and 2006 the World Bank funded more than 300 privatization projects in the developing world with the goal of full cost recovery of the investments and profits for the investors (Barlow 2007: 39). Water privatization is central to the World Bank and IMF poverty reduction and debt relief programs. These are intended to make progress toward the UN Millennium Development Goals. In 2000 189 UN member nations proposed eight Millennium Development Goals to (1) eliminate extreme poverty and hunger; (2) achieve universal primary education; (3) promote gender equality and women empowerment; (4) reduce childhood mortality; (5) improve maternal health; (6) combat HIV/AIDS, malaria, and other diseases; (7) ensure environmental sustainability; and (8) create a global partnership for development (www.undp.org/mdg). Of the eight goals six relate to water scarcity (Palaniappan 2009: 57–59). For example, target ten of goal seven asserts the following mandate: "Halve by 2015, the proportion of people without sustainable access to safe drinking water and basic sanitation."

A study, entitled "Financing the Water Crises," published in India by the Research Foundation For Science, Technology & Ecology, confirms that the World Bank requires privatization as a condition for its loans (www.navdanya.org. 2005: 1). As a result of accepting World Bank loans, water utilities in India have supplied water primarily to the industrial and wealthy urban sectors, diverted scarce groundwater from rural to urban areas, and forced utilities to raise rates. Water resource management has shifted from the government to private corporations through management and "build-operate-transfer" contracts (www.navdanya.org. 2005: 10). This type of contract involves a private firm contracting to build a dam or water treatment plant, operating it for several years, and then giving up rights to the public utility (www.navdanya.org. 2005: 17). Meanwhile, the government pays the company for its construction and operating costs, as well as a financial return, but the utility pays for specific amounts of water. This privatization contract is the consequence of India's joining the WTO, which promotes deregulation and privatization, and treats water as a tradable commodity.

The Indian study finds that contracts with the World Bank or Asian Development Bank(ADB) increase property taxes by 200% in some cases, in order to pay for sewer drainage, sanitation, and investment return (www.navdanya.org. 2005: 11). This trend has forced small and marginal farmers with fewer than two acres of land to go out of business. They represent 82% of all farmers.

The study documents widespread failures of water privatization. Between 1991 and 2005 the World Bank financed water sector restructuring projects at US\$ 3,621,000,000 for which India has had to pay US\$ 397,000,000 in annual interest (www.navdanya.org. 2005: 35). For example, one project proposal was for the improvement of the water supply to Madras, a metropolis with the fewest water resources and a high susceptibility to drought. The project was supposed to encourage conservation and improve the distribution of water by running a pipe line from the Veeranam irrigation tank across a distance of 235 kilometers. The total cost was US\$ 421,000,000. The project failed, however, to provide an adequate supply of water to Madras and to encourage conservation.

The study also points out that in the last 50 years India has invested in infrastructure for the storage of surface water in small, medium, and large dams. By 2005 there were about 4,050 large dams with 475 under construction, along with numerous small dams. Most of the dams have inadequate flood management mechanisms, and the increased sedimentation has diminished their storage capacity, thereby limiting economic benefits (www.navdanya.org. 2005: 50). The dams lack appropriate regulatory and legislative guarantees for safe, sustainable operations. The World Bank believes that India's poverty is due to its inability to store surface water (www.navdanya.org. 2005: 53), This implies that poverty should be eliminated by expanding the areas of stored water with the building of more dams.

By 2006 it became apparent that water privatization had failed. Privatization has not conserved water or protected water sources. Under privatization corporations have minimal accountability to local officials; they impose foreign controls upon local communities and create monopolies (Barlow 2007: 60). Under privatization water is not distributed equitably to all people, particularly to the poor from whom there is no profit. In the world today water flows to the rich and the powerful.

The Plan of This Book

The primary aim of this book is to affirm a human right to water and to support that right by considering the views of water in selected religious traditions of the world. The right to water is imposed upon all governments with the imperative to provide their citizens affordable, accessible access to safe drinking water. The dominance of water corporations with their policies of commodification and privatization, their sales of bottled water, and their unsustainable projects of water diversion signify the failure to implement the right to water.

In current legal discussions, however, the status of the right to water is not entirely clear. Is the right to water fundamental or does it derive from other rights, such as those of an adequate standard of living, food, or housing? Is the right to water explicit or is it implied in other rights? The contention of this book is that the right to water is fundamental, free-standing, and the precondition for other basic human rights. This study draws upon some of the major religious traditions of the world that make water a central element in ritual and theology and that bear witness to the fact that water represents the sacred. The sanctity of water indicates a direct participation in the sacred; and therefore it is primal. Recognizing the primal quality of water in religious experience makes the right to water fundamental and compelling.

Chapters one and two review several religious traditions of water. Chapter one explores ancient religious traditions that flourished around river banks and that developed symbolic meanings of water, some of which have survived to the present day. Chapter two discusses rituals at river banks, large bodies of water, and wells, and it shows how these religions developed motifs of crossing over water.

Chapters one and two rely upon myths and symbols in the respective religions. In this study myth is understood as a story that narrates an ultimate truth or primordial event that is inaccessible to human memory or knowledge, such as the creation of the world or the end of the world. As a story, myth has characters, plot, and context, but it lacks linear time. Myth is a symbolic narrative that universalizes its subject, so that the ultimate truth or primordial event becomes meaningful and accessible to human consciousness in the present time. Symbols are the components of myth. A symbol is a term or figure that combines opposites into a new reality which points beyond itself and reorients one's view of the world. Symbols are polysemous, that is, they yield multiple meanings that open up new and unique relationships to the world and to the sacred. The term "living water," which is found in the Gospel of John (7:38), refers to pure running water that participates in the sacred.

Chapter three presents the principal themes of water in the Bible. One of the central motifs is that of the cross-over, beginning with the Spirit of God passing over the primal waters of creation, followed by the Hebrew people passing through the sea in the Exodus, their crossing the Jordan River in Israel, and finally Jesus crossing over waters in his ministry. Water carries multiple meanings in the Bible, such as punishment of sin by the flood, care of the people through rainfall, and rivers of blessing, all of which revealing different modes of divine activity in nature.

Chapter four discusses the principal water ritual in Christianity, namely, the Sacrament of Baptism. The chapter surveys the basic meanings and rituals of baptism, beginning with the New Testament and extending into the history of Christianity, including the apostolic writers, selected Church Fathers, Medieval Catholicism, the Protestant Reformation, two post-Reformation theologies, and a contemporary ecumenical approach to baptism.

Chapter five develops the idea of natural sacramentality, as presented by an Anglican theologian and a Roman Catholic ethicist, and it focuses on the latter's model of the sacramental commons. The commodification and privatization of water collide with the sacramental and commons understanding of nature. The chapter illustrates the sacramental commons by reviewing the Roman Catholic bishops pastoral letter on the Columbia River watershed in the Pacific Northwest. The Columbia River is the site of a conflict between a hydropower conception of the river and that of a fish habitat as held by Native American tribes. The chapter suggests a few criticisms of Roman Catholic sacramental theology and appeals to the Anglican Communion as a source for a natural sacramentality. The Anglican Communion also produced the English common law as a legal framework for a global sacramental commons.

Chapter six explains the standard of water law in the English common law, known as the riparian doctrine, and shows how this standard shaped the water laws in the eastern United States. With the settling of the American frontier the prior appropriation doctrine superseded riparian law in the western mountain states. Some of the western states, such as California, have combined the two doctrines into hybrid water systems. The chapter concludes by discussing four groundwater concepts in American law.

Chapter seven appeals to the public trust doctrine as the legal standard for the sacramental commons, and it explains how the public trust has evolved in the western legal tradition. The chapter finds a public trust doctrine in Islamic water law, and it discusses how the Islamic and Roman law standards came together into a unique synthesis in Spanish water law. This system entered into the American Southwest during the Spanish colonial era and shaped the Hispanic tradition of water sharing known as the *acequia*. The chapter concludes by evaluating the public trust principles in the recently enacted Great Lakes Compact.

Chapter eight presents evidence for the right to water within international human rights law. The chapter reviews several international treaties, conventions, charters, and ecumenical church policies. The chapter examines specific contents of the right to water and the proposals for the quantification of the right. Special attention is devoted to the water crises in the Palestinian Occupied Territory and the controversial aspects of Israeli water policies and practices.

Finally, the conclusion proposes a cooperative or relational attitude toward bodies of water and waterways, and it rejects any attitude based on the domination of nature. The chapter discusses the rules of international law that guide nations in water sharing and in the resolutions of conflicts over surface water and groundwater. The chapter explores the federal doctrine of reserved water rights, as a corollary to the public trust, and suggests that imperiled bodies of water be placed under a reserved water right, both domestically and internationally. The last section of the conclusion recapitulates the central theses of this study, summarizes the religious meanings of water, and reaffirms the human obligation to care for water as a symbol of the sacred and revere it as a primal reality.

Chapter One: Riparian Religions

The Tigris and Euphrates Rivers

The primary states of the Old World civilizations were Sumer, Old Kingdom Egypt, Shang Dynasty China, and the Indus Valley, and all of these states arose out of the banks of great rivers (Scarborough 2003: 140). The respective religions of these rivers developed symbols, myths, and rituals dealing with water. I propose to designate those religions as riparian. The term riparian derives from the Latin noun *ripa*, which means "river bank" or "shore."

Sumer was the first culture of Mesopotamia, and it flourished in the early fourth millennium or about 3100 BCE. Sumer was succeeded by Akkad after 2340 BCE and later by Babylon between 2000 and 1500 BCE. Sargon of Akkad established the first world empire about 2300 BCE, and his exploits took shape as legends. His first legend was that of his birth. As an infant, Sargon was abandoned by his mother who placed him in a reed basket, sealed the lid, and set the sealed basket in a river. The king's gardener discovered the baby, and through the love goddess Ishtar Sargon prevailed. I cite the birth legend in pertinent part:

> I am Sargon the great king, king of Agade.
> My mother was a high priestess, I did not know my father.
> My father's brothers dwell in the uplands.
> My city is Azupiranu, which lies on Euphrates bank.
> My mother, the high priestess, conceived me, she bore me in secret.
> She placed me in a reed basket, she sealed my hatch with pitch.
> She left me to the river, whence I could not come up.
> The river carried me off, it brought me to Aqqi, drawer of water.
> Aqqi, drawer of water, brought me up as he dipped his bucket.
> Aqqi, drawer of water, raised me as his adopted son.
> Aqqi, drawer of water, set (me) to his orchard work,
> During my orchard work, Ishtar loved me.
> Fifty-five years I ruled as king (Foster 2003: 461).

Mesopotamia arose in the valley of the twin rivers, the Tigris and the Euphrates. The term Mesopotamia means "between the rivers," and it derives from two Greek terms, *mesos*, which means "middle" or "between" and *potamos* or "river." The Euphrates flows from Turkey in a winding course through the present-day countries of Syria and Iraq for 1800 miles and then empties into the Persian Gulf. The Tigris also originates in Turkey and flows in more of a straight course for 1500 miles to the Persian Gulf. In their upper or northern regions the two rivers flow through mountains until they reach the semi-arid alluvial plain in central Iraq and then finally through the lakes and marshes of southern Iraq before reaching the Persian Gulf.

The two rivers are not exactly identical twins due to the different times of their annual floods. Since antiquity, the major rivers of Iraq have changed their courses, because heavy deposits of new soil hide the ancient river- and canal-beds (Jacobsen 1960: 174). Therefore, archaeologists must use special methods to reconstruct the water courses of antiquity. As acknowledged by one contemporary archaeologist, the Tigris was fast-flowing and unpredictable, cutting into the alluvium three meters, but the Euphrates had a longer and slower flow, losing 40% of its water by evaporation and by carrying more silt than the Tigris (Gibson 1974: 7). The Euphrates flowed above the plain, building up high levees without cutting into the alluvium. In antiquity six major branches flowed from the Euphrates (Jacobsen 1960: 176).

Snow melted in the mountains in the spring, and the two rivers flooded between March and May or June (Driver and Miles 1952: 151). The main flood of the Euphrates arrived in April, frequently washing away young plants and field gardens (Gibson 1974: 7). The Tigris flood arrived about one month earlier. The Tigris waters began to recede in June, allowing the start of the farming season, and they continued to recede throughout the summer months. The spring floods could be violent, as they were often driven by the spring tides and gales from the Persian Gulf. The Tigris with its swift and straight flow tended to be more dangerous than the Euphrates.

Difficulties in maintaining irrigation systems and surviving violent floods, along with shifts in the river beds, aroused a deep sense of insecurity among the peoples of Mesopotamia (Hawkes 1973: 23). Mesopotamians regarded these natural forces as laws enacted by the gods and goddesses who had to be worshipped (Nigosian 2008: 44). The deities comprised a monarchy, consisting principally of Anu, Enlil, and Enki, who came together in the divine assembly and decreed the fates for humans (Bottero 1992: 213–214). Anu was the father, Enlil the son, and Enki was the adviser. The deities were also guardians of cities, and shifts in political power led to the rise of specific urban gods. For example, the ascent of Babylon brought forth the supremacy of Marduk over other deities.

Mesopotamian religion featured unique water-related motifs. The worldview consisted of a vertical and bipolar universe (Bottero 1980: 29). The globe comprised two symmetrical hemispheres, the one above was the sky, the other below was the earth. The earth contained a vast underground ocean called Apsu, which was the source of lakes, marshes, and the water of the subsoil (Wilson 1961: 14). In Mesopotamian mythology Apsu was a male deity, whose name related to the Greek *abussos* or "bottomless pit" and which survives as "abyss" in English. The upper hemisphere or sky was occupied by gods in their respective zones. Within the lower hemisphere or earth was the underworld where the sun was hidden and which was connected to the Apsu Ocean.

This universe was the stage for the Babylonian Creation story. In the beginning all was water. Apsu and Tiamat were the primeval couple who embodied two great seas, the former saline and the latter freshwater (Bottero 1992: 220). A third god was Mummu who was an adviser to Apsu and who represented other forms of water, such as ice, mists, or clouds.

> Tablet 1
> When on high no name was given to heaven,
> Nor below was the netherworld called by name;
> Primeval Apsu was their progenitor,
> And matrix-Tiamat was she who bore them all,
> They were mingling their waters together,
> No cane brake was intertwined nor thicket matted close.
> When no gods at all had been brought forth,
> None called by names, none destinies ordained.
> Then were the gods formed within the (se two). (Foster 2003: 391).

The gods were brothers whose constant reveling and dancing disturbed their parents Apsu and Tiamat. Tiamat remained "silent before them. Their actions were noisome to her. Their behavior was offensive, (but) she was indulgent." Apsu summoned Mummu for legal counsel concerning his offspring gods. Apsu said to Tiamat in a loud voice: "Their behavior is noisome to me! By day I have no rest, at night I do not sleep! I wish to put an end to their behavior, to do away with it! Let silence reign that we may sleep."

Tiamat became enraged and cried out angrily and bitterly: "What? Shall we put an end to what we created? Their behavior may be most noisome, but we should bear it in good part." Mummu agreed, however, with Apsu. "Whatever they plotted between them, was reported to the gods their offspring. The gods heard it as they stirred about. They were stunned, they sat down in silence."

Ea, one of the offspring gods, cast a spell upon his father Apsu, causing him to fall asleep, and Ea killed him. Ea also kidnapped and locked up Mummu. To avenge the murder of her husband Tiamat prepared for battle. She brought forth eleven monstrous species and shaped them into an army under the command of Qingu. Ea and Anu advanced against Tiamat, but in terror they retreated. In the course of these confrontations Marduk was born out of the waters of Apsu. Although young, Marduk was persuaded to lead an assault against Tiamat. He agreed on condition that he be granted supreme authority; so the gods appointed Marduk as king.

Marduk armed himself with a bow, arrows, mace, and a net held by the four winds. He mounted his chariot and moved against Tiamat.

> Tiamat and Marduk, sage of the gods, drew close for battle,
> They locked in single combat, joining for the fray.
> The Lord spread out his net, encircled her,
> The ill wind he had held behind him he released in her face.
> Tiamat opened her mouth to swallow,
> He thrust in the ill wind so she could not close her lips.
> The raging winds bloated her belly,
> Her insides were stopped up, she gaped her mouth wide.
> He shot off the arrow, it broke open her belly,
> It cut her innards, it pierced the heart.
> He subdued her and snuffed out her life,
> He flung down her carcass, he took his stand upon it (Foster 2003: 398).

Marduk cut Tiamat's body in two, turning the upper half into the sky and the lower half into the earth. He released the waters of the Tigris and Euphrates to flow through her eyes.

> He opened underground springs, a flood was let flow (?).
> From her eyes he undammed the Euph[rates] and Tigris,
> He stopped up her nostrils...
> He heaped up high- peaked mo[unt]ains from(?) her dugs.
> He drilled through her waterholes to carry off the catchwater (Foster 2003: 399).

After disposing of the eleven monstrous species Tiamat had borne, Marduk created humankind from blood. Finally, the gods constructed Marduk's house on the earth above the subsoil waters of Apsu. In the house the divine assembly convened and set the eternal, unchangeable destinies of all things.

The story of the Great Flood was in Tablet XI of the Epic of Gilgamesh, which evolved from Sumerian sources through successive Akkadian translations and adaptations until reaching its final form. Utnapishtim was the heroic survivor of the flood, and he told the story to Gilgamesh. The divine assembly decided to punish humanity with a flood, and the gods informed Utnapishtim and his boatman Puzur-Amurri of their decision. The boatman built and caulked the vessel in seven days, according to specific measurements. Utnapishtim brought into the vessel his possessions, "living creatures," "family and kin," and "all skilled craftsmen." Shamash, the sun god, appointed the time for the rains to begin.

Six days and [seven] nights
The wind continued, the deluge and wind storm leveled the land.
When the seventh day arrived, the wind storm and deluge left off their assault,
Which they had launched, like a fight to the death
The sea grew calm, the tempest grew still, the deluge ceased.
I looked at the weather, stillness reigned (Foster 2003: 459).

The boat landed on Mount Nimush; and after seven days Utnapishtim released a dove, but it came back without finding a resting place. He released a swallow which also returned. Then he released a raven which flew around, saw the water recede, and did not return. Utnaptishtim set free all the inhabitants of the boat and made an offering on top of the mountain. The god Enlil blessed Utnaptishtim and his wife and conferred immortality upon them.

Then Enlil came up into the ship,
Leading me by the hand he brought me up too.
He took my wife up and made her kneel beside me.
He touched our brows, stood between us and blessed us,
"Hitherto Utnapishtim has been a human being,
Now Utnapishtim and his wife shall become like us gods,
Utanpishtim shall dwell afar-off at the source of the rivers."
Thus it was they took me afar-off and made me dwell at the source of the rivers (Foster 2003: 460).

In Mesopotamian mythology Shamash was the sun god who arose from the underworld in the East, travelled across the sky, and in the evening sank into the western horizon. After descending into the West, Shamash passed through the underworld and reemerged in the eastern horizon to start the cycle all over again. Mesopotamians believed that before the sun set in the evening, it crossed a vast, desolate desert, which bordered the land in the West and touched a large body of water called Hubur (Bottero 1980: 31). The waters of Hubur encircled the earth, separating the dark shores of the beyond that were so distant and indiscernible that no one could know whether they were above or below the cosmic ocean (Bottero 1980: 31−32). Beyond the Hubur was the land of no return, where the dead dwelled in silence, darkness, and motionlessness. The land of no return was a vast cavern whose occupants were sad, gloomy, mournful, and the Hubur was the last boundary before the cavern (Bottero 1983: 192). In the Babylonian Creation story the waters were addressed as mother Hubur (Tablet 2, line 19).

The Nile River

Unlike the turbulent Tigris and Euphrates rivers the Nile had a more serene and predictable flow. The upper part, or White Nile, flowed out of central African lakes for more than a 1000 miles before becoming the Blue Nile, as it carried a blue-green silt, and then emptied into the Mediterranean Sea in southern or lower Egypt.

Between 10,000 and 7000 BCE a pastoral group settled along the fertile Nile valley, and they organized themselves in independent villages, living in buildings, made of wood, brick, and stone (Nigosian 2008: 28). The Nile flooded annually. Beginning with the monsoonal rains in the Ethiopian highlands, the flood waters reached Aswan in southern Egypt by mid-August, and from there the river flowed to the south until reaching the Nile delta at the Mediterranean Sea six months later (Postel and Richter 2003: 11). After the flood waters receded, between early October and late November, farmers planted their crops. The flood plain contained enough moisture for growing crops until mid-April or early May of the following year, when the flood cycle resumed again.

The Nile ecosystem supported flood-recession agriculture. Peak river flows released about ten million tons of nutrient-rich silt into the flood plain as well as an additional 90 million tons into the delta (Postel and Richter 2003: 11). The force of the flooding washed out the salt that had accumulated in the soil and prevented salinization, the traditional plague of farming in dry regions.

The predictability of the Nile flooding allowed Egyptians to live in relative contentment. Continuous flooding meant that the farmers did not have to irrigate during the summer months. Looking across the Nile in either direction, Egyptians could see the boundaries of their self-contained world— the wide deserts to the West and the East. Egyptians believed that the gods had given them the Nile for continuous moisture and that strangers and foreigners had to rely on rain water which was seasonal (Hawkes 1973: 27).

A brief description of the creation of the world appeared in the Coffin Texts compiled about 2050 BCE. After the first verse, the speaker is Atum the creator god:

> I am the waters, unique, without second.
> That is where I evolved,
> On the occasion of my floating that happened to me.
> I am the one who once evolved—
> Circlet, who is in his egg.
> I am the one who began therein, (in) the waters,
> See, the Flood is subtracted from me:

See, I am the remainder.
I made my body evolve through my own effectiveness.
I am the one who made me.
I built myself as I wished,
According to my heart (Allen 2003: 6–7).

As in Mesopotamia, ancient Egypt affirmed the solar myth in the order of the world. Egyptians believed that Re, the sun god, arose in the morning in the East, travelled across the sky in the day, and then set in the West in the evening. During the 12 hours of the night, the sun god journeyed through the underworld canals in a boat called the Bark of Re (Geyer 2004: 41). In the sixth hour after sunset the open sea appeared as a source of life and chaos. In Egyptian mythology, however, the sea was not a threat; instead sand and the desert were more dangerous (Geyer 2004: 55). By navigating the waters the sun god completed the underworld journey and achieved the renewal of life, when arising from the East in the morning of the next day.

After 3000 BCE, when upper and lower Egypt had been united politically under Menes, Egyptian religion recognized the king or pharaoh as the incarnation of the sun god and, therefore, as a god himself. The will of the sun god was discharged through the decrees of the pharaoh. At his death the pharaoh's mummified body was placed in a tomb, and he was addressed as Horus. As his soul ascended to the sun god after death, the pharaoh was addressed as Osiris (Lesko 1989: 38).

The cult of the pharaoh was based on the story of Osiris. The oldest Egyptian version of the story appeared in the Pyramid Texts, which were compiled from funerary hymns and rituals about 2700 BCE (Nigosian 2008: 29, 34). Osiris, a benevolent god-king, was murdered by his brother Seth. After killing Osiris, Seth escaped and took with him Osiris' "third eye," which was a symbol of kingship. Osiris' sister-wife Isis looked for Osiris' body and, finding it, wept and embraced the corpse. Osiris came back to life briefly to impregnate Isis, who later gave birth to their son Horus. When Horus came of age, Isis asked him to avenge his father's death.

Horus charged Seth with the murder of his father before the Court of Deities. Since the court did not respond in a timely manner, Horus killed Seth and recovered his father's "third eye." When Horus replaced the "third eye" on his father's corpse, Osiris arose and became the Lord of the Dead. Osiris bequeathed his "third eye" to Horus, who bore it as the ruler of Egypt. In his reign Pharaoh identified with Horus.

The Hymn to Osiris was the fullest Egyptian account of the story, and I cite it in pertinent part:

Mighty Isis who protected her brother,
Who sought him without wearying.

Who roamed the land lamenting,
Not resting till she found him,
Who made a shade with her plumage,
Created breath with her wings,
Who jubilated, joined her brother,
Raised the weary one's inertness,
Received the seed, bore the heir,
Raised the child in solitude,
His abode unknown.

They gave to Isis' son his foe,
His attack collapsed,
The disturber suffered hurt,
His fate overtook the offender.
The son of Isis who championed his father,
Holy and splendid is his name,
Majesty has taken its seat,
Abundance is established by his laws (Lichtheim 2003: 42).

The Greek version of the story appeared in Plutarch's *Moralia* in the first century CE, and I follow the text as published in the Loeb Classical Library (Plutarch, Babbit, trans., 1962). Osiris was born first, followed by Typhon or Seth, and then by Isis and Nephthys. The name Typhon represented conceit due to ignorance and self-deception (351. F). Isis was the goddess of moisture, vegetation, the Nile, and the sea. She was the sister-wife of Osiris, and Nephthys was the sister-wife of Typhon. When Osiris returned home, after civilizing the earth, Typhon conspired against him, along with 72 co-conspirators. Typhon had secretly measured Osiris' body and built a beautifully decorated chest with the size and shape of Osiris. At a festival Typhon promised to give the chest to any man, who could fit into it. Some tried, but they did not fit. When Osiris lay down in the chest, Typhon closed the lid and fastened it with nails and molten lead. The conspirators carried the chest to the Nile River where the flowing water took it out to sea (356. C).

When Isis learned of the disappearance of Osiris, she grieved deeply, wandered everywhere, and asked people about the chest. She learned from children that the chest had washed up on the land of Byblos or the Phoenician coast (357. A). She found the chest and brought it back home. One night, while hunting, Typhon discovered the chest, opened it, dismembered Osiris' body into 14 pieces, and scattered them (358. A). Isis searched for the parts and had a funeral for each one that she found. She did not find, however, the male organ, which had been thrown into the Nile and eaten by fish (358. B). Isis made a replica of Osiris' phallus and consecrated it. Osiris appeared from the otherworld to his son Horus and prepared him to avenge his murder by Typhon. Horus confronted Typhon in combat and prevailed.

Plutarch explained that since Osiris's phallus was thrown into the Nile, then its floods were effusions of Osiris (365. B). The flood waters carried the germinal powers of the god. In contrast, Typhon had the power of heat and drought, and the receding of the flood waters represented his enclosing Osiris into the chest. The receding of the waters occurred in November, and Isis began grieving on the 17th for four days. On the night of November 19 the priests took the chest to the sea, poured water on it, and shouted with joy that Osiris had been found (366. E-F).

The myth of Osiris lay behind the coronation of the pharaoh, a ceremony that included a ritual washing or baptism. According to temple scenes and their accompanying hieroglyphic legends, a priest personifying divinity and witnessed by two gods, typically Horus and Thoth the moon god, poured water over the head of the pharaoh and then led him into the sacred precinct of Re the sun god, who placed a crown on the head of the kneeling king. While pouring the water, the priest recited the following verse: "I purify thee with life and dominion, that thou mayest grow young like thy father Re and make Sed-festival like Atum, being arisen gloriously as prince of joy" (Gardiner 1950: 7-8). Although temple scenes presented the two gods with the priest, accompanying texts cited Nephthys and Seth of upper Egypt and Isis and Osiris of lower Egypt. The pouring of water was a purification and a transfer of power from the four gods to the pharaoh (Gardiner 1950: 9). The gods could represent one another, for example Horus for Osiris. The water symbolized the *ankh* or the principle of life. Thus, the sacred water, flowing forth from the primordial sea from which the world was created, conferred dominion upon the baptized king and elevated him to eternal life (Milgrom 1991: 959).

The Indus River

The Indus River originates in the glacier waters of southern Tibet at an altitude of 1700 feet and flows toward the West for 650 miles; then it cuts through the Himalayan Mountains in a series of gorges and enters the plane of Attock in Pakistan (Hawkes 1973: 28). The Indus takes in five major tributaries, as it flows to the South toward the delta, which spans 60,000 hectares in southern Pakistan and empties into the Arabian Sea (Husain 2003).

In ancient times the climate was dominated by uncontrollable monsoons in the spring, both ravaging and renewing nature (Basham 1967: 3). The average annual flow of the Indus was about the same as that at the middle of the 20th century, that is, about 100 million acre-feet (Raikes 1965: 199). The Indus carried abundant water and heavy silt loads along a shallow gradient, after plunging from the Himalayan Mountains (Scarborough 2003: 140). Great annual floods blanketed the ancient flood plains, releasing nutrient-rich sediment. With the melting of the snow and glaciers in the mountains the flood waters reached their peak in March and then receded to their lowest levels in September. The silt-bearing floods nurtured the growth of wheat, barley, and peas (Hawkes 1973: 267).

Between 2600 and 2000 BCE a civilization flourished in the Indus Valley in what is now Pakistan and northwest India (Miller 1985: 35). The civilization had two main cities, Harappa and Mohenjo-daro, and these cities were built on a grid pattern of straight streets and cardinal directions. The area was larger than Egypt and Mesopotamia combined, and it comprised a semi-circle with the center at the Indus River and with the communities spreading eastward and westward (Miller 1985: 40). Mohenjo-daro was in the Sindh region of southern Pakistan, next to the Indus, and it had a population of 40,000 (Miller 1985: 42). It had both residential and commercial buildings. Harappa was located north of Mohenjo-daro on the Indus.

At Mohenjo-daro three 30-feet wide streets ran north and south, and with two crossing at right angles they made 12 blocks measuring 1200 by 800 feet (Hawkes 1973: 271). The larger blocks were divided into alleys extending up to ten feet wide, and the streets and houses were made of bricks. Commercial buildings and houses were functional without architectural decoration, and in Mohenjo-daro private homes accounted for 77% of the buildings (Miller 1985: 48). Every house had a bathroom with drainage channels and chutes linking it to the street, and water for sanitation came from brick-lined wells (Scarborough 2003: 144). Toilets discharged effluent into soak pits dug into and under streets. The drains were constructed of bricks, and they included inspection holes (Hawkes 1973: 276).

Mohenjo-daro had the Great Bath for public bathing, and it was housed in a building with small cubicles for washing. In Harappa there was also a large bath about 40 feet long, and it was waterproofed with bitumen. Flights of steps descending into the water meant that it was used for public bathing (Hawkes 1973: 273). The focus of the Indus Valley civilization was on cleanliness and ritual purity, as well as social homogeneity and the non-display of wealth (Scarborough 2003: 145).

The name India derives from the Indus River (Aitken 1992: 1). Hinduism, one of the major religions of the world, arose out of the context of the Indus Valley civilization. A distinctive characteristic of Hinduism was the establishment of the caste system of social stratification unlike the egalitarian homogeneous social structures of Indus Valley cities. On top of the Hindu caste system was the priestly caste (*Brahmin*), whose members performed sacrifices and other rituals. The second caste consisted of the warriors (*kshatriya*) who were a kind of nobility that maintained armed forces and defended the country. The merchant caste (*vaisya*) contained farmers, merchants, traders, and artisans who promoted the well-being of society. Finally, the servants (*sudra*) provided manual labor and other services for the upper three castes. Membership in a particular caste was determined by birth.

Hinduism maintained the authority of divine revelation derived from a collection of sacred writings, beginning with the Vedas. The first text, the RgVeda, was compiled about 1000 BCE, and it contained 1000 hymns of praise and prayer to the Vedic gods. The RgVeda portrayed several gods who collectively comprised heaven, from where water descended to the earth. Since ancient times, Hindus have worshipped seven rivers as sacred, four arising in the Himalayan watershed in the North and three in the South (Aitken 1992: 5). The seven were the Ganges, Yamuna, Godavari, Sarasvati, Narmada, Indus, and the Kaveri.

Book One of the RgVeda affirms the adoration of water: "I call the Waters, Goddesses, wherein our cattle quench their thirst; oblations to the streams be given. Amrit [nectar of immortality] is in the waters: in the waters there is healing balm: Be swift ye Gods, to give them praise" (Griffith, trans.. 1973. 1. 23: 17–19).

The same hymn ascribes healing power to water: "O Waters, teem with medicine to keep my body safe from harm, so that I long may see the sun. Whatever sin is found in me, whatever evil I have wrought. If I have lied or falsely sworn, waters remove it from me. The Waters I this day have sought, and to their moisture have we come" (1. 23: 21–23a).

Belief in the cleansing power of water, the ability to wash away spiritual and material impurities, is age-old in Hinduism. That is why even to this day Hindus chant the names of the seven sacred rivers, as they do their daily baths: "May you all be pleased to manifest in these waters with which I shall purify myself" (Shiva 2002: 133).

For devout Hindus rivers are goddesses (1. 56: 4b). Waters possess knowledge: "The Waters listen as they flow along: they know the origin of heaven and earth" (7. 34: 2). Some hymns invoke the refreshing, purifying qualities of water: "May we obtain this day from you, O Waters, that wave of pure refreshment.... All-purifying, joying in their nature, to paths of Gods the Goddesses move onward. They never violate the laws of Indus. Present the oil-rich offering to the Rivers" (7. 47: 1a, 3).

Within the Hindu pantheon Indra was the thunder god, who served as the model and champion of the warriors (Nigosian 2008: 144). He received appeals from the warriors in combat against their enemies. Indra co-existed with other atmospheric gods: Vayu the wind god, Parjanya the rain and cloud god, Maruts a group of storm gods, and Rudra the god of death, disease, and destruction who controls atmospheric catastrophes. In later epic Hinduism Rudra was known as Shiva the destroyer of worlds.

The relation between Indra and water is portrayed in the RgVeda as follows:

> Forth from the middle of the flood the
> Waters—their chief the Sea—flow
> cleansing, never sleeping.
> Indra, the Bull, the Thunderer, dug their
> Channels: here let those Waters, Goddesses,
> Protect me.
> Waters which come from heaven, or those
> that wander dug from the earth, or
> flowing free by nature,
> Bright, purifying, speeding to the Ocean,
> Here let those Waters, Goddesses, protect
> me (7. 4a: 1–2).

The waters nourish Indra:

> Ye wealthy Waters, hear mine invocation.
> Send forth the rapture-giving wave, O
> Rivers, which Indra drinks, which sets
> The Twain [heaven and earth] in motion;
> The well that springeth from the clouds,
> Desirous, that wandereth triple-formed,
> Distilling transport.
> These winding Streams which with their
> Double current, like cattle-raiders, seek
> the lower pastures.... (10. 30; 9–10a).

Hinduism has always revered its rivers as goddesses sent to earth to help humanity (Aitken 1992: 1).

> The singer, O ye Waters...shall tell your grandeur forth
> That is beyond compare.
> The Rivers have come forward triply, seven
> And seven. Sindhu [Indus River] in might surpasses all
> the streams that flow.
> Varuna [sky god] cut the channels for thy forward
> Course, O Sindhu, when thou rannest on

To win the race.
Thou speedest o'er precipitous ridges of
the earth, when thou art Lord and
Leader of these moving floods.
His roar is lifted up to heaven above the
Earth: he puts forth endless vigour with
a flash of light.
Like floods of rain that fall in thunder
From the cloud, so Sindhu rushes on
bellowing like a bull (10. 75: 1–3).

This hymn mentions the Ganges River in verse 5a: "Favour ye this my laud, O Ganga...." In modern Hinduism the Ganges is the most sacred of the seven sacred rivers (Aitken 1992: 35). It originates in Tibet and flows through the Himalaya Mountains in an eastward direction and then after 1500 miles empties into the Bay of Bengal near Calcutta. Although briefly mentioned in the RgVeda, it became the holiest river, as the priestly caste transferred the sanctity of water from the Indus to the Ganges. Whereas the Indus Valley civilization cultivated a relatedness with nature, the priestly caste considered nature as an abstraction, claiming that the river water was not as important as the sacred element within it (Aitken 1992: 100). Consequently, the priests emphasized sacrificial rituals at the Ganges.

According to Hindu mythology, Indra's enemy, Vrtra the demon of chaos, withheld and hoarded water, thereby inhibiting creation. When Indra defeated Vrtra, the heavenly waters were released, and they rushed to earth, permitting life to spring forth (Shiva 2002: 131). Since the Ganges descended from heaven, she became a sacred "bridge" to the realm of the gods. Hindus believe that the Ganges possesses antiseptic minerals that kill bacteria, including cholera germs (Shiva 2002: 134). The Ganges is the all-nurturing, mysterious, healing mother, and her healing qualities are lauded in a hymn that appears near the end of the RgVeda: "The Waters have their healing power, the Waters drive disease away. The Waters have a balm for all: let them make medicine for thee" (10. 137: 6).

After death, the corpse is washed, wrapped in a cloth, placed on a bier, and carried to the municipal fire which is burning all the time. A flame is purchased by the family of the deceased to ignite the funeral pyre, on which the corpse rests (Justice 1997: 105, 108). In the cremation fire the elements of the body disintegrate and the soul, or technically the subtle-self, fuses with the god Shiva who resides in Banaras, a city which sits on the west bank of the Ganges River. The hope of every Hindu is to die in Banaras, and the terminally ill must be taken to that city as a pilgrimage. The cremains are cast into the Ganges to ensure a passage to the heavenly realm. If water is the source of life, then water is also the element to which the dead return (LaFleur 1992: 22).

Historically, the Vedic stage of Hinduism, with its emphasis on sacrificial rituals and the dominance of the priestly caste, gave way to a new approach in the sacred texts called the Upanishads. The warrior caste rebelled from the priestly control of rituals and in the ninth century BCE began a contemplative search for the meaning of life. The anti-Brahmanical movement achieved fundamental new insights, and they expressed them in the Upanishads which were compiled about 800 BCE.

The central affirmation of the Upanishads is the *Brahman* or the Absolute, a transcendent ground of being that pervades all of the world and even extends beyond time, space, and causality. At the same time the warrior contemplatives identified the *Atman* or Self that dwells in the inner core of humans and is one with the *Brahman*. The Self has the same attributes as the Absolute. They are indissolubly one, indefinable, transcendent, and infinite. The Self is differentiated from the body-ego, subtle-self, and supreme soul, which wrap around and conceal the Self in the course of human existence. The aim of the Hindu, according to the Upanishads, is to achieve Self-realization or oneness with the Absolute. If this identity should be achieved, one would escape the bodily and individualistic limitations of human existence, including the cycle of rebirth and death, and fuse with the Absolute.

One of the Upanishadic metaphors of Self-realization is that of a river flowing into the sea. Just as rivers originate from the sea as precipitation and then flow back into the sea, so does one's Self originate from the Absolute and return to it. In a Chandogya Upanishad passage (6. 10: 1–3) a son asks his father for further clarification, and the father replies: "The rivers of the east, my son, flow eastward, the rivers of the west flow westward. From ocean they merge into ocean, it becomes the same ocean. Just as they then no longer know that they are this river or that one, just so all these creatures, my son, know no more, realizing only when having come to the Existent [Absolute] that they have come to the Existent" (Deutsch and van Buitenen 1971: 14).

Reverence for water did not survive in Buddhism, however, one of the other great religions that came out of India. According to his legend, the founder Siddhartha Gautama was born into the warrior caste about 563 BCE. Seven days after his birth, Siddhartha's mother died. He was raised by his maternal aunt, whom his father had married. In his teenage years Siddhartha married and had one son.

In his late 20s Siddhartha renounced his family and its high social status and took up the way of a homeless wanderer. After wandering alone for about seven years, during which he rejected the extremes of asceticism and ritualism, he ceased his wandering and sat down under a rose-apple tree in a cross-legged yoga posture. He entered into a deep state of meditation throughout the hours of the night under a full moon in May, 524 BCE, when he was 36 years old (Nakamura 1977: 58). He passed through a series of four meditative stages: (1) beholding the law of karma; (2) seeing his own transmigrations through many previous lives; (3) grasping the interrelated field of being called dependent co-origination; and (4) entering into a state of total awareness or enlightenment. As the fully awakened one, he acquired the title of the Buddha.

After his enlightenment, Siddhartha resumed his travels as a homeless wanderer, clothed in a monk's robe, wearing sandals, and carrying a begging bowl. He came to a wide river and stepped into a ferry boat without paying the fare. This was an exemption granted to the religious (Nakamura 1977: 73). When he arrived on the distant shore, he looked back to the previous shore and could not see it.

Siddhartha's crossing the river and arriving on the distant shore became a metaphor of enlightenment in the Buddhist tradition. The previous shore, from which Siddhartha had embarked, signified ordinary, unenlightened consciousness as confined to the subject-object cognitive structure and conditioned by sensory experience. The ferry boat became a metaphor of Siddhartha's new teaching, the *Dharma*, that conveys people across the waters of life. Thus, Buddhism subordinated the flowing stream to the *Dharma*. Water was neither sacred nor an element of intrinsic value. Water was purely instrumental.

The Buddha preached two sermons at Banaras, and the second one altered the elemental view of the world. In his Fire Sermon Siddhartha proclaimed that "all is burning. And what is the all that is burning?" He answered: "The eye is burning, visible forms are burning, visual consciousness is burning, visual impression is burning ...." He asks—burning with what?—and he answers: "Burning with the fire of lust, with the fire of hate, with the fire of delusion...." (Rahula 1974: 95)

He proceeds through the other senses, declaring that they are all burning with the fires of lust, hate, and delusion. He concludes by urging his audience to become dispassionate, detached from sensory experiences and their driving forces of lust, hate, and delusion. "Being dispassionate, he becomes detached; through detachment he is liberated" (Rahula 1974: 96).

Liberation means extinguishing the flames of passion and becoming fully awakened. This is the experience of Nirvana.

Siddhartha's fire sermon made fire the fundamental element and displaced the sanctity of water in Hinduism. Buddhism did not link water to the origin of life, to fertility, and to blessing as Hinduism did (LaFleur 1992: 17–18). After Siddhartha's death at age 80, his body was cremated; but his teeth, collar bone, and hair were retained as relics and enshrined in stupas or pagodas (Nigosian 2008: 194). Consequently, Buddhism promoted pilgrimages to stupas instead of rivers, as had been encouraged in Hinduism (Aitken 1992: 91).

The Yellow River

The fourth great Old World civilization developed in the valley of the Yellow River in China, the river known affectionately to the Chinese as its "mother river" (Postel and Richter 2003: 5). Artifacts excavated from the Yellow River Valley date the beginning of Chinese history with the rule of the Shang Dynasty about 1500 BCE (Nigosian 2008: 233). The Yellow River originates in the Qinhai-Tibetan plateau in western China and flows in a kind of zig-zag pattern through the vast North China Plain before emptying into the Bo Hai or North China Sea. The Yellow is the second longest river in China. The longest is the Yangtze River, which also begins in western China, but it flows south until turning east and continuing a winding course to the East China Sea.

In the Chinese religion of Taoism water is the primary element (Saso 1990: 6). The primacy of water is attested in chapter eight of the *Tao Te Ching*: "The highest good is like that of water. The goodness of water is that it benefits the ten thousand creatures; yet itself does not scramble, but is content with the places that all men disdain. It is this that makes water so near to the Way" (Waley 1958: 151).

The Way refers to the Tao, pronounced Dao, which is the ultimate unity of nature and primordial reality. Water is the principle means of understanding the Tao as the way of nature. Since water flows gently and low ground and is not assertive, then a corresponding passive attitude opens humans up to the Tao. The ideal attitude toward nature is that of non-interference, known as *wu-wei*, and this is preferable to an aggressive, dominating approach.

Metaphorically speaking, the Tao dwells in low places, not in high places like mountains, and therefore the Valley Spirit expresses the experience of the Tao. Chapter six of the *Tao Te Ching* explains that spirit;

"The Valley Spirit never dies. It is named the mysterious Female and the Doorway of the Mysterious Female is the base from which Heaven and Earth sprang. It is there within us all the while; draw upon it as you will, it never runs dry" (Waley 1958: 149). The same principle is applied to rivers in the opening lines of chapter 66: "How did the great rivers and seas get their Kingship over the hundred lesser streams? Through the merit of being lower than they; that was how they got their kingship" (Waley 1958: 224).

The attributes of water fit the yin principle of Chinese thought. The ancient Chinese developed the yin-yang complementarity as a proto-scientific ordering system of the world. Yin means passivity, receptivity, coolness, darkness, fall-winter, valleys, femininity; and yang means activity, creativity, warmth, light, hills, spring-summer, masculinity. Each component has multiple metaphorical equivalents applicable to all domains of the universe. Yin and yang cohere in a harmonious whole that constitutes all natural entities and processes. They stand in foreground and background relationships. For example, as the light of day comes out and night fades away, the yang ascends into the foreground, and the yin recedes into the background. The yin remains in the background until the light of day recedes, and it ascends into the foreground again at night.

The nature of water is discussed in the 39th chapter of the Taoist text *Kuan Tzu*. "Now water is the blood and breath (*chhi hsü*) of the earth, flowing and communicating (within its body) as if in sinews and veins. Therefore we say that water is the preparatory raw material of all things (*chǔ tshai*)." (Needham 1969: 42).

The *Kuan Tzu* correlates water flows with the shared characteristics of populations. The water of chhi flows rapidly, and its streams turn around in rocky gorges; so its people are rough, brave, and covetous (Needham 1969: 45). The water of chhu is soft, weak, pure, and its people are light and self-confident. The water of yüen is heavy and turbid; and its people are dirty, foolish, and unhealthy. The water of chin has sediment, mud, and dust; so its people are greedy and deceptive. The water of yen is slow-moving and turbid; and its people are simple, chaste, and humble. The water of sung is light, strong, and pure; and its people are quiet, easy-going, and orderly.

Water also serves as a model for a nation. "If the water is pure and clean the heart of the people will readily be unified and desirous of cleanliness. If the people's heart is changed their conduct will not be depraved. So the sage's government does not consist of talking to people and persuading them family by family. The pivot (of his work) is water" (Needham 1969: 45).

From ancient times to the present Chinese folk religion has believed that spiritual beings or deities pervade the universe. One type, the shen or benevolent spirit, animates the rivers and seas (Nigosian 2008: 237). The Chinese have built temples and shrines dedicated to deities connected to the regulation of water, either by bringing rain during periods of drought or by controlling rivers in times of floods (Yang 1961: 65). These were mainly dragon gods who governed rain clouds and rivers, as well as a variety of water gods. In 1869 an imperial edict bestowed an honorary title on the river god Golden Dragon because, "when the dikes of the Yellow River were in imminent danger of collapse, the repeated apparition of the Golden Dragon saved the situation" (Yang 1961: 67).

Similar edicts were made in the 19th and early 20th centuries, as honors were given to river and rain gods for saving rural areas from floods and droughts. This is illustrated by the stele inscription in a temple of the goddess of sailing: "The flood is rampaging...The means of men have come to an end, and upon what except the goddess can we depend" (Yang 1961: 68).

Summary

The riparian religions exemplify an assessment made by a distinguished historian of religion that "immersion is equivalent to dissolution of forms. This is why the symbolism of the water implies both death and rebirth. Contact with water always brings a regeneration—on the one hand because dissolution is followed by a new birth, on the other hand because immersion fertilizes and multiplies the potential for life" (Eliade 1959: 130). The riparian civilizations experienced the dissolution of forms in the floodings of their respective rivers and regeneration in their agricultural practices.

The riparian religions attested to the ultimacy of water, either through their mythologies of the primordial seas from which they would take shape or in the rituals of purification which washed away spiritual and material impurities. Mesopotamian and Egyptian religions derived the authority of their respective kings from water. Among the surviving riparian religions only Hinduism worships rivers as goddesses and imparts the sanctity of water through a divinely revealed scripture. Both Hinduism and Taoism draw upon river flows to symbolize union with ultimate reality. Taoism finds a unique set of moral virtues in different kinds of water, and Chinese folk religion displays adoration to the benevolent deities active in rivers and rainfall.

Chapter Two: Bridges, Crossings, Holy Wells

Sacrifice at the River

Ancient peoples felt awe and reverence toward rivers and believed they were functions of the divine scheme of separating boundaries or designating frontiers. The ancients also recognized that rivers were obstacles in getting to the other side or distant shore. As sacred flows, rivers had their own gods or goddesses; and, therefore, crossing rivers was a transgression into the deities' territories. Consequently, ancient peoples offered sacrifices in order to appease the river deities (Knight 1953: 848). According to Heraclitus, for example, virgins were thrown into the Nile River to facilitate fruitful flooding (Knight 1953: 849).

The ancient Greeks believed that rivers were gods and springs divine nymphs (Burkert 1985: 174). The Naiads were the water nymphs that dwelled in brooks, springs, and fountains. Ocean was the Lord of Ocean River, a great river that encircled the earth. His wife was Tethys. Their daughters, the Oceanids, were nymphs of Ocean River, and the gods of all the rivers were the sons of Ocean and Tethys. Poseidon, the Lord of the Mediterranean and Black seas, ruled the underground rivers. Nereus, the Old Man of the Mediterranean Sea, was married to Doris, a daughter of Ocean, and they had fifty nymphs of the sea called Nereids.

Each Greek city worshipped its river or spring and even built temples to them. When they came of age, boys and girls dedicated their hair to the river. Votive offerings were brought, and animals were slaughtered in the rivers and springs. In these ritual settings the sacrifices meant that water was so precious that it could not be used without divine assistance.

In order to cross a river to the other side ancient peoples built bridges. By building bridges they displayed not only technical ingenuity but also curiosity and a desire to explore unknown lands. The role of the bridge was that it connected separate lands with a means of communication (Bleeker 1963: 180). Bridge building promoted, therefore, the expansion of culture.

In ancient Rome the *Pontifex Maximus* was the priest-engineer who supervised the building of *Pons Sublicius*, the first bridge over the Tiber River. The term *pontifex* derived from the Latin noun *pons* or "bridge" and from the verb *facere* for "to do" or "to make." To ensure the sanctity of the bridge it had to be constructed of wood (Knight 1953: 855). In the *Roman Antiquities* Dionysius Halicarnassus reported that in ancient times humans were sacrificed at the Tiber River but that instead the Romans threw effigies into the Tiber to appease the anger of the river god (1. 35.2). The Romans conducted this ritual every year after the vernal equinox in the middle of May (1. 25.3).

The ritual was the Feast of the Argei which took place in two stages on March 16–17 and on May 14. The feast involved a procession in March, when mannequins made of rushes were carried through the city to 27 chapels (Schilling 1989: 205). On May 14 the mannequins were removed from the chapels and carried to the *Pons Sublicius* in the Tiber River. From there, according to Ovid in his *Fasti* (95. 621), the mannequins were thrown from the bridge into the Tiber in the presence of the *Pontifex Maximus* and Vestal Virgins. The mannequins had human shapes, and their being cast into the river symbolized human sacrifices. The itinerary of the procession moved through the four quarters of the city and then circled the Roman Forum before heading to the Tiber. The Feast of the Argei was a foundation sacrifice for the development of Rome.

Rainbow Bridge

Within the mythologies of some ancient peoples a bridge took the shape of a rainbow. In the myths of northern Europe the center of the world was Yggdrasil, the great ash tree where the gods convened every day to hold a court (Zaleski 2000: 93). The branches of the tree spread out all over the world, even reaching up to heaven, while the roots extended deeply and widely in the earth. Under one root that pointed toward the frost ogres, there was the spring of Mímir, which contained wisdom and understanding. Mímir, the owner of the spring, drank water from it with the Gjöll horn and was filled with wisdom.

Another root of the world tree extended up to the sky, and under it was the spring of destiny, where the gods held their court. They rode to that spring every day over the Bifröst Bridge, which was a quivering rainbow bridge. The god Thór walked to the court every day, and he had to wade through three rivers. "…when he goes to give judgment at Yggdrasil's ash, since the Bridge of the Aesir [Bifröst] is flaming with fire the sacred waters glow. Then Gangleriõ asked; 'Does fire burn over Bifröst?' High One replied: 'The red you see in the rainbow is flaming fire.'" (Zaleski and Zaleski 2000: 94).

Near the spring under the ash tree was a beautiful hall occupied by the three maidens of fate called the Norns: Urõ (past), Verõandi (present), and Skuld (future). Nearby was the spring of Urõ from which the Norns drew water every day to sprinkle Yggdrasil, so that its branches would neither whither nor decay. The water that came from the spring of Urõ was sacred, and everything that touched it became as white as an egg shell (Zaleski and Zaleski 2000: 96).

Nordic mythology featured darkness, desolate forests, rivers, and bridges. The Germanic world of the dead lay beyond the sea, and this belief was implied in the ritual of placing the dead in burning ships and sending them out on the waves of the sea (Patch 1980: 61). Entrance into the otherworld occurred by a descent into the sea. At the end of time fire and water will destroy the world in a catastrophe, and the rainbow bridge will burn as a vast wall of fire (Davidson 1988: 171, 188).

A variation on the theme of the rainbow bridge may be found among the Native Americans in the American Southwest. The Pueblos live in northern New Mexico and practice wet farming by irrigation; and to their West the Hopi and Navajo tribes occupy the desert regions of Arizona and southern Utah, and they practice dry farming by raising sheep and other livestock. Southern Utah is the location of the Rainbow bridge which has a central place in Navajo life and ritual.

According to Navajo mythology, a rainbow appeared at the time of creation after the emergence of clouds. At creation a large body of water was in the East, from where the sun rose, and a mountain stood out from the water. Water flowed up the sides of the mountain and turned into clouds. At sunset a rainbow appeared facing West, and at sunrise a rainbow appeared facing East. The ancestral gods or Holy People determined that the primeval rainbow should take a permanent shape, lest its moisture evaporate and it disappear forever (Luckert 1977: 109–110, 117). Consequently, the Holy People created the rainbow bridge in the form of rock.

The actual rainbow bridge is a rock-arch spanning a canyon in southern Utah near the Arizona border. It is located southeast of the place where the Colorado and San Juan rivers diverge. The Navajo view the earth as continuous and not divided by state boundaries. Their only boundaries are the Colorado and San Juan rivers, the former being male and the latter female (Luckert 1977: 43). The Navajo make pilgrimages to the rainbow bridge and give offerings in order to receive blessings and healings.

Rainbow bridge symbolizes the primordial rainbow of the creation. The Navajo believe that every rainbow, appearing anywhere in the world, is a reenactment of the primordial rainbow. In Navajo mythology water is sacred

(Luckert 1977: 134). All life originates in the primordial rainbow and, therefore, life emerges from water.

Heavenly Suspension Bridge

Shinto is the native religion of Japan, and the word means the "way of the gods" (Spae 1972: 18). The gods are the *kami* or the innumerable, invisible spiritual beings or deities that pervade all of nature. In Japanese folk religion the mountains are at the center of the world, and walking up to a mountain top is a pilgrimage from the profane world to the sacred (Hori 1968: 141). Rivers that surround the mountains are boundaries of the sacred (Hori 1968: 165–166). Thus, one must cross the waters before reaching the sacred.

According to ancient folk custom, whenever a bridge had washed away or a new one was difficult to build over a river, the people believed the river *kami* had been displeased and demanded a sacrifice called a "human pillar" (Seward 1968: 24). This is illustrated in the legend of Iwafuji, a village chief. A bridge was washed away repeatedly, and the villagers had to select someone to sacrifice himself or herself to appease the river *kami*. Iwafuji requested that the first man who happened to pass by the ruins of the bridge should be offered as a sacrifice. The village elders accepted his suggestion. Iwafuji was so pleased that his idea had been accepted that he went to the bridge site the next morning to see whom the victim would be. The village elders came as well, and they all cried out in loud voices. "Iwafuji shalt offer thyself, because ye hast come the first" (Seward 1968: 24). Hence, Iwafuji had to sacrifice himself. This custom of a human sacrifice at a bridge was the original basis of *seppuku* or ritual suicide in Japan.

The Shinto creation story functions as a foundation narrative for Japanese religion and culture. The story is known as the *Kajiki*, and it is the oldest recorded document of Japanese mythology. In the beginning heaven and earth were a non-differentiated mass that contained the life principle. Three *kami* came into being, and they were invisible "reed-shoots" who produced two more invisible deities. Altogether, the five were called "Separate Heavenly Deities" (Earhart 1974: 15). Deities continued to come forth, culminating in the birth of Izanagi and his wife Izanami. So far the deities comprised the "Seven Generations of the Age of the Gods."

The heavenly deities commanded Izanagi and Izanami to complete the creation and solidify the land, which was "young, resembling floating oil and drifting like a jelly fish." The *kami* gave Izanagi and Izanami the "Heavenly Jeweled Spear" to fulfill their mission. "Thereupon, the two deities stood on the Heavenly Floating Bridge and, lowering the jeweled spear, stirred with it.

They stirred the brine with a churning-churning sound, and when they lifted up [the spear] again, the brine dripping down from the tip of the spear piled up and became an island. This was the island Onorago" (Earhart 1974: 15).

After descending from the bridge to the island, Izanagi asked his wife: "How is your body formed?" She replied, saying:

"My body, formed though it be formed, has one place which is formed insufficiently." Then Izanagi said; "My body, formed though it be formed, has one place which is formed to excess. Therefore, I would like to take that place in my body which is formed to excess and insert it into that place in your body which is formed insufficiently, and [thus] give birth to the land. How would this be?" (Earhart 1974: 18).

She replied: "That will be good." Izanagi and Izanami walked in a circle and had "conjugal intercourse." They gave birth to a "leech-child" which they placed in a "boat made of reeds and floated it away." Then they gave birth to the island of Apa, which they also did not consider their own child. After consulting with the heavenly deities about their failures, they resumed their sexual union.

When Izanami gave birth to the fire *kami*, she was burned to death and descended into the underworld. The enraged Izanagi decapitated his son and journeyed into the underworld to retrieve his deceased wife. Her rotting body was covered with maggots and worms and, feeling ashamed, she told her husband to return to the land of the living. Arriving on the surface of the earth, he went to a river and purified himself. When washing his left eye, the sun goddess Amaterasu came into being; and when washing his right eye, the moon god Tsukiyami came into being.

Izanagi fathered three noble children, the sun goddess, the god of the night, and the god of the ocean. The sun goddess Amaterasu was commanded to rule the land. Her heir, the *kami* Masakatu, born of Amaterasu and Takakino, was commanded by them as follows: "Now it is reported that the pacification of the Central Land of the Reed Plains has been finished. Therefore, descend and rule it as you have been entrusted with it" (Earhart 1974: 17). Other *kami* were born in the lineage of the sun goddess. The symbols of her authority were a beaded necklace, given to her by Izanagi, the mirror, and the spear. Her shrine took shape at Ise, where she has been worshipped until this day.

In modern Japan the imperial household has descended from the sun goddess. Prior to World War Two the emperor of Japan was venerated as divine, because he had united with the sun goddess in a heavenly marriage, and he gave offerings to her (Bix 2000: 193). From the perspective of the imperial household Japan is pure, but other nations are impure and in need of purity. Within Japan the *kami* are worshipped in shrines and access to those shrines occurs by crossing bridges. The bridge spans the profane and sacred realms and represents the heavenly suspension bridge of the creation.

For the Japanese the sea is the source and receptacle of life (LaFleur 1992: 25). In its primordial state life is water, and water is comforting, maternal, psychically positive, and sacred. Each individual originates as liquid life. When a baby is born he or she is not automatically human but liquid. To become human the infant must undergo a process of thickening or densification of being (LaFleur 1992: 33). The process involves passing through a series of rituals at ages three, five, and seven, and then finally at 15 one becomes fully human or densified. The reason why odd numbers are used is that the Japanese view nature asymmetrically. Even numbers represent a rational, harmonious worldview, which is absent in Japan.

The primordial sanctity of water is present in one of the oldest Shinto shrines which survives today. The Nachi Waterfall in Wakayama prefecture is an object of pilgrimage and a place for reciting sacred prayers and making offerings to the *kami* (Earhart 1974: 20). Water is also a means of purification, and one Shinto ritual involves standing under a waterfall to receive its cleansing power. The ritual of purification reenacts Izanagi's washing himself after leaving his decomposing wife in the underworld. From the creation story Japanese culture derives a moral polarity of shame and purification.

Since life comes from water in the beginning, it returns to water at the end. After middle age humans begin to lose their densities, and they gradually melt back into the primal state of liquidity. At death the de-densification process is completed. The body is cremated, and the soul lingers four days before beginning the otherworld journey lasting 33 years and culminating in one becoming an ancestral *kami* (Spae 1993: 295).

Every summer the family of the deceased participates in a festival of the dead known as the O-Bon. The dead temporarily interrupt their otherworld journeys and return to their earthly homes in mystical seances. The festival begins on July 15 and ends on July 18. For three days the family shares a joyous reunion with their deceased loved one. Offerings and prayers are made at family shrines for the benefit of the dead (Gilday 1993: 295).

On the evening of the 18th the entire community assembles at the sea coast or, if inaccessible, at a river, pond, or lake. Family members construct lanterns of paper, candle, and wood. If the death occurred during the previous year, the lantern is white; otherwise it is red, blue, or green (Gilday 1993: 293). Ritual dancing entertains the dead before their departure, and choirs sing laments. The candles inside the lanterns are lit from a common fire and carried in a procession to the water. The lanterns are set adrift on the water, and amid the fires of the night the family bids farewell. When the candles go out inside the lanterns, drifting on the waves of the water, the dead return to the otherworld (Gilday 1993: 296).

Crossing the Waters

The ancestors of the Australian aboriginal people came to Australia across the sea more than 40,000 years ago (Flood 1988: 30–31). During the Ice Age, water was frozen around Australia creating ice bridges to southeastern Asia. Between Asia and Australia there were also many islands that served as bridges where the waters were open, due to a temporary rise in temperatures and consequent melting of the ice. The settlers made their passage by means of canoes constructed of bamboo and animal cord available in Asia which had abundant rainfall (Flood 1988: 36–37). When they reached Australia, they did not return to Asia, as they suffered high death rates. These settlers were early representatives of *Homo Sapiens*, who had descended from their Asian predecessor, the species *Homo Erectus* which had evolved over two million years (Flood 1988: 74).

At the end of the Ice Age temperatures rose, melting the ice and causing the rising waters to drown the coastal areas. Mountains became islands, and about one seventh of the land mass of Australia was flooded by the rising glacial-melt water (Flood 1988: 179). Fertile lands were turned into lakes, and the continent of Australia became a large island in the Pacific Ocean.

These ecological changes took place between 9000 and 7000 years ago, and they were commemorated in myth and symbol and preserved in oral traditions. Myths memorialized the original aboriginal settlers and transformed them into supernatural beings or spirit ancestors who dwell in the Dreamtime (Eliade 1973: 42–43). One of the most revered supernatural beings was the Rainbow Serpent, whose story belonged to the myth of the encroaching sea (Flood 1988: 133–134).

> The giant Rainbow Serpent emerged from beneath the earth and as she moved, winding from side to side, she forced her way through the soil and rocks, making the great rivers flow in her Path, and carving through mountains she made the gorges of northern Australia. From the Rainbow Serpent sprang many tribes, and tales about her are told all over Arnhem land—over to Western Australia, in central Australia, and even to New South Wales (Marika 1980: 5).

The Rainbow Serpent was the Creator Spirit and great fertility mother who gave birth to humans as well as to other life forms. She brought forth wet seasons after periods of drought. As the spirit of the rainbow, she stood up on her tail and reached high into the sky forming a bridge between earth and the Dreamtime. The Rainbow Serpent lived in the deep waters of the Alligator and Liverpool rivers, and she was the supernatural being most feared by the people (Isaacs 1980: 62). If she were not revered, she would punish people with flash floods, torrential rains, or droughts. Whether taking beneficial or destructive forms, the Rainbow Serpent made water sacred.

Another cultural migration across the sea occurred independently of Australia in the central Pacific Ocean. Between 1700 and 800 BCE Polynesians known as the "Vikings of the Sunrise" emigrated out of islands in the southwestern Pacific, crossing in large out-rigger canoes with tall sails, and settled islands in the central Pacific region. In particular people from Tahiti migrated to Hawaii (Daws 1968: xiii). Tahiti has always been the ancestral home of Hawaiians and known as Kahiki.

As with the Australian immigrants, the Hawaii settlers were commemorated mythically as spirit ancestors who dwelled in the Dreamtime. In Hawaii the ancestors are known as the *Aumakua*, who are present invisibly in the lives of Hawaiians and are known through dreams and visions. The *Aumakua* are spirits of the dead who, because of their special qualities, have been transfigured into gods after death (Knipe 1989: 24). The *Aumakua* send messages and omens to people through rainbows, particularly in times of trauma, pregnancy, or death (Pukui 1972: 53–54). Within traditional tribal society Hawaiian chiefs wore rainbow figures on their head dresses, displaying the fact that they were privileged bridges between the people and the Dreamtime.

Traditional Hawaiian religion features a quaternity of gods: Ku, Lono, Kanaloa, and Kane. Ku is the ancestral god of the Dreamtime who rules the morning and is associated with storms and clouds. His signs are thunder, lightning, earthquakes, dark clouds, rainbows, rain and wind, and "whirlwinds that sweep the earth, rocks washed down ravines by 'the red mountain streams [stained with red earth] rushing to the sea,' waterspouts, the clustering clouds of heaven, gushing springs on the mountains" (Beckwith 1970: 31–32).

Kanaloa is the god of Squid, an angry, poisonous being that opposes Kane (Beckwith 1970: 60). Kane is the leading god of the Hawaiian pantheon and is associated with water. The "Water of Kane" is an ancient hula chant that portrays water with a question and answer format. The chant begins with

A query, a question.
I put to you:
Where is the water of Kane?
At the Eastern Gate

Where the Sun comes in at Hae bae;
There is the water of Kane (Emerson 1909: 258).

The chant links Kane "with the floating Sun, where the cloud-forms rest on Ocean's breast." The chant continues to sing of the water of Kane in the mountains, valleys, and rivers.

A question I ask of you:
Where, pray, is the water of Kane?
Yonder, at sea, on the ocean,
In the driving rain.
In the heavenly bow,
In the piled-up mist-wraith,
In the blood-red rainfall,
In the ghost-pale cloud-forms,
There is the water of Kane (Emerson 1909: 259).

The chant concludes:

One question I put to you:
Where, where is the water of Kane?
Deep in the ground, in the gushing spring,
In the ducts of Kane and Lua [Kanalua]
A well-spring of water, to quaff,
A water of magic power—
The waters of life!
Life! O give us this life (Emerson 1909: 259).

Kane protects water and gives it power for life, healing, and resurrection (Knipe 1989: 11). The water of Kane flows in the otherworld or Dreamtime, where the spirit ancestors of the first settlers dwell. Known as paradise, the otherworld represents the lower zone of the sky-worlds amid the clouds (Beckwith 1923: 40). The water of Kane also flows in the distant horizon where it is sacred and always fresh.

Holy Wells

Polynesians shared similar views of water and the otherworld with the Celts (Beckwirh 1923: 29, 54). The Celts were the ancestors of the Irish and the Welsh in the British Isles. After 12,000 BCE, the last Ice Age came to an end, and with the increase in temperatures sea levels rose, and forests grew on the prairies of Western Europe (Hutton 1991: 13). The rising of the sea caused Ireland and Britain to break off from the European continent and become islands. Previously, Europe had been a vast, continuous land mass.

Celtic mythology featured the solar myth. The sun arose in the East in the morning, moved across the sky, and set in the West in the evening. The solar arc was represented graphically by the Celtic Cross, that is, a cross inside a circle. The circle symbolized the route of the sun, travelling from East to West during the day and journeying in the underworld from West to East by night. The four-pointed cross represented the spokes of the wheel of a wagon on which the bodies of the dead were carried to the West for burial. As with other ancient religions, Celtic mythology identified the East with life and the West with death.

The Celts maintained the practice of throwing precious objects into rivers, pools, or bogs (Hutton 1991: 184–187). The rivers chosen all flowed to the East. Rivers flowing to the West have been dredged, but no precious objects have been found in their beds. Shields and vessels were thrown into bogs and pools, but swords and stripped skeletons were cast into rivers. The swords were always broken in two pieces. These customs implied sacrificial offerings given to sacred waters, and the sanctity of water has survived in the term *latis* which means "pool-goddess" (Hutton 1991: 230). Sacrificial offerings appeased the river deities.

Celtic worship took place out of doors at rivers, streams, pools, and springs. Cult sites were identified by stone circles connected to nearby rivers by streets between 2500 and 1000 BCE (Bord 1985: 4). Several river names have come from Celtic river gods, such as the Clyde River from Clota the divine washer and the Severn River from Sabrina, a princess who drowned in a river (Bord 1985: 5–6). Water bubbling up from the earth was thought to have great potency. Drinking water from springs and wells was for healing purposes. Healing was accelerated if the water were drunk from a human skull, a practice common in Ireland and Wales (Bord 1985: 8–9). Some wells were associated with the healing of specific illnesses, and eye wells were the most common (Bord 1985: 35). The Welsh term for river or stream is *Llygad* or "eye," implying that wells were the eyes of the god. One should not look directly into running water, because that would be the same as gazing into the god's eye.

Visits to wells on certain days were customs of ancient water worshippers. Visitors arrived in the early morning and dropped coins or bent pins into a well, walking sun-wise around it, drinking the water, bathing parts of the body, and attaching a cloth to a nearby tree, thereby transferring one's illness to the cloth (Bord 1985: 60, 67, 71). Walking around the well should done be three, seven, or nine times in order to live in harmony with the cosmic force of the sun. Walking opposite to the route of the sun meant death.

Several Irish wells were on tops of hills and mountains, in mountain passes, or near bogs and seashores. All were open to the sky, and many were located under trees. Most wells produced water spontaneously, and consequently people ascribed supernatural powers to them. Lakes, especially in Scotland, had water deities, and some holy wells were thought to be inhabited by fairies or little people (Bord 1985: 111–112).

Generally, river deities required sacrifices, either of animals or humans. The Welsh River Dee, home of the war goddess, required three human sacrifices a year to ensure success in battle (Bord 1985: 124). In Scotland the River Spey needed one human sacrifice a year. The same belief was found in British rivers but not lakes. Where the belief prevailed, some people answered the call of the river deity by plunging into the water in apparent suicides. After those deaths, hauntings frequently occurred near the running waters. Hauntings were recurrent, intentional energy forces that split off from the death sites as afterimages.

The Test Bridge

Several major religious traditions of the world have appealed to the bridge symbol at an advanced state of their development. Typically, these religions view the bridge as the testing point of the self in its highest level of self-knowledge and moral responsibility. Crossing the bridge over a river would be a process of judgment.

In Hinduism five passages of the Upanishads contain the bridge as a symbol of the Self or *Atman* (Brih. 4. 4.22; Chand. 8.4. 1; Mund. 2.25; Svet. 6.19; Katha 32). For example, the *Atman* "is the bridge that serves as the boundary to keep the different worlds apart" (Brih. 4. 4.22). The compilers of the Upanishads believed that Self-realization had a higher religious value than sacrifices. Crossing the bridge symbolized the ultimate achievement of *Brahman-Atman* or the fusion of the Self with the Absolute.

Long before the era of the Upanishads, however, in the ninth century BCE, the classical conception of the bridge appeared in the Persian religion of Zoroastrianism between 5000 and 3000 BCE. The Chinvat Bridge, also called the "Bridge of the Separator" or "Account-Keeper's Bridge," spanned this world and the next world, and it was crossed by the soul of the deceased person after death. The Chinvat Bridge was guarded by two supernatural dogs and ruled by Yima, the Lord of the Dead. In the earlier Zoroastrian scriptures the prophet Zoroaster escorted the souls of the dead across the Chinvat Bridge to the otherworld. As the prophet declared in the oldest text (Yasna 46:10): "Whosoever, Lord, man or woman will grant me those things thou knowest best for life-recompense for truth, power with good purpose— and those whom I shall bring to your worship, with all these I cross over the

Chinvat Bridge" (Boyce 1990: 42). Zoroaster addressed his God Ahura Mazda.

In the Avestan texts of the Parthian period, compiled between 141 BCE and 224 CE the soul of the deceased was met by a 15-year old being of the opposite sex. If the figure were attractive, then it signified that one had lived a righteous life of good thoughts, good words, and good deeds; but if the figure were unattractive, then it signified that one had lived an unrighteous life of evil thoughts, evil words, and evil deeds. The 15-year old being was the soul or conscience (*Daena*) of the person, which was awakened at initiation conducted at age 15, and it granted one knowledge of immortality (Molé 1960: 170).

In its mature form, as portrayed in Dadestan i denig, question 20: 3–7, a ninth century CE text, the Chinvat Bridge

> Is like a sword ... one of whose surfaces is broad, one narrow and sharp. With its broad side, it is so ample that it is twenty-seven poles wide; with its sharp side, it is so constructed that it is narrow as a razor's edge. When souls of the just and the wicked arrive ... it becomes a broad crossing for the just ... for the wicked it becomes a narrow crossing, just like a razor's edge (Boyce 1990: 83).

A river flows beneath the Chinvat Bridge, and it represents the abyss of hell into which the souls of the unrighteous fall. The souls of the righteous will pass over the bridge into paradise which is a place of great beauty, light, and joy. Neither paradise nor hell is final, as each is preparatory for the apocalyptic end of the world. The end will include a bodily resurrection, a three-day purification by molten metal, the final defeat of the forces of evil in a cosmic conflagration, followed by immortality on a regenerated earth.

The active test-bridge of mature Zoroastrianism passed into Islamic eschatology. At the end of the world, after the judgment and resurrection, the saved and the damned will be organized into groups, depending on whether they submitted to God or not throughout their lifetimes. Human life is a probationary period. The prophet Muhammad will escort them across the al-Sirat Bridge to their respective destinations, either to the Garden or to the Fire. The eschatological bridge in Islam is "finer than a hair and sharper than a sword; on its edges are metal hooks that grab onto one. If a person falls it involves a 3000 year journey—1000 climbing back up, another 1000 trying to travel along the bridge, and again another falling down" (Smith and Haddad 1981: 215). The hellish water beneath the bridge is stagnant and festering, as the Qur'an states: "Those souls disgraced by what they earned shall have boiling water to drink, and painful torment, because of their blasphemy" (6:70).

They who cross the bridge into the Garden or Paradise experience "cooling rivers, fresh rain and fountains of flavored drinking water" (De Chatel 2002). Water flows through the Garden, making it green and quenching thirst. As the Qur'an says

> The likeness of the Garden promised to the pious is this: in it are rivers of water, not brackish, and rivers of milk, unchanging in taste, and rivers of wine, delicious to them who drink it, and rivers of honey, pure and limpid. Therein they shall enjoy all kinds of fruits, and forgiveness from their Lord.
>
> Can this be compared to one abiding eternally in the Fire, where they are given boiling water to drink, which rends their innards? (47:15).

An equally distinguished bridge tradition appeared in classical Christian thought. In 593 CE Pope Gregory the Great introduced the bridge of death in the context of a night vision. A soldier died; his soul left his body in an otherworld journey. He recovered, returned to bodily consciousness, and recalled that: "He saw a river whose dark waters were covered by a mist of vapors that gave off an unbearable stench. Over the river was a bridge. It led to pleasant meadows beyond, covered by green grass and bathed with scented flowers. These meadows seemed to be the gathering places for people dressed in white robes" (Gregory 4:37).

During his reign Pope Gregory the Great appropriated the title of *Pontifex Maximus*, which Caesar Augustus had adopted in 12 BCE, and he applied the title to the Roman Catholic papacy. The papacy became the pontificate, and the *Pontifex* was the one who made a pathway into the unknown and defended the crossing against danger (Bleeker 1963: 184). The papacy or pontificate became the exclusive bridge between heaven and earth, this world and the next. For the ancient Roman Catholic Church bridges were sacred, and the maintenance and repair of bridges served as a means of penance (Dinzelbacher and Kleinschmidt 1984: 255). Persons in full communion with the church would cross the sacred bridge safely in death and not fall into the fiery river below. The flowing water beneath the bridge represented hell, because the church associated the Roman river deity with the devil (Knight 1953: 852). When the Vatican was constructed in the 16th century, it faced the *Pons Sublicius*, the first bridge over the Tiber River, demonstrating the everlasting conquest of the devil in the river.

Gregory's bridge did not rotate as did the Chinvat Bridge, but it provided a test. The unrighteous would fall into the polluted river below, while the righteous would cross over to everlasting life. In the post-Gregorian tradition the river became a flow of fire into which sinners were immersed by degrees, as in the following example from the Vision of Wenlock at 716 CE:

He sees a pitchy river boiling and flaming, over which was placed a piece of timber for a bridge. Over this the holy and glorious souls strove to pass. Some went securely, others slipped and fell into the tartarean stream, some were wholly submerged in the flood, others to the knees, some to the middle of the body, and some to the ankles. All eventually came out of the fire rendered bright and clean to ascend to the other shore (Patch 1980: 101).

The tenth century Vision of Adamnan described "a fiery river, which is unlike all other rivers, for in the midst of it is a strange kind of whirlpool, wherein souls of the wicked keep turning round and round …." (Zaleski and Zaleski 2000: 214). In the 12th century Legend of St. Patrick's Purgatory Owen enters a cave after 15 days of prayer and fasting. He passes through various levels until he arrives on the mountain top, where he "sees a fiery pit, and a broad fiery river filled with demons over which is a slippery bridge so narrow that one could not stand on it and so high that it makes one dizzy to look downward" (Patch 1980: 115).

Throughout the classical Roman Catholic era the church banned the worship of rivers, wells, and other bodies of water. As early as 452 CE the Second Council of Arles decreed: "If in the territory of a bishop infidels light torches or venerate trees, fountains, or stones, and he neglects to abolish this usage, he must know that he is guilty of sacrilege" (Bord 1985: 19). Several decrees in later times banned water worship in particular. For example, in 960 CE, during Saxon King Edgar's reign, the following canon appeared: "That every priest industriously advance Christianity, and extinguish heathenism, and forbid the worship of fountains" (Bord 1985: 19). Edicts prohibiting water worship continued to come out into the 12th century as well.

Nevertheless, as Christianity spread it attempted to integrate water reverence into the faith instead of banning it. Consequently, churches and baptisteries were built over or at wells, and many of these were dedicated to Christian saints. People also linked the bubbling water of wells to supernatural powers of the saints or the Virgin Mary. Drinking the water of the holy wells was a way to unite with the saints or with the Holy Mother. Wales has 500 holy wells with saints or Christian names, and Ireland and England have more than 8000 holy wells (Bord 1985: 24).

The history of Europe and the British Isles demonstrates a profound duality of water. On the one hand, Celtic people worshipped water, but on the other hand classical Christianity demonized bodies of water and linked river deities to the devil. This duality of demonic and holy waters invites an investigation into the meanings of water in the Bible, as well as a discussion of the sacramentality of water. These themes appear in the next three chapters.

Summary

Ancient peoples revered rivers and other bodies of water, and they performed sacrifices to appease water deities before erecting bridges. Since ancient times, bridges have taken various forms in different mythologies. In Nordic and Navajo religions the bridge is a rainbow, and water is sacred. Japanese folk religion reveres water and builds bridges for access to the sacred. In Shinto life is water, and humankind emerges from water in the beginning and returns to water at the end of the human life span.

Religions of the Pacific evolved from ancient migrations across the ocean, and their oral traditions memorialized those immigrants as spirit ancestors who dwell in the Dreamtime. In Australia the Rainbow Serpent spans earth and the Dreamtime, and she is worshipped as a Creator Spirit. In Hawaiian religion the rainbow is the bridge to the Dreamtime, and water is sacred. Polynesian mythology shares the theme of crossing the water with Celtic religion. The Celts and their descendants the Irish and the Welsh locate the divine in wells, and they drink the sacred water for healing.

The Indo-Persian religious tradition introduced the bridge as a symbol of the self, and its mythic narratives portrayed crossing the bridge as a moral test prior to death. The Zoroastrian test-bridge entered into Islamic eschatology, and the Roman Catholic Church made the bridge the symbol of the papacy and the exclusive access to the otherworld. Catholic vision literature rejected the sanctity of wells and demonized rivers, thereby promoting a dualism of divine and demonic waters.

Chapter Three: Biblical Waters

Primal Cross-Over

The Bible does not contain the bridge symbol, as such, but it includes several variations on the cross-over theme, starting in the creation story: "In the beginning when God created the heavens and the earth, the earth was a formless void and darkness covered the face of the deep ...." (Gen. 1:1–2a) The "face of the deep" refers to the primal waters or ocean, and it appears elsewhere in the Old Testament or Hebrew Bible: "The waters of the great deep" (Isa. 51:10b), and "when I bring up the deep over you, and the great waters cover you" (Eze. 26:19b). The Hebrew term for ocean (*tehom*) never has an article in the biblical text, and it bears a primordial power with a mythic quality. *Tehom* represents the primeval ocean, the waters encircling the earth after creation, which continually threaten the world and yet serve as a source of blessing for the earth (Tromp 1969: 59). The primeval ocean is dark and uncreated.

The creation began when "a wind from God swept over the face of the waters" (Gen. 1:2b). The wind represented the Spirit or breath of God crossing over the primal ocean to make a dramatic announcement. "Then God said, 'Let there be light'; and there was light" (Gen. 1:3). The divine Spirit passed over the watery chaos to create the world by the word. Creation was a separation of the elements from one another, as with light from darkness, but it was not a cause. In the Hebrew account creation meant dividing or separating (Westermann 1994: 35).

Creation as separation of the elements came out of the primal waters, as the psalmists declared: "for he has founded it on the seas, and established it on the rivers" (Ps. 24:2), and "you cover it [the earth] with the deep as with a garment; the waters stood above the mountains" (Ps. 104:6). God separated the light from the darkness (Gen. 1:4b), and the light became day and the darkness night. "And there was evening and there was morning, the first day" (Gen. 1:5b). In the biblical tradition, as represented in modern Judaism, the day began in the evening and ended in the morning.

The creation continued as God spoke again: "Let there be a dome in the midst of the waters, and let it separate the waters from the waters" (Gen. 1:6). The dome was the sky, and God "separated the waters that were under the dome from the waters that were above the dome" (Gen. 1:7b). The waters under the dome were gathered into one place, allowing the dry land to appear (Gen. 1:9). The dry land was the earth, and the waters became the seas. The waters were assigned boundaries, as indicated by the following parallels: "If I take the winds of the morning and settle at the farthest limits of the sea" (Ps. 139:9), and "when he assigned to the sea its limits, so that the waters might not transgress his command" (Prov. 8:29a).

On the fifth day God said: "Let the waters bring forth swarms of living creatures, and let birds fly above the earth across the dome of the sky. So God created the great sea monsters and every living creature that moves ...." Gen. 1:20−21a). The psalmists regarded the sea monsters as the mythic personifications of the primal ocean: "You divided the sea by your might; you broke the heads of the dragons in the waters" (Ps. 74:13), and: "Yonder is the sea, great and wide, creeping things innumerable are there, living things both small and great. There go the ships, and Leviathan that you formed to sport in it" (Ps. 104:25−26). Leviathan was the mythological sea monster.

The process came to a climax with the creation of humankind in the image of God: "Let us make humankind in our image, according to our likeness; and let them have dominion over the fish of the sea ...." (Gen. 1:26ab) The use of the plural of majesty—as with "our image"— strengthened the form of the image of God. Bearing the image, humanity was given the fertility mandate: "Be fruitful and multiply, fill the earth and subdue it; and have dominion over the fish of the sea ...." (Gen. 1:28bc) The meaning of dominion will be discussed below in chapter five and the conclusion, but whatever it meant in biblical times it imparted a hierarchy of humanity over nature.

Chapter two of Genesis featured the creation of the man from the ground by means of the divine Spirit or breath. At the same time "a stream would rise from the earth, and water the whole face of the ground ...." (Gen. 2:6) The watering turned the ground into Eden, a garden of delight, containing rivers and trees.

> A river flows out of Eden to water the garden, and from there it divides and becomes four branches. The name of the first is Pishon; and it is the one that flows around the whole land of Havilah, where there is gold; and the gold of that land is good; bdellium and onyx stone are there. The name of the second river is Gihon; it is the one that flows around the whole land of Cush. The name of the third river is Tigris, which flows east of Assyria. And the fourth river is the Euphrates (Gen. 2:10−14).

The Gihon was the main source of water for the city of Jerusalem: "This same Hezekiah closed the upper outlet of the waters of Gihon and directed them down to the west side of the city of David" (2 Chron. 32:30). When expecting the Assyrian siege, King Hezekiah ordered the building of a tunnel under Jerusalem, causing the waters of Gihon to flow into the Pool of Siloam, or *Shiloah* in Hebrew, on the other less vulnerable side of the city (Shanks 2005: 16–18). The Gihon was the source of the gently flowing waters of Shiloah that symbolized for the prophet Isaiah a quiet trust in God in contrast to the mighty waters of the Euphrates that symbolized Assyrian military power (Levenson 2006: 87).

> The Lord spoke to me again: Because this people have refused the waters of Shiloah that flow gently, and melt in fear before Rezin and the son of Remaliah; therefore, the Lord is bringing up against it the mighty flood waters of the River [Euphrates], the King of Assyria and all his glory; it will rise above all its channels and over flow all its banks; it will sweep on into Judah as a flood .... (Isa. 8:5–8a)

In the story of Noah the "Lord saw that the wickedness of humankind was great in the earth, and that every inclination in the thoughts of their hearts was only evil continually" (Gen. 6:5). God was deeply grieved that he had created humankind on the earth and said: "I will blot out from the earth the human beings I have created—people together with animals and creeping things and birds of the air, for I am sorry that I have made them" (Gen. 6:7). God instructed Noah to build an ark and bring into it two of every living thing. "For my part, I am going to bring a flood of waters on the earth, to destroy from under heaven all flesh in which is the breath of life; everything that is on the earth shall die" (Gen. 6:17). The biblical story of the flood paralleled Tablet XI of the Epic of Gilgamesh and the Mesopotamian story of the flood (Foster 2003: 458).

Rain fell for seven days, and the flood lasted 40 days and 40 nights (Gen. 7:4a). The "fountains of the great deep burst forth, and the windows of the heavens were opened" (Gen. 7:11b). The force of the waters threatened to reduce the earth to the chaos of the primeval ocean. The waters of the flood "swelled so mightily on the earth that all of the high mountains under the whole heaven were covered; the waters swelled above the mountains, covering them fifteen cubits deep" (Gen. 7:19–20). The waters flowed on the earth for 150 days (Gen. 7:24), and all living beings perished.

In the manner of the primal cross-over, "God made a wind blow over the earth, and the waters subsided; the fountains of the deep and the windows of the heavens were closed, the rain from the heavens was restrained" Gen. 8:1b–2). Noah sent out a raven and a dove, but they found no resting place. Seven days later he sent out the dove which came back with a freshly picked olive leaf. Knowing that the flood had receded, Noah sent out the dove again, and it did not return (Gen. 8:12).

God determined that never again would a flood destroy all life on earth, and God established a covenant with humankind and all other living beings: "I have set my bow in the clouds, and it shall be a sign of the covenant between me and the earth" (Gen. 9:14). In the Ancient Near East the rainbow represented the bow of the warrior storm god (Ps. 7:12–13; Lam. 2:4; Hab. 3:9–11), and in the Noah story God set his warrior bow aside as a divine disarmament, promising to withhold a final destruction (Knauth 2000: 1107–1108). When the rainbow appeared in the clouds, that was a sign of God's everlasting covenant with all life (Gen. 9:16).

The flood story co-existed with the creation story as monumental events in primeval time, and they reflected an ancient consciousness that life was subject to creation and destruction (Westermann 1994: 50–52). The two stories witnessed to the fact that water gave life and brought death. The Noah story, in particular, demonstrated that when water took the form of the primal ocean, it became an element of death (Bleeker 1963: 133).

Water and the Exodus

Following the drama of the flood, the story of Abraham inaugurated biblical history. As with Noah, God made a covenant with Abraham, promising a land in which his numerous descendants would prosper: "To your descendants I give this land, from the river of Egypt to the great river, the river Euphrates" (Gen. 15:18b).

The narrative portrays the patriarchs Abraham, Isaac, and Jacob and the latter's 12 sons as the ancestors of the Hebrew tribes. Genesis 46:8–27 lists the names of Jacob's offspring as immigrants in Egypt. Altogether, "the persons of the house of Jacob who came into Egypt were seventy" (Gen. 46:27). After settling in Egypt, the Hebrews increased in numbers and power, threatening pharaoh and the Egyptians. Consequently, Egyptian authorities forced the Hebrew people to do hard labor; and in order to reduce their population pharaoh decreed the following policy: "Every boy that is born to the Hebrews you shall throw into the Nile, but you shall let every girl live" (Ex. 1:22).

Moses was born into the family of Levi, which included two older siblings, Miriam and Aaron. For three months after his birth Moses' mother hid him at home. When she could no longer hide him, "she got a papyrus basket for him, and plastered it with bitumen and pitch; she put the child in it and placed it among the reeds on the bank of the river" (Ex. 2:3). The daughter of pharaoh went to the river to bathe, and, finding the baby, she took him home and raised him as her adopted son. The story paralleled the legend of the birth of Sargon I as an etiological explanation of the miraculous origin of Moses (Beegle 1972: 53).

When Moses had grown up, he saw an Egyptian beating a Hebrew to death. Moses intervened, killed the Egyptian, and buried his body in the sand (Ex. 2:12). After the crime had become known and pharaoh had sought to kill him because of the murder, Moses fled from Egypt into the land of Midia, where he worked as a shepherd for Jethro, a Midianite priest. While tending the flock one day on Mount Sinai, Moses beheld a vision of the burning bush, out of which God spoke, revealing the divine name and commissioning him to return to Egypt and lead the Hebrews out of bondage (Ex. 3:6, 10). At first Moses resisted, but then he submitted to God's summons. With his brother Aaron Moses went back to Egypt and confronted pharaoh with God's demand: "Let my people go ...." (Ex. 5:1c) Pharaoh adamantly rejected God's demand.

God instructed Moses to meet pharaoh on a bank of the Nile River and, holding a staff in his hand, strike the river water: "and all the water in the river was turned to blood, and the fish in the river died. The river stank so that the Egyptians could not drink its water, and there was blood throughout the whole land of Egypt. And all the Egyptians had to dig along the Nile for water to drink, for they could not drink the water of the river" (Ex. 7:20b–21, 24).

Seven days passed, and Moses struck the river water again and brought out frogs all over Egypt, including its rivers, canals, and pools (Ex. 8:5). The struggle continued, as God released additional plagues through Moses, but pharaoh remained adamant. Finally, on the night of the tenth plague God instructed the people to sacrifice one year-old unblemished male lambs, eating their roasted flesh with unleavened bread and bitter herbs and smearing some of the sacrificial blood on the doorposts and lintels of their houses (Ex. 12:7–8). During the night, God passed over Egypt, striking down all the first born of the Egyptians (Ex. 12:29).

The Hebrews left Egypt in the night under Moses' leadership, and when arriving at the Red Sea, or technically in Hebrew the Reed Sea, Moses stretched out his hand over the sea, and the "Lord drove the sea back by a strong east wind all night, and turned the sea into dry land, and the waters were divided" (Ex. 14:21). After the people passed through the sea, Moses extended his hand again, causing the waters to come back, and drown the chariots of the pursuing Egyptian army. "Thus the Lord saved Israel that day from the Egyptians; and Israel saw the Egyptians dead on the seashore" (Ex. 14:30).

The deliverance of the people from bondage in Egypt, known as the Exodus in the Hebrew-Christian tradition, reenacted the primal cross-over of the creation (Gen. 1:1–2). Salvation at the Red Sea was a conquest of the primal waters at the beginning of creation (Tromp 1969: 61). The salvation was celebrated in the Hymn to the Divine Warrior in Exodus chapter 15: "The Lord is a warrior; the Lord is his name. Pharaoh's chariots and his army he cast into the sea; his picked officers were sunk in the Red Sea. The floods covered them; they went down into the depths like a stone" (Ex. 15:3–5).

When moving from the Red Sea into the wilderness, the people found no water after journeying for three days. "When they came to Marah, they could not drink the water of Marah because it was bitter" (Ex. 5:23a). The people complained against Moses, who cried out to God, "saying 'What shall we drink?'" God showed Moses a piece of wood, and "he threw it into the water, and the water became sweet" (Ex. 15:25). The quality and the quantity of the water in the Sinai desert varied seasonally, so that a spring might be drinkable at one time but not at another. A long-standing tradition has maintained that brackish water could be made drinkable by putting a bitter thornbush into it (Beegle 1972: 171).

When the water became sweet to drink, God enacted a statute and an ordinance as a test and said: "If you will listen carefully to the voice of the Lord your God, and do what is right in his sight, and give heed to his commandments and keep all his statutes, I will not bring upon you any of the diseases that I brought upon the Egyptians; for I am the Lord who heals you" (Ex. 15:26). In the Jewish tradition Marah was the place where the earliest instructions were given for observing the Sabbath (Wilbanks 2000: 855).

The people continued on their journey, but once again they found no water and blamed Moses. He said to them: "Why do you quarrel with me? Why do you test the Lord?" (Ex. 17:2b) They replied: "Why did you bring us out of Egypt, to kill us and our children and livestock with thirst?" (Ex. 17:3b) Moses asked God what he should do with the people. God told him to carry the staff with which he had struck the Nile and, accompanied by some of the elders, stand in front of the rock at Horeb: "Strike the rock, and water will come out of it, so that the people may drink" (Ex. 17:6b) "Moses did so, in the sight of the elders of Israel. He called the place Massah and Meribah, because the Israelites quarreled and tested the Lord, saying 'Is the Lord among us or not?'" (Ex. 17:7). Massah meant "testing" and Meribah "fault-finding," and this was probably located in the limestone region of Qadesh-barnea, where water flowed from porous limestone (Beegle 1972: 184).

The drama resumed with the promulgation of the Law or *Torah* on Mount Sinai. The Law contained three systems of divine positive law: The

Covenant Code (Ex. 20:22–23; 33), The Holiness Code (Lev. 17–26), and The Deuteronomic Law (Deut. 12–26). The Holiness Code prescribed ethical duties for the people who were set apart for a special relationship with God. The following prescription is one example: "If you follow my statutes and keep my commandments and observe them faithfully, I will give you your rains in their season, and the land shall yield its produce, and the trees of the field shall yield their fruit" (Lev. 26:3–4).

The purpose of the people's journey through the desert was to acquire and occupy the land promised to them by God through Abraham. The promised land differed from that of Egypt, where the Nile Valley was irrigated by the annual flooding of the river for the production of crops. "But the land that you are crossing over to occupy is a land that the Lord your God looks after" (Deut. 11:11). The people were instructed to obey God's commandment, by loving the Lord "with all your heart and with all your soul" (Deut. 11:13). The succeeding verse served as the paradigm of rain in ancient Israel: "Then he will give the rain for your land in its season, the early rain and the later rain, and you will gather in your grain, your wine, and your oil ...." (Deut. 11:14). In Palestine the early rains came in October, often with violent thunderstorms, and rainfall continued sporadically throughout the winter until ending with the later rains in April (Meyers and Meyers 1993: 181–182). Thus, the ancient Israelites practiced rainfall agriculture in which crops were dependent on seasonal rains rather than on water from springs, lakes, or rivers. The Bible equated the granting of rain with divine blessing and the withholding of rain, as in periodic droughts, with divine wrath.

On arriving at the boundary of the promised land, Moses and Aaron were not permitted to enter it, "because both of you broke faith with me among the Israelites at the waters of Meribath-kadesh in the wilderness of Zin, by failing to maintain my holiness among the Israelites" (Deut. 32:51). As explained in Numbers chapter 20, there was no water for the people at Kadesh, and the people complained. "The Lord spoke to Moses, saying: 'Take the staff, and assemble the congregation, you and your brother Aaron, and command the rock before their eyes to yield its water. Thus you shall bring water out of the rock for them; thus you shall provide drink for the congregation and their livestock'" (Numb. 20:7–8a).

Moses did as the Lord commanded, but the Lord said to Moses. "Because you did not trust in me, to show my holiness before the eyes of the Israelites, therefore you shall not bring this assembly into the land that I have given them" (Numb. 20:12). At God's command Moses died in the land of Moab and was buried in an unmarked grave (Deut. 34:5–6).

Water and the Rites of Purity

The book of Leviticus contains ancient priestly writings that clarify the distinction between purity and impurity. As an example, Leviticus prescribes purification rituals with water for leprosy and bodily discharges. To be cleansed the leper has to "wash his clothes, and shave off all his hair, and bathe himself in water, and he shall be clean" (Lev. 14:8). Some water rituals also deal with seminal emissions;

> All who sit on anything on which the one with the discharge has sat shall wash their clothes, and bathe in water, and be unclean until evening (Lev. 15:6).

> All those whom the one with the discharge touches without his having rinsed his hands in water shall wash their clothes, and bathe in water, and be unclean until evening (Lev. 15:11).

> When the one with a discharge is cleansed of his discharge, he shall count seven days for his cleansing; he shall wash his clothes and bathe his body in fresh water, and he shall be clean (Lev. 15:13).

Unlike Israel's neighbors in the Ancient Near East the Israelites believed that water was purification only by the will of God and not regenerative by magical means. Water did not possess inherent purification qualities. Bathing in water did not require that water be pure; and in the 36 places that the priestly writings called for bathing in water only one, Leviticus 15:13 cited above, specified running or spring water (Milgrom 1991: 963). In ancient Israelite law purification followed healing. Purification was not a precondition for healing, as it was in the Ancient Near East. In Israel purification set in by the evening of the day of the ablution. Impurity wore off gradually.

Elsewhere in the Bible sanctification was the equivalent of purification effected on the day before receiving a revelation from God (Milgrom 1991: 465). In preparation for the promulgation of the Law on Mount Sinai God instructed Moses:

> Go to the people and consecrate them today and tomorrow. Have them wash their clothes and prepare for the third day, because on the third day the Lord will come down upon Mount Sinai in the sight of all people. You shall set limits for the people all around, saying, "Be careful not to go up the mountain or to touch the edge of it. Any who touch the mountain shall be put to death."

> So Moses went down from the mountain to the people. He consecrated the people, and they washed their clothes. And he said to the people, "Prepare for the third day; do not go near a woman" (Ex. 19:10–12, 14–15).

Thus, purification through washing and laundering also entailed a prohibition against sexual intercourse.

Sanctification on the day preceding divine revelation was illustrated further in the people's crossing the Jordan River. The Jordan was the boundary the people had to cross over to reach the promised land. They camped near the river before crossing over, and Joshua, Moses' successor, commanded the people to "Sanctify yourselves; for tomorrow the Lord will do wonders among you" (Josh. 3:5). Then God said to Joshua: "This day I will begin to exalt you in the sight of all Israel, so that they may know that I will be with you as I was with Moses. You are the one who shall command the priests who bear the ark of the covenant, 'When you come to the edge of the waters of the Jordan, you shall stand still in the Jordan'" (Josh. 3:7–8).

Joshua invited the people to hear the words of the Lord: "By this you shall know that among you is the living God" (Josh. 3:10a), who will drive out the enemies of Israel. Joshua continued to say that: "When the soles of the feet of the priests who bear the ark of the Lord, the Lord of all the earth, rest in the waters of the Jordan, the waters of the Jordan flowing from above shall be cut off; they shall stand in a single heap" (Josh. 3:13).

The image of the waters standing "in a single heap" was a quotation of a verse in the Song of Moses that the people sang after passing through the Red Sea in the Exodus: "At the blast of your nostrils the waters piled up. The floods stood up in a heap, the deeps congealed in the heart of the sea" (Ex. 15:8). As in the Exodus, God led the people through the dried up river bed of the Jordan to the promised land.

God commanded Joshua to select 12 men, representing the 12 tribes of Israel, to place 12 stones on the river bank to commemorate the people's crossing the Jordan River (Josh. 4:1–7). Joshua explained to the people: "For the Lord your God dried up the waters of the Jordan for you until you crossed over, as the Lord your God did to the Red Sea, which he dried up for us until we crossed over so that the peoples of the earth may know that the hand of the Lord is mighty, and so that you may fear the Lord your God forever" (Josh. 4: 23–24).

Water and Justice

In the perspective of the Hebrew Bible God was sovereign over nature and history, and God disclosed his transcendent intentions to his prophets. The prophets were the spokespersons for God, and their vocation was two-fold. First, when God revealed a punitive judgment on the people, the prophet would announce this to them with the phrase, "thus says the Lord." Second, then the prophet would turn around and become a defender of the people, arguing against God's determination to punish the people and changing

God's wrath into God's love (Muffs 1992: 9). The prophet was both a messenger of God and a defender of the people. The Hebrew term for prophet was *nabi*, and its root, derived from Akkadian, meant "the called one" (Blenkinsopp 1983: 37).

Amos, a shepherd, was called to be a prophet during the middle of the eighth century BCE (Am. 1:1; 7:14). He brought indictments against Israel for its sins and injustices in violation of The Covenant Code (Blenkinsopp 1983: 96). Amos charged the people for not serving God in acts of love and kindness, and as a result of those failures God's punishment included seasons of water scarcity: "And I also withheld the rain from you when there were still three months to the harvest; I would send rain on one city, and send no rain on another city; one field would be rained upon, and the field on which it did not rain withered; so two or three towns wandered to one town to drink water, and were not satisfied; yet you did not return to me, says the Lord" (Am. 4:7).

Amos rejected, in particular, the people's preference for sacrifices and festivals as substitutes for justice. This criticism appeared in chapter five and culminated in the following declaration: "But let justice roll down like waters, and righteousness like an ever flowing stream" (Am. 5:24). With water imagery Amos correlated the fundamental ideals of justice and righteousness. Justice was a ruling made by a judge, and it meant norm, ordinance, legal right, or law (Heschel 1962: 200). Justice was a specific juridical holding and formal balance of claims, in which persons received what was due to them. Righteousness was an act of kindness, generosity, or compassion flowing out to persons beyond the formality of law (Heschel 1962: 201). Righteousness brought compassion to the oppressed. While justice and righteousness were conceptually distinct, they always had to come together in legal decisions.

Amos affirmed the sovereignty of God over nature and history. "The Lord, God of hosts, he who touches the earth and it melts, and all who live in it mourn, and all of it rises like the Nile, and sinks again, like the Nile of Egypt ... who calls for the waters of the sea, and pours them out upon the surface of the earth—the Lord is his name" (Am. 9:5–6cd).

From the creation story the Hebrews believed that water was always present, due to the primal ocean out of which the earth was created, and the people feared that the earth might fall back into the void and chaos of the ocean (Barr 1998: 60). This fear was expressed by the prophet Jeremiah, who said: "I looked on the earth, and lo, it was waste and void ...." (Jer. 4:23a)

Jeremiah referred to God as "the fountain of living water," and he charged that the people had abandoned God "and dug out cisterns for themselves, cracked cisterns that can hold no water" (Jer. 2:13). Jeremiah's declaration implied that clean, running water was pure and stagnant water impure. The prophet went on to lament a catastrophic drought coming over Jerusalem. The "cry of the city goes up," and her "nobles send their servants for water; they come to the cisterns, they find no water, they return with their vessels empty" (Jer. 14:2c–3abc). The people are troubled, and they hang their heads in shame, "because the ground is cracked ... and there has been no rain on the land the farmers are dismayed; they cover their heads" (Jer. 14:4). Lack of rainfall means the land has no grass on which the animals can graze. Jeremiah's indictment culminates in the following charge: "O hope of Israel! O Lord! All who forsake you shall be put to shame; those who turn away from you shall be recorded in the underworld, for they have forsaken the fountain of living water, the Lord" (Jer. 17:13).

The prophet Isaiah, proclaiming the wickedness of the tribe of Judah, drew upon ablution imagery in his exhortation of justice: "Wash yourselves; make yourselves clean; remove the evil of your doings from before my eyes; cease to do evil, learn to do good; seek justice, rescue the oppressed, defend the orphan, plead for the widow" (Isa. 1:16–17).

Isaiah appealed to the theme of "mighty waters" as a metaphor of judgment upon the nations. Whether used in parallel with rivers, the deep, or the sea, the mighty waters expressed a primal force of chaos over which God asserted control (Knauth 2000: 854). "Ah, the roar of nations, they roar like the roaring of mighty waters! The nations roar like the roaring of many waters, but he will rebuke them ...." (Isa. 17:12b–13a) Isaiah's oracle against Sidon had the same motif: "Be still, O inhabitants of the coast, O merchants of Sidon, your messengers crossed over the sea and were on the mighty waters .... Be ashamed O Sidon, for the sea has spoken ...." (Isa. 23:2,4a).

Isaiah foresaw a peaceful reign of God centered in Jerusalem: "But there the Lord in majesty will be for us a place of broad rivers and streams, where no galley with oars can go, nor stately ship can pass" (Isa. 33:21). Thus, the land will be watered for people's needs but not for warships. For Isaiah water also signified hope for the renewal of creation at the end of time: "For waters shall break forth in the wilderness, and streams in the desert; the burning sand shall become a pool, and the thirsty ground springs of water; the haunt of jackals shall become a swamp, the grass shall become reeds and rushes" (Isa. 35:6c–7).

The prophet of the Babylonian Exile, known as the Second Isaiah, envisaged God as the creator who has assigned boundaries to the creation. "Who has measured the waters in the hollow of his hand and marked off the heavens with a span, enclosed the dust of the earth in a measure …?" (Isa. 40:12abc) As creator, God preserves the life of the people. "When the poor and the needy seek water, and there is none, and their tongue is parched with thirst, I the Lord will answer them, I the God of Israel will not forsake them. I will open rivers on the bare heights, and fountains in the midst of the valleys; I will make the wilderness a pool of water, and the dry land springs of water" (Isa. 41:17–18).

Reflecting the Exodus story of the deliverance of the people through the Red Sea, the Second Isaiah declared:

> When you pass through the waters, I will be with you; and through the rivers, they shall not overwhelm you …. (Isa. 43:2ab)

> I am about to do a new thing; how it springs forth, do you not perceive it? I will make a way in the wilderness, rivers in the desert, to give drink to my chosen people …. (Isa. 43:19–20)

> Was it not you who cut Rahab in pieces, who pierced the dragon? Was it not you who dried up the sea, the waters of the great deep, who made the depths of the sea a way for the redeemed to cross over? (Isa. 51:9c–10)

The Second Isaiah also made water a metaphor of God's life-giving word: "For as the rain and the snow come down from heaven, and do not return there until they have watered the earth, making it spring forth and sprout, giving seed to the sower and bread to the eater, so shall my word that goes out from my mouth; it shall not return to me empty, but it shall accomplish that which I purpose, and succeed in the thing for which I sent it" (Isa. 55:10–11).

Similarly, Habakkuk's hymn in chapter three celebrated God's triumphant march through the desert: "Was your wrath against the rivers, O Lord? Or your anger against the rivers, or your rage against the sea, when you drove your horses, your chariots to victory? You split the earth with rivers. The mountains saw you and writhed; a torrent of water swept by ….You trampled the sea with your horses, churning the mighty waters" (Hab. 3:8, 9b–10, 15). In the vision of Habakkuk God conquered the watery chaos of rivers and the sea in a cosmic battle (Knauth 2000: 854).

Rivers as Blessings

The Bible maintains that water is both spiritual and nourishing, as illustrated in Psalm 42:1: "As a deer longs for flowing streams, so my soul longs for you, O God." Rivers, in particular, represent the blessings of God, originating with those in the creation story that spring up from the primal sea and flow across the land (Gen. 2:11–14).

According to the prophet Ezekiel, the Temple on "God's holy mountain" in Jerusalem was identified with the Garden of Eden (Eze. 28:13). This connection grew out of the ancient conception of the Temple as paradise or the ideal state of the world as intended by God the creator (Levenson 2006: 85). From the throne of God in the Temple water flowed to the east toward the Dead Sea, making its saline waters fresh. Ezekiel declared:

> Then he [God] brought me back to the entrance of the Temple; there, water was flowing from below the threshold of the Temple toward the east .... Then he led me back along the bank of the river. As I came back, I saw on the bank of the river a great many trees on the one side and on the other. He said to me, "This water flows toward the eastern region and goes down into the Arabah [valley south of the Dead Sea]; and when it enters the sea, the sea of stagnant waters, the water will become fresh (Eze. 47:1ab, 6b–8).

Ezekiel reflected a theme that Isaiah had stated, namely, that the water of the Temple was for people's needs and not for ships of war (Isa. 33:21). Similarly, the caring of the people by the Temple was celebrated by the psalmist: "There is a river whose streams make glad the city of God, the holy habitation of the Most High" (Ps. 46:4).

In the apocalyptic vision of the prophet Zechariah the renewal of the waters will occur at the end of time: "On that day living waters shall flow out from Jerusalem, half of them to the eastern sea and half of them to the western sea; it shall continue in summer as in winter" (Zech. 14:8). Zechariah maintained the tradition of Jeremiah (2:13) and Leviticus (15:13) of fresh water flowing from a natural spring rather than that collected in a cistern. By claiming that streams of freshwater will flow from the Temple he identified Jerusalem with the Garden of Eden in the creation story (Myers and Myers 1993: 435). The eastern sea is the Dead Sea (cf. Eze. 47:18), and the western sea is the Mediterranean (cf. Deut. 11:24; 34:2). In Zechariah's vision of the end water will be uniformly available throughout the entire year. There will be no seasonal variation between summer and winter. This claim reversed the concept of the heavenly storehouse of waters (Deut. 28:12) that provided rainfall seasonally (Meyers and Meyers 1993: 438). According to Deuteronomy (28:23–24) God could withhold rain depending upon the people's obedience to the Law.

Unlike Zechariah, however, Ezekiel and the prophet Joel envisioned that in the eschatological future the waters will flow abundantly from the Temple, and the waters will have fructifying qualities (Meyers and Myers 1993: 435–436). As cited above, Ezekiel foresaw trees flourishing on both sides of the river and the Dead Sea becoming fresh. Similarly, Joel foresaw: "In that day the mountains shall drip sweet wine, the hills shall flow with water; a fountain shall come forth from the house of the Lord and water the Wadi Shittim" (Joel 3:18).

For these prophets the saline and arid regions will become productive. Since the lands around Jerusalem were infertile and poorly watered, the prophetic vision of the abundance of freshwater was eschatological and not actual or realistic (Meyers and Meyers 1993: 437–438). Palestine has only two seasons, summer and winter, and rain has not always come during the growing seasons. Consequently, the prophets distinguished between the early rain and the later rain, or the early rain in October and November and the later rain in March and April (Jer. 5:24; Hos. 6:3; Joel 2:23; Zech. 10:1). The early rains came about the time of the Festival of Tabernacles or Booths (*Sukkoth*), and Zechariah threatened the withholding of rainfall for those who did not celebrate that festival: "Then all who survive of the nations that have come against Jerusalem shall go up year after year to worship the King, the Lord of Hosts, and to keep the festival of booths. If any of the families of the earth do not go up to Jerusalem to worship the King, the Lord of hosts, there will be no rain upon them" (Zech. 14:16–17).

Likewise, at the end of the New Testament the apocalyptic visionary John proclaimed the divine triumph over the watery chaos of the sea: "Then I saw a new heaven and a new earth; for the first heaven and first earth had passed away, and the sea was no more" (Rev. 21:1). John continued to declare: "Then the angel showed me the river of the water of life, bright as crystal, flowing from the Throne of God and of the Lamb through the middle of the street of the city" (Rev. 22:1–2a). In the holy city, as foreseen by John, there will be no temple but on each side of the river the Tree of Life will stand for the healing of the nations (Rev. 22:2bc). In the dramatic climax of John's vision the Risen Lord appeared and announced: "And let everyone who is thirsty come. Let anyone who wishes take the water of life as a gift" (Rev. 22:17cd).

Water and Women

In biblical times it was customary for women to fetch water from wells for their families. This practice was attested in the story of Isaac and Rebekah:

> He [Abraham's servant] made the camels kneel down outside the city by the well of water; it was toward evening, the time when women go out to draw water. And he said, "O Lord, God of my master Abraham, please grant me success today and show steadfast love to my master Abraham. I am standing here by the spring of water, and the daughters of the townspeople are coming out to draw water (Gen. 24:11–13).

Rebekah came to the spring, filled her jar, and approached Abraham's servant. "'Drink, my Lord,' she said, and quickly lowered her jar upon her head and gave him to drink" (Gen. 24:18). She drew water for all the camels. Later, Isaac went out for a walk in the evening and, seeing Rebekah, fell in love with her and took her for his wife.

In the next generation of the family Jacob, son of Isaac and Rebekah, travelled a dangerous desert journey and arrived at a well.

> As he looked, he saw a well in the field and three flocks of sheep lying there beside it; for out of that well the flocks were watered. The stone on the well's mouth was large, and when all the flocks were gathered there, the shepherds would roll the stone from the mouth of the well, and water the sheep, and put the stone back in its place on the mouth of the well (Gen. 29:2-3).

Rachel, a shepherdess, came with her father's sheep, and Jacob fell in love with her. Jacob's love for Rachel was immediate and impulsive, for she was a woman of mercy, caring, and independence (Dresner 1994: 30-34).

The same custom appeared in the story of Moses. After fleeing Egypt and entering into the land of the Midianites, Moses came to a well. The seven daughters of Jethro, the priest of Midian, "came to draw water, and filled the trough to water their father's flock. But some shepherds came and drove them away. Moses got up and came to their defense and watered their flock" (Ex. 2:16b-17). On hearing that Moses had helped his daughters, Jethro offered him hospitality. Moses agreed to stay with Jethro as a shepherd, and he took Jethro's daughter Zipporah as his wife.

In the Gospel of John Jesus travelled through Samaria and, becoming tired, sat down at Jacob's well in the middle of the day. A Samaritan woman came to the well, and Jesus asked her for a drink of water (Jhn. 4:7). She asked why a Jew would request water from a Samaritan woman, since the Jews regarded the Samaritans as their enemies. The theological reason for the enmity was that the Samaritans worshipped God and the gods (2 Kings 17:33) on hill tops in direct violation of the First Commandment of the Law of Moses (Ex. 20:1-3). "Jesus answered her, 'If you knew the gift of God, and who it is that is saying to you, 'Give me a drink,' you would have asked him, and he would have given you living water" (Jhn. 4:10). Thinking that Jesus meant actual, flowing water, the woman asked him where she could get the living water, since she had no bucket, and the well was deep. "Jesus said to her, 'Everyone who drinks of this water will be thirsty again, but those who drink of the water that I will give them will never be thirsty. The water that I will give will become in them a spring of water gushing up to eternal life'" (Jhn. 4:13-14).

She asked him for his water, so that she would never be thirsty or draw water again. Speaking in the tradition of Jeremiah's metaphor of "the fountain of living water" (Jer. 2:13), Jesus affirmed that the spirituality of water led to eternal life. In the Gospel of John the phrase "living water" refers to Jesus' revelation of eternal life and the Spirit given by Jesus (Brown 1966: 178–179).

As reported in the seventh chapter of the Gospel of John, Jesus spoke on the last day of the Festival of Tabernacles, which commemorated the Hebrews wandering in the desert after receiving the Torah on Mount Sinai.

> On the last day of the festival, the great day, while Jesus was standing there, he cried out, "Let anyone who is thirsty come to me, and let the one who believes in me drink. As the scripture has said, "Out of the believer's heart shall flow rivers of living water." Now he said this about the Spirit, which believers in him were to receive; for as yet there was no Spirit, because Jesus was not yet glorified ((Jhn. 3:37–39).

In ancient Israel the Festival of Tabernacles was linked to the Day of the Lord, when the messianic king would enter Jerusalem. As portrayed in Zechariah 9–11, God would open up the fountain for the house of David to cleanse Jerusalem, and living waters would flow out from Jerusalem to the Mediterranean Sea and the Dead Sea (Zech. 14:8). In the background of the festival was the expectation of abundant rainfall in late September or early October, the time of the festival, assuring fertile crops for the following year (Brown 1966: 326).

On each of the seven days of the festival a solemn ceremony took place. A procession went down to the Gihon Spring on the southwest side of the Temple hill. This was the spring that supplied the waters of the Pool of Siloam. As discovered by archaeologists, the Pool of Siloam measured 225 feet wide, and it had three sets of stairs that descended into the water which was used for ritual bathing (Shanks 2005:19–20, 22). At the pool a priest filled a golden pitcher with water, and the choir recited: "With joy you will draw water from the wells of salvation" (Isa. 12:3). Then the procession went up to the Temple through the Water Gate, as the accompanying crowd carried the symbols of the festival, myrtle and willow twigs tied with a palm and a lemon. They sang the Hallelujah Psalms (Pss. 113–118). When arriving at the altar in front of the Temple, the crowd circulated it carrying the twigs and singing Psalm 118:25: "Save us, we beseech you, O Lord! O Lord, we beseech you, give us success!" Finally, the priest went up the ramp to the altar and poured water into a silver funnel through which it flowed into the ground. On the seventh day the participants walked around the altar seven times.

In the gospel story after the seven-fold circumambulation Jesus stood up in the Temple and proclaimed that he was the source of living water. On the backdrop of Zechariah 14:8 and Ezekiel 47:1, cited above, Jesus said the rivers of living water will flow from his body (Brown 1966: 327). The Gospel of John identified Jesus' body with the Temple (Jhn. 2:21). Whereas in the desert Moses struck a rock to bring forth water, now they who thirst need only to come to Jesus to receive his revelation and the Spirit of eternal life.

Jesus' Cross-Over

The primal cross-over of the creation was renewed not only in the Exodus but also in Jesus' ministry, as recorded in the Gospel of Mark. His ministry began when he was baptized by John the Baptist in the Jordan River. "And just as he was coming up out of the waters, he saw the heavens torn apart and the Spirit descending like a dove on him" (Mk. 1:10). Literally, in the Greek text the Spirit descended into [*eis*] Jesus, thereby possessing him. After the ascending and descending parallel, a voice from heaven sounded: "You are my Son, the beloved; with you I am well pleased" (Mk. 1:11). The splitting of the heavens was a common motif in apocalyptic situations, and it occurred in the context of visions (Husser 1999: 131).

Following the baptism, the author of Mark used the water metaphor in the form of the sea (*thalassa*) 19 times, by my count, in order to characterize Gennesaret, or the Sea of Galilee, as a large body of water. "As Jesus passed along the Sea of Galilee, he saw Simon and his brother Andrew casting a net into the sea—for they were fishermen" (Mk. 1:16). The Greek text reads literally "casting a net in [*en*] the sea." This implies that Simon and Andrew were standing in the sea, because they did not have a boat. Further, to develop the cross-over motif the Markan author combined the sea with the images of moving or travelling. "Jesus went out again beside the sea; the whole crowd gathered around him, and he taught them" (Mk. 2:13). "Jesus departed with his disciples to the sea, and a great multitude from Galilee followed him ...." (Mk. 3:7)

In the first verse of Mark chapter four the term for sea appeared three times. "Again he began to teach beside the sea. Such a very large crowd gathered around him that he got into a boat on the sea, and sat there, while the whole crowd was beside the sea on the land" (Mk. 4:1). Further, in the story Jesus rebuked the sea while riding in a boat during a storm: "A great windstorm arose, and the waves beat into the boat, so that the boat was already swamped. But he was in the stern asleep on the cushion .... He woke up and rebuked the wind, and said to the sea, 'Peace! Be still!'" (Mk. 4:37–38a, 39a). In the ancient Mediterranean world mastery of the sea was ascribed to the Roman emperors, and Mark transferred such mastery to Jesus (Bolt 2003: 132). Storms at sea brought threats of death and a source of grief due to a lack of proper burial for those who drowned (Bolt 2003: 137).

The Markan author extended Jesus' cross-over motif in his sea journeys:

> On that day, when evening had come he said to them, "Let us go across to the other side" (Mk. 4:35).

> When they had crossed over, they came to land at Gennesaret and moored the boat (Mk. 6:53).

> And immediately he got into the boat with his disciples and went to the district of Dalmanutha (Mk. 8:10).

Both the cross-over and the sea motifs converged in Jesus' healing of the Gerasene Demoniac. "They came to the other side of the sea, to the country of the Gerasenes" (Mk. 5:1). The demoniac came out of the tombs where he lived, howling and bruising himself with stones. Jesus healed him from possession by unclean spirits and sent them into a herd of swine grazing nearby. "And the unclean spirits came out and entered the swine; and the herd, numbering about two thousand, rushed down the steep bank into the sea, and were drowned in the sea" (Mk. 5:13). Then Jesus made another cross-over. "When Jesus had crossed again in the boat to the other side, a great crowd gathered around him, and he was by the sea" (Mk. 5:21).

Jesus' cross-overs in the gospel story frequently occurred in the darkness or the night. In the New Testament the night was the time of the revelation of nature and of the will of God (Bleeker 1963: 79–80). The gospel story ended with the crucifixion of Jesus, when he cried out in agony and abandonment in the darkness (Mk. 15:33–37). In the older Hebrew tradition the desert, the sea, and the darkness were the zones of death, where *Sheol*, the underground realm of death, appeared on the surface of the earth (Keel 1985: 62). Jesus passed through all of those zones in his ministry, thereby demonstrating his conquest of death.

At the center of the gospel story loomed the mystery of darkness (Grayston 1952: 123–126). The darkness reenacted that at the creation when the Spirit passed over the waters of the primeval ocean (Gen. 1:2). Since Jesus' cross-overs mainly responded to the cries of the sick and afflicted, when the sun had set (Mk. 1:32, 34), the darkness also represented that of the Exodus (Ex. 12:29–32), when God passed over Egypt, amid the cries of death, and delivered his people through the sea into freedom.

Summary

In the biblical narratives the cross-over theme originated in the creation story, when the Spirit of God passed over the dark, chaotic waters of the primordial ocean and separated the elements of the world. The story culminated in the creation of humankind in the image of God which established human dominion over nature. The climactic setting of the creation was the Garden of Eden through which rivers flowed from the primal sea. The creation narrative also included Noah's flood in which waters became a destructive force in punishment of human evil. Unlike the riparian religions water was a means of creation and destruction, blessing and curse, according to the divine command.

The Exodus story included the miraculous birth legend of Moses, as a parallel with that of Sargon, and a renewal of the primal cross-over in the people's passage from slavery through the sea to freedom. The people journeyed through the wilderness to the promised land of Israel where water came from seasonal rainfall. God granted rain as a blessing for obedience to divine commandments and withheld rain as a curse for disobedience. Water was also an agent of purification in the healing of disease and in preparation for receiving divine revelation.

The prophets were spokespersons for God who frequently called for justice with water imagery. Jeremiah identified God as the fountain of living water, and he distinguished between pure flowing water and impure stagnant water. Isaiah foresaw a future age of peace when the land would be watered for people's needs and not for warships. The Second Isaiah and Habakkuk portrayed a future salvation as a reenactment of crossing the sea in the Exodus. Ezekiel, Zechariah, and Joel envisioned a future when water would be abundantly available all year and not only during seasonal rainfall. For Ezekiel and Joel water would flow from the Temple, as it did in the Garden of Eden.

The Bible preserved the ancient custom of women going to a well to fetch water. The Gospel of John developed the theme of living water in Jesus' encounter with the Samaritan woman at Jacob's well. John identified Jesus as the source of living water on the backdrop of the eschatological vision of water flowing from the Temple for Ezekiel and Joel. Unlike the prophets, however, Jesus' body replaced the Temple. In the Gospel of Mark Jesus' ministry reenacted the cross-over motif of creation and the Exodus, as he crossed over the waters and through the desert in the darkness or the night. Jesus' ministry responded to the cries of the sick and the oppressed, and his passage through the waters, the desert, and the darkness demonstrated his mastery of death.

Chapter Four: Sacrament of Baptism

Biblical Origins

Within the Christian faith the Sacrament of Baptism is a water ritual that initiates members into the church. Historically, the decisive event was the baptism of Jesus by John the Baptist, as recorded in the Synoptic Gospels. Mark, the earliest gospel, reported that as Jesus "was coming up out of the water, he saw the heavens torn apart and the Spirit descending like a dove into him. And a voice came from heaven, 'You are my Son, the Beloved; with you I am well pleased'" (Mk. 1:9−11). After the baptism, the Spirit drove Jesus into the desert for 40 days, when he was tempted by Satan and wild beasts, but he prevailed (Mk. 1:12−13).

The two other synoptics reported Jesus' baptism, and they emphasized the Spirit descending upon him (Matt. 3:16; Lk. 3:22). All three gospels stated that John baptized people for repentance and the remission of sin (Mk. 1:4; Matt. 1:6, 8; Lk. 3:3). The Gospel of John neither stated explicitly that John the Baptist baptized Jesus nor that the Baptist preached a baptism of repentance for the forgiveness of sin. The probable reason for the omission was that by the end of the first century, when John was written, saying Jesus was baptized for remission of sin would have been an embarrassment (Mitchell 1995: 243). John portrayed Jesus as the Word made flesh, the Lamb of God, the one who came from heaven, and the source of living water leading to eternal life. Such titles were hardly compatible with repentance and the remission of sin.

All the gospels proclaimed that John the Baptist baptized with water and that he would be followed by a more eminent figure who would baptize with the Holy Spirit (Mk. 1:8; Matt. 3:11; Lk. 3:22; Jhn. 1:26, 33). All the gospels also reported John's proclamation of Isaiah 40:3, as a messenger crying out in the wilderness, to prepare the way of the Lord (Mk. 1:2−3; Matt. 3:3; Lk. 3:4−6; Jhn. 1:23). Matthew and Luke clarified that Jesus as the imminent divine agent would baptize with Spirit and fire to escape the wrath to come: "His winnowing fork is in his hand, and he will clear his threshing floor and will gather his wheat into the granary; but the chaff he will burn with unquenchable fire" (Matt. 3:12; cf. Lk. 3:17). Thus, John the Baptist was a forerunner of Jesus, anticipating Jesus as a divine agent who would intervene in the world in the prophetic-apocalyptic tradition (Collins 1995: 38).

Of all the gospels, however, only Matthew presented the command of Jesus as the Risen Lord after his resurrection: "Go therefore and make disciples of all nations, baptizing them in the name of the Father and of the Son and of the Holy Spirit ...." (Matt. 28:19). This commandment connected preaching and baptism, and it reaffirmed the same connection at the beginning of the gospel, namely, the preaching of repentance and baptizing for the remission of sin by John the Baptist (Johnson 1993: 8).

The Acts of the Apostles confirmed that Christian baptism originated in John's baptism of Jesus (1:21–22; 16:37). Whereas John baptized for repentance, the early Christians baptized in or into the name of Jesus or in the name of God the Father, the Son, and the Holy Spirit, thereby conferring an identity and ownership (Spinks 2006: 5–6). As an example, Peter made an invitation to Jews in Jerusalem on Pentecost: "Peter said to them, 'Repent, and be baptized every one of you in the name of Jesus Christ so that your sins may be forgiven; and you will receive the gift of the Holy Spirit'" (Acts 2:38). Thus, the fundamental meaning of baptism for the early Christians was a washing or cleansing of sin, and this meaning originated in the preaching of John the Baptist.

Within the gospel tradition two sayings ascribed to Jesus associated baptism metaphorically with his death (Collins 1995: 54):

> But Jesus said to them, "You do not know what you are asking. Are you able to drink the cup that I drink, or be baptized with the baptism that I am baptized with?" They replied, "We are able." Then Jesus said to them, "The cup that I drink you will drink; and with the baptism with which I am baptized, you will be baptized ...." (Mk. 10:38–39)
>
> I have a baptism with which to be baptized, and what stress I am under until it is completed! (Lk. 12:50)

The apostle Paul also said that baptism was associated with Jesus' death and resurrection:

> Do you not know that all of us who have been baptized into Christ Jesus were baptized into his death? Therefore we have been buried with him by baptism into death, so that, just as Christ was raised from the dead by the glory of the Father, so we too might walk in newness of life. For if we have been united with him in a death like his, we will certainly be united with him in a resurrection like his (Rom. 6:3–5).

Paul's question in verse three, cited above, was rhetorical, and he assumed that baptism was an established ritual of initiation (Spinks 2006: 3).

In another passage Paul elaborated on his view of death:

> For we know that if the earthly tent we live in is destroyed, we have a building from God, a house not made with hands, eternal in the heavens. For in this tent we groan,

longing to be clothed with our heavenly dwelling—if indeed, when we have taken it off, we will not be found naked. For while we are still in this tent, we groan under our burden, because we wish not to be unclothed but to be further clothed, so that what is mortal may be swallowed up by life (2 Cor. 5:1–4).

Paul's references to death, stripping of clothing, burial, and reclothing into a new life reflected the stages of the Greek funeral (Johnson 1993: 7). The first stage of the Greek funeral was the *prosthesis* or the laying out of the body, stripping the clothing and washing the body, followed by a reclothing in new clothes. The second stage was the *ekphora* or carrying out to the place of burial and funeral with a banquet (Burkert 1985: 190–194). The banquet or the third stage culminated a three day period of fasting, and the deceased in a disembodied spiritual form hosted the banquet (Davies 1999: 15).

Although baptism was principally performed in the name of Jesus or into Jesus' death and resurrection, it had other meanings as well. In his first letter to the Corinthians Paul linked baptism to the Exodus: "I do not want you to be unaware, brothers and sisters, that our ancestors were all under the cloud, and all passed through the sea, and all ate the same spiritual food, and all drank the same spiritual drink. For they drank from the spiritual rock that followed them, and the rock was Christ" (1 Cor. 10:1–4). These Exodus allusions meant that God had led the people out of Egypt under a cloud by day (Ex. 13:21), and they went into the Red Sea (Ex. 14:22); then God provided them food in the wilderness (Ex. 16:4–35) and water in the rock which Moses had to strike (Ex. 17:6).

In the same letter Paul also said that baptism conferred equality upon members of the church as the Body of Christ: "For just as the body is one and has many members, and all the members of the body, though many, are one body, so it is with Christ. For in the one Spirit we were all baptized into one body—Jew or Greek, slaves or free—and we were all made to drink of one Spirit" (1 Cor. 12:12–13). Paul asserted a new humanity in Christ as a body in the Spirit. By virtue of baptism, therefore, the Corinthians belonged to a new humanity unified by the mind of Christ (Lee 2006: 153, 160). For Paul mind was the equivalent of Spirit (1 Cor. 2:10–16).

Baptism conferred equality upon Christians as descendents of Abraham: "As many of you as were baptized into Christ have clothed yourselves with Christ, there is no longer slave or free, there is no longer male and female, for all of you are one in Christ Jesus. And if you belong to Christ, then you are Abraham's offspring, heirs according to the promise" (Gal. 3:28–29).

Paul understood equality in Christ as a rejection of slavery in the Roman Empire (Crossan 2007: 162). Baptism ensured freedom within the Christian community and independence from the social hierarchies and patronage systems of Roman society. Baptism as a washing ritual separated Christians from the unclean world and made them pure (Meeks 1983: 154). Paul insisted that "you were washed, you were sanctified, you were justified in the name of the Lord Jesus Christ and in the Spirit of our God" (1 Cor. 6:11bc).

Another reference to baptism as death and resurrection occurred in Colossians whose author, probably not Paul, connected stripping of the body with the Jewish rite of circumcision: "In him [Christ] also you were circumcised with a spiritual circumcision, by putting off the body of the flesh in the circumcision of Christ; when you were buried with him in baptism, you were also raised with him through faith in the power of God, who raised him from the dead" (Col. 2:11–12).

Additional interpretations of baptism came from the pastoral epistles. The author of First Peter viewed baptism in terms of Noah's flood:

> who in former times did not obey, when God waited patiently in the days of Noah, during the building of the ark, in which a few, that is, eight persons, were saved through water. And baptism, which this prefigured, now saves you—not as a removal of dirt from the body, but as an appeal to God for a good conscience, through the resurrection of Jesus Christ .... (1 Pet. 3:20–21).

Hence, water destroyed then, but now it saves.

Themes of washing and salvation appeared in several other passages: "let us approach with a true heart in full assurance of faith, with our hearts sprinkled clean from an evil conscience and our bodies washed with pure water" (Heb. 10:22). Titus, an important companion of Paul (cf. Gal. 2:1–3), testified in a similar way that "he saved us, not because of any works of righteousness that we had done, but according to his mercy, through the water of rebirth and renewal by the Holy Spirit" (Titus 3:5). This passage summarized the motifs of washing and rebirth among early Christians.

The author of Ephesians stipulated that baptism be done only once: "...one Lord, one faith, one baptism ...." (Eph. 4:5) In the same letter the author compared baptism to the ritual bath of purification taken by Jewish women prior to their weddings: "Husbands, love your wives, just as Christ loved the church and gave himself up for her, in order to make her holy by cleansing her with the washing of water by the word ...." (Eph. 5:25–26)

The Gospel of John related baptism to the Holy Spirit. Jesus said to Nicodemus: "Very truly, I tell you, no one can enter the Kingdom of God without being born of water and the Spirit" (Jhn. 3:5). The intent of the statement was to emphasize the gift of the Holy Spirit through baptism (Brown 1966: 140, 144). Linking water and the Spirit reflected the same relationship in the Hebrew Bible: "I will pour out my spirit on all flesh ...." (Joel 2:28a, 29b). "I will sprinkle clean water upon you, and you shall be clean from all your uncleannesses, and from all your idols. I will cleanse you. A new heart I will give you, and a new Spirit I will put within you .... I will put my Spirit within you, and make you follow my statutes and be careful to observe my ordinances" (Eze. 36:25−26a, 27).

John added further historical data concerning the relationship between Jesus and John the Baptist. "After this Jesus and his disciples went into the Judean countryside, and he spent some time there with them and baptized. John also was baptizing at Aenon near Salim because water was abundant there; and people kept coming and were baptized ...." (Jhn. 3:22−23).

The reference to Aenon and Salim meant that John was baptizing in Samaria (Brown 1966: 151). The assertion that Jesus baptized was contradicted in a subsequent verse: "Now when Jesus learned that the Pharisees had heard, 'Jesus is making and baptizing more disciples than John'—although [*kaitoive*] it was not Jesus himself but his disciples who baptized ...." (Jhn. 4:1−2). While the assertions in 3:22 and 4:2 appear contradictory, authoritative scholarship indicates that 4:2 gives evidence of another, final redactor, since the term for "although" is highly unusual for the Gospel of John (Brown 1966: 164; Dodd 1968: 311). My judgment is that the two passages are not so much contradictory as chronological. At one time Jesus baptized, but he stopped baptizing for two reasons. One was that John was sent to prison, and the other was that Jesus went on to conduct his own ministry. The fact that Jesus' ministry did not include baptism was the reason why the Synoptic Gospels neglected to state that Jesus baptized in his lifetime (Mk. 3:13−19; Matt. 10:1−15; Lk. 9:1−6; 10:1−12). The decisive aspect of Jesus' ministry was his proclamation of the coming of the Kingdom of God, beginning after the arrest and imprisonment of John the Baptist (Mk. 1:14−15).

In summary, the gospel tradition presented Jesus' baptism by John the Baptist in the prophetic-apocalyptic tradition. Originally, baptism as immersion was a washing ritual for the cleansing of sin, and this idea was maintained in Acts chapter two, presupposed by Paul (1 Cor. 6:9−11), and expressed by Ephesians (5:25−27). (Collins 1995: 53). On the basis of the fundamental washing motif the Pauline letters correlated baptism with the experiences of death and resurrection, the Exodus, a renewed humanity, and equality within the Christian community. The Gospel of John correlated baptismal water with the Holy Spirit for the purpose of rebirth, and this understanding reflected the older Hebrew tradition of the pouring of water as a means of conferring the Spirit. First Peter drew upon the analogy of baptism with Noah's flood and linked them to death and resurrection.

Apostolic Fathers

The second level of development began in the late first or early second
century with the *Didache*, a manual of communal discipline that preserved
Matthew's teaching of Jesus authorizing baptism in the name of God the
Father, Son, and Holy Spirit which would become the doctrine of the Trinity
in later centuries. The community of the *Didache* was that of Christian Jews
who observed the Jewish Law or *Torah* as taught by Jesus (Mitchell 1995:
232). The community was not egalitarian, because one had to be a Jew to
become a Christian (Spinks 2006: 16).

Unlike the New Testament writings the *Didache* offered practical
instructions to the candidates for baptism.

> Now about baptism: This is how to baptize. Give public instruction on all these
> points, and then "baptize" in running water, "in the name of the Father and of the
> Son and of the Holy Spirit." If you do not have running water, baptize in some
> other. If you cannot in cold, then in warm. If you have neither, then pour water on
> the head three times "in the name of the Father, Son, and Holy Spirit." Before the
> baptism, moreover, the one who baptizes and the one being baptized must fast, and
> any others who can. And you must tell the one being baptized to fast for one or two
> days beforehand (*Didache* 7:2–4).

The phrase "running water" or "living water" in the Greek text is a
Hebrew metaphor for "fresh, flowing water which has been taken from a
spring (rather than water which is collected in a cistern)" (Mitchell
1995:251–252). Such water reflected prescriptions for cleansing rituals in
Leviticus (e.g. 14:50; 15:13). Cold water meant water taken from a natural
source such as a stream or spring with a natural temperature, and warm water
was that which had lost its natural temperature due to standing in a cistern
(Mitchell 1995: 252). The requirement to fast continued Matthew's emphasis
on fasting (Matt. 4:2; 6:16–18; 9:14–15), but neither Matthew nor the
Didache mentioned clothing worn before, during, or after baptism (Johnson
1993: 9).

By the second century baptism was the universally accepted rite of
admission into the church, and it was administered with water and the Trinity
(Kelly 1960: 193–194). The second century apostolic father Justin Martyr
explained in his *First Apology* that baptism involved repentance of sin and
rebirth in the name of the Trinity. "This washing is called illumination, since
those who learn these things are illumined within. The illumined is also
washed in the name of Jesus Christ ... and in the name of the Holy Spirit
....." (61) To be illumined meant to be regenerated, following Isaiah 1:16–20
and John 3:3. Justin also clarified what happened after baptism. "We,
however, after thus washing the one who has been convinced and signified

his assent, lead him to those who are called brethren, where they are assembled. They then earnestly offer common prayers for themselves and the one who has been illumined and all others everywhere .... On finishing the prayers we greet each other with a kiss" (65). Justin's community consisted of Syrian and Palestinian immigrants living in Rome, but his information did not represent all the churches in Rome (Spinks 2006: 26).

In his *Against Heresies* Irenaeus of Lyon reported that the Gnostics rejected the Christian belief in baptism as a means of rebirth. They thought that the baptism of Jesus was inferior to a heavenly or spiritual baptism that came from the ineffable Godhead (I. 21:2−3). Irenaeus also reported that some Gnostics believed that the use of water was superfluous and that a mixture of water and oil poured on the head of the initiated one was sufficient (I. 21. 4). Thus, Irenaeus defended the spiritual integrity of water. For Irenaeus the washing of baptism was an imparting of the Holy Spirit, a seal of eternal life, and a rebirth with God (Kelly 1960: 195).

Church Fathers

Tertullian was born to pagan parents about 160 CE, and he became a Christian in 190 CE. He lived in Carthage and was one of the founding fathers of African Latin theology. Tertullian established the term s*acramentum* or "soldier's oath," and it meant that a sacrament was an oath or a sign-act of faith (White 2000: 181). The Greek Fathers preserved the New Testament Greek term *mysterium* or mystery instead of using sacrament. In 200 CE Tertullian wrote an essay entitled "On Baptism" in which he said that baptism washed away sins and admitted one into eternal life. Following the example of Jesus' baptism by John the Baptist, Tertullian declared that humans "are born in water, nor have we safety in any other way than by permanently abiding in water ...." (Tertullian 1903: 669) He posed the question as to why water had such high cleansing power. He answered that water was present at creation before the earth took shape, and so water had age and dignity. Water was a simple, pure element that served as the seat of the Divine Spirit. Water was the first element in the creation story that received the divine command to "bring forth swarms of living creatures" (Gen. 1:20a). Thus, for Tertullian the sanctity of water was located in creation and not Jesus' baptism (Spinks 2006: 32).

Just as the Spirit of God hovered over the primeval waters at creation, so does it linger over baptism. According to Tertullian, where one was baptized did not matter, whether at sea, in a lake, pool, or fountain. He rejected the biblical distinction between cold and warm water, or natural water, and water which stands in a cistern, a position held by the *Didache* (Mitchell 1995: 252). "All waters, therefore, in virtue of the pristine privilege of their origin, do, after the invocation of God, attain the sacramental powers of sanctification ...." (Tertullian 1903: 671). The Spirit came down from heaven, stayed upon the waters, and sanctified them. The baptismal formula of the Trinity (Matt. 28:19) meant that the Church was present in the baptismal rite.

During the third century the Church grew rapidly, so that bishops delegated baptism to presbyters or elders, and it added secondary rites of chrismation or anointing with the sign of the cross and the laying on of hands (Kelly 1960: 207). Tertullian clarified the details for administering those secondary rites. After the person came up from the baptismal water, he or she was anointed with oil, reenacting Moses' anointing of Aaron and his sons to serve as priests (Ex. 30:30), and signifying that Jesus had been spiritually anointed by the Holy Spirit at his baptism. In the New Testament the Spirit descended as a dove, a simple innocent creature which became a sign of peace after Noah's flood had subsided. The benediction for baptism was done by the laying on of hands, a ritual derived from Jacob's blessing his grandsons (Gen. 48:14).

The bishop was the primary officiant at baptism, followed by the presbyters and deacons. Passover was the most solemn day for a baptism, since the baptismal waters reenacted the Hebrews' passage from bondage in Egypt through the waters of the Red Sea. Actually any day was suitable; but whenever baptism was conducted, candidates had to pray, fast, attend vigils, and confess their sins. The fast symbolized the wandering of the Hebrews in the desert for forty years as well as Jesus' temptation in the desert for 40 days after his baptism.

Hippolytus wrote *The Apostolic Tradition* about 217 CE and was martyred in 235 CE. He represented a dissident group in Rome, consisting of resident aliens, and he provided a ritual initiation that functioned as a rite of passage from Roman society into the church (Finn 1989: 70). Hippolytus also added more details to the secondary rites of baptism. He said that newcomers to the faith had to be questioned as to whether they were capable of hearing the Word of God and about their status in life (15). Brothel-keepers, charioteers who competed in athletic contests, gladiators, creators or keepers of idols, and prostitutes were excluded from baptism. They who were chosen for baptism were examined to determine if they had lived good lives. "From the time that they were set apart, let hands be laid on them daily while they are exorcised. And when the day of their baptism approaches, the bishop shall exorcise each one of them ...." (20) Candidates were instructed to wash themselves on Thursday, fast on Friday, and on Saturday be exorcised by the bishop while kneeling and praying. They spent the entire night in vigil receiving instruction before being baptized. Hippolytus directed that

> At the time when the cock crows, first let prayer be made over the water. Let the water be flowing in the font or poured over it. Let it be thus unless there is some necessity; if the necessity is permanent and urgent, use what water you can find. They shall take off their clothes.
>
> And at the time fixed for baptizing, the bishop shall give thanks over the oil, which he puts in a vessel: one calls it "oil of thanksgiving." And he shall also take other oil and exorcise: one calls it "oil of exorcism."
>
> And when the priest takes each one of those who are to receive baptism, he shall bid him renounce, saying: I renounce you, Satan, and all your service and all your works.
>
> And when each one has renounced all this, he shall anoint him with the oil of exorcism, saying to him: Let every spirit depart from you (22).

The deacon descended into the water with the naked candidate and assisted him or her to say: "I believe in one God, the Father almighty." Then the bishop or priest placed his hand on the person and baptized him or her, while asking: "Do you believe in Christ Jesus, the Son of God, who was born from the holy Spirit from the Virgin Mary, and was crucified under Pontius Pilate, and died, and rose again on the third day alive from the dead, and ascended into heaven, and sits on the right hand of the Father, and will come to judge the living and the dead?"

The answer—"I believe"—brought a second immersion in the water. The officiant asked again; "Do you believe in the holy Spirit and the holy Church and the resurrection of the flesh?" When answering, "I believe," the person was immersed a third time. After coming up out of the water, candidates were anointed with the oil of thanksgiving with these words: "I anoint you with holy oil in the name of Jesus Christ." The baptized persons dried themselves, dressed, and entered the church, where the bishop laid his hands on them and invoked the Holy Spirit for the remission of sin and regeneration. He anointed them with the oil of thanksgiving, kissed them, and said: "The Lord be with you." They replied: "And with your spirit." The baptism then concluded with the Holy Communion. The result of baptism was to incorporate the new Christians, separated from Roman society, into a kinship network with God as the father and Christ as the brother (Finn 1989: 78).

During the fourth century, the Church changed from a dissident persecuted group to the established church of the Roman Empire. The fourth century Church Fathers organized baptism into two stages: commitment to Christ and the baptismal bath. They also acknowledged metaphorically that baptism was a transition from Adam or the old humanity to Christ and a new humanity (Riley 1974: 155). Among the fourth century Church Fathers Cyril, bishop of Jerusalem between 349 and 387, had a comprehensive account of baptism that reflected Romans chapter six (Spinks 2006: 38–39). Emperor Constantine had rebuilt Jerusalem, locating buildings over Jesus' place of death. As a resident of Jerusalem, Cyril had an "on the scene" perspective on baptism as a participation in Jesus' death and resurrection.

Cyril emphasized that baptism had three effects: (1) remission of sin and passage from the filth of sin to the cleanliness of righteousness: (2) a positive blessing of sanctification, illumination, indwelling of the Holy Spirit, or union with Christ in his resurrection; and (3) an impressing a seal of the Holy Spirit upon the recipient through the water (Kelly 1960: 428–429). These effects were represented in the theologies of baptism among the fourth and fifth century Church Fathers.

In his introductory catechetical lecture Cyril insisted that baptism be done only once (para. 7) in light of the biblical declaration of "one Lord, one faith, one baptism" in Ephesians 4:5. In his third catechetical lecture, entitled "On Baptism," Cyril explained that the baptismal font did not hold ordinary water but rather "the spiritual grace that is given with the water" (III. 3). The water acquired its sanctifying power by the invocation of the Trinity. The baptismal cleansing was two-fold. The water washed the body, and the Holy Spirit sealed the soul.

Cyril posed the question: Why was water used in the sacrament? He answered that water was the fundamental element in the Bible. "Heaven is the angels' home, yet heavens were made from waters. Earth is man's place, and earth arose from waters …. As water was the foundation of the world, so Jordan was the foundation of the Gospel. Israel was set free from Pharaoh by means of the sea, and the world was freed from sins "with the washing of water by the (divine) word" (III. 5).

Cyril explained that when a covenant was made between two parties, water was a part of it. For example, God established a covenant with Noah after the flood. Baptism ended the old covenant and inaugurated the new covenant through John the Baptist, who was the greatest of all the prophets (III. 6). By being baptized by John, Jesus hallowed baptism. Although he had no sin to be forgiven, nevertheless, Jesus' baptism imparted grace and dignity to water.

Cyril knew the mythic idea of water as the element where the power of evil lurked. As in Job 40:15–24, the dragon thought it could swallow the

Jordan River. When Jesus descended into the Jordan at his baptism, he conquered the dragon and conferred on the baptized "the power to tread upon serpents and scorpions" (Lk. 10:19). Jesus' baptism also destroyed the sting of death (1 Cor. 15:55). Just as Jesus faced temptation after his baptism, so the baptized received the power to wrestle with demonic forces and to prevail with the weapons of righteousness.

In the following generation Saint Augustine introduced such basic sacramental phrases as "visible form" and "invisible grace," and he contended that the source of the sacrament was divine agency, according to the Latin phrase *ex opere operato* (White 2000: 182–183). With reference to baptism in particular, Augustine stated in his *Tractates on the Gospel of John*:

> "Now you are clean by reason of the Word that I have spoken to you." Why does he not say, "You are clean by reason of the baptism by which you were washed," but say, "by reason of the Word that I have spoken to you," except that in the water also the Word cleansed?" Take away the Word, and what is water except water? The Word is added to the elemental substance, and it becomes a sacrament, also itself, as it were, a visible Word (80. 3).

Elsewhere in the same work Augustine clarified that the baptism of Jesus was one of "water in the Word. Take away the water; there is no baptism. Take away the Word; there is no baptism" (15. 4. 2).

Augustine provided a theological summary of baptism in his *Enchiridion*, which he wrote toward the end of his life in 421 CE:

> This is the meaning of the great sacrament of baptism, which is celebrated among us. All who attain to this grace die thereby to sin—as he himself is said to have died to sin because he died in the flesh, that is, "in the likeness of sin"—and they are thereby alive by being reborn in the baptismal font, just as he arose from the sepulcher. This is the case no matter what the age of the body (XIII. 42).

In the same work Augustine insisted that children and the elderly could be baptized and that no one should be rejected. When baptized, infants "die to original sin only; adults, to all those sins which they have added, through their evil living, to the burden they brought with them at birth" (XIII. 43). Children inherit the sin of Adam and Eve, as explained by Paul in Romans 5:12, that sin "entered into the world by one man and so spread to all men." Hence, all must be reborn by baptism in order to absolve sins both before birth and after birth (XIII. 46).

While infant baptism became widespread in the Western Church, the Greek Fathers did not ascribe sin to babies. Instead they emphasized that baptism provided the gift and the seal of the Holy Spirit (Kelly 1960: 430).

After Augustine in the Western Church, therefore, baptism became salvation from original sin rather than reception of the Holy Spirit.

Catholic Middle Ages

In the mid-12th century Hugh of Saint Victor began the Medieval tradition of a systematic theology of the sacraments. Hugh wrote that a sacrament in the tradition of Augustine had "one thing which is treated visibly without and is seen, and there is another which is believed invisibly within and is received" (Hugh of St. Victor 1951: 154). He went on to define a sacrament as follows: "A sacrament is a corporeal or material element set before the senses without, representing by similitude and signifying by institution and containing by sanctification some invisible and spiritual grace" (Hugh of St. Victor 1951: 155). Thus, every sacrament has a similitude, institution, and sanctification.

In baptism water possesses a similitude with the Holy Spirit in the sense that the former washes the body, and the latter cleans the soul. Jesus instituted baptism as an invisible cleansing of the soul through grace. The Word of sanctification completes the sacrament, and the Word is the recitation of the Trinity.

Baptism has primacy among all the sacraments (Hugh of St. Victor 1951: 282). Historically, baptism was the successor to circumcision. Whereas circumcision signified the covenant with Abraham, baptism conferred rebirth and entry into the Kingdom of God. Previously, circumcision signified justification, but with Christianity baptism brought justification and salvation. Baptism could be administered only once, following Ephesians 4:5, and only water could be used sacramentally. Water "alone has full and perfect cleanness. All other liquids indeed are purified by water" (Hugh of St. Victor 1951: 301).

In the late 12th century Peter Lombard worked out a synthesis of sacramental theology in his Distinctions I–XXVI, which were the earlier chapters of the *Fourth Book of Sentences* (Rogers 1976). In Distinction I.II he defined a sacrament as "the visible form of an invisible grace," following Augustine. Lombard was the first theologian in the history of the church to list seven sacraments (White 1992: 123). "Let us now come to the sacraments of the new covenant; which are baptism, confirmation, the blessing of bread, that is the eucharist, penance, extreme unction, ordination, marriage. Of these some offer remedy for sin, and confer helping grace, as baptism ...." (Distinction II.I) The seven sacraments conferred the seven-fold grace of the Holy Spirit. Lombard believed that Jesus had instituted baptism and the eucharist, but that the apostles had established the other five (White 2000:185–186).

Lombard acknowledged that baptism was "first among sacraments of the new grace" (II.II). Following Augustine, Lombard defined baptism as "an immersion, that is, an exterior cleansing of the body and administered under a prescribed form of words. For if the cleansing takes place without the Word, there is no sacrament, but with the addition of the Word to the element, it becomes a sacrament; not that the *element* itself becomes the sacrament, but the cleansing performed in the element" (III.I).

Lombard meant that the Trinity was the form. When the apostles baptized "in the name of Christ" (Acts 8:12), they affirmed the Trinity (III.III). Baptism was instituted by Jesus when he was baptized by John the Baptist, and his baptism "bestowed regenerating power on the waters," so that thereafter whoever were immersed would be cleansed from sin (III.V). Since water was a cleansing agent, baptism could only be done by immersion. Immersion should occur three times, symbolizing the Trinity and Jesus' three-day entombment (III.VII).

In the late 13th century Saint Thomas Aquinas explained that the sacraments were necessary for salvation and that they were the instruments of divine grace (*Summa Theologica* III, Quest. 62, Art. 4). Jesus instituted baptism, and so by divine institution water was the matter and the Trinity the form (Spinks 2006: 146). The dualism of form and matter, which characterized Medieval sacramental theology, was refined by "The Decree for the Armenians" of 1439. "The matter of this sacrament is water, pure and natural: it does not matter if it be cold or warm" (White 1992: 165). The form is: "I baptize you in the name of the Father and of the Son and of the Holy Spirit." Baptism received its power, when the minister invoked the Trinity.

Protestant Theologies

As an Augustinian monk, Martin Luther studied the Bible, the writings of the Church Fathers, and the *Sentences* of Peter Lombard (Genthe 1996: 68). From Lombard's Distinctions Luther learned that Jesus had instituted baptism and the eucharist, but that the apostles had established the other five. Therefore, he posed the following question: Where was the evidence of the sacraments? Luther believed that the sacraments required clear and explicit evidence in the biblical text, according to the rule of Scripture alone. Consequently, he found that only baptism and the eucharist came directly from Jesus and that only they had dominical authority. He rejected the other five as non-biblical.

In 1519 and 1520 Luther wrote two polemical essays in which he attacked the *ex opere operato* formula and instead emphasized the divine promise. In his 1519 essay on "The Holy and Blessed Sacrament of Baptism" Luther said that to be baptized meant to plunge fully into water (*Luther's Works*, Vol. 35: 29). The German term for baptism *taufe* derived from that for deep *tiefe*. Plunging into the water meant that flesh and blood were completely drowned. In the biblical narrative Noah's flood prefigured baptism as a drowning.

As a sacrament, baptism had three parts: the sign, significance, and faith (*Luther's Works*, Vol. 35: 30). The sign consisted of going into and coming out of the water in the name of the Trinity. The significance was that of dying and rising with Christ, and these were not fulfilled until death. One was baptized unto death, and the sooner one died, the earlier baptism would be fulfilled. Faith meant that one believed in these things.

When coming out of the baptismal water, one became pure, sinless, and guiltless. Since the flesh was sinful, baptism began God's plan for renewing the flesh. One became sinless sacramentally, but the process was not yet completed. Through baptism one entered into a covenant, giving up oneself with the desire to die, and pledging to continue living with that desire (*Luther's Works*, Vol. 35: 34).

After baptism, sin remained in the flesh; but the sin was not imputed to the person. One had to struggle against the evil impulse, vow to slay evil, and become holy (*Luther's Works*, Vol. 35: 37, 41). No vow was higher than that of baptism, and no vow could be taken after baptism. When dying, one should remember one's baptism and remind God of the covenant. At that moment baptism would be fulfilled.

In his 1520 essay on *The Babylonian Captivity of the Church* Luther denied that there were seven sacraments. In the beginning of his discussion he said there were three—baptism, penance, and eucharist—but toward the end he admitted that there were only two, baptism and the eucharist (*Luther's Works*, Vol. 36: 18, 124). He explained that penance or more properly repentance was a return to the power of baptism; and that when the ancient Hebrews repented, they remembered the Exodus (*Luther's Works*, Vol. 36: 60). Luther also refuted the Roman Catholic duality of form and matter in Medieval sacramental theology. These terms, which aligned water with matter and the Trinity with form, neglected the truth of faith and the divine promise (*Luther's Works*, Vol. 36: 62). God was the originator of baptism, and the administrator was the divine instrument. One baptized in the name of the Triune God and not in terms of form and matter. He reiterated that the divine promise was the first part of baptism, the sign or immersion in the water the second, and faith which justified and fulfilled the sign was the third part (*Luther's Works*, Vol. 36: 58–66). Baptism was not a once-for-all event but a life-long process of dying and rising with Christ.

Luther's preferred biblical model of death was Noah's flood, and he commemorated this in his flood prayer of 1526:

> Almighty eternal God, who according to thy righteous judgment didst condemn the unbelieving world through the flood and in thy great mercy didst preserve believing Noah and his family, and who didst drown hard hearted Pharaoh with all his host in the Red Sea and didst lead thy people Israel through the same on dry ground, thereby prefiguring this bath of thy baptism, and who through the baptism of thy dear child, our Lord Jesus Christ, hast consecrated and set apart the Jordan and all water as a salutary flood and a rich and full washing away of sins: We pray through the same thy groundless mercy that thou wilt graciously behold this N. and bless him with true faith in the spirit so that by means of this saving flood all that has been born in him from Adam and which he himself has added thereto may be drowned in him and engulfed, and that he may be sundered from the number of the unbelieving, preserved dry and secure in the holy ark of Christendom, serve thy name at all times fervent in spirit and joyful in hope, so that with all believers he may be made worthy to attain eternal life according to thy promises; through Jesus Christ our Lord. Amen (*Luther's Works*, Vol. 53: 107–108).

In the words of a contemporary theologian the entire world is covered with the "flood of wrath," which has become through baptism a "flood of grace" submerging the entire world in God's mercy (Stewart 2011: 25).

In 1529 Luther wrote "The Small Catechism," advising pastors that they should instruct children on the Ten Commandments, Lord's Prayer, Apostles Creed, and the sacraments. Not to esteem the sacraments highly was captivity by the Devil. Luther clarified that baptism, in particular, bestowed forgiveness of sins, deliverance from death and the Devil, and eternal life (Tappert 1959: 348–349). Water and the Word produced those effects. Water baptism signified the drowning and death of the old man and a rising to a new life with God, as Paul said in Romans 6:4 (Tappert 1959: 349).

Luther also wrote "The Large Catechism" for the instruction of adults, and he emphasized that God justified baptism through his command and ordinance of Matthew 28:19 and Mark 16:16 (Tappert 1959: 437). God sanctified the water and baptism, and through faith the recipients of the sacrament accepted the blessed water. Since baptism came from God's command, the sacrament included children in the expectation that they would believe. Luther clarified a recurrent theme in his writings. He reduced penance to baptism, making the two one (Tappert 1959: 445). Baptism should not be understood as a past event but as a daily process.

In 1540 Luther preached a sermon at the baptism of an infant, entitled "Sermon at the Baptism of Bernard von Anhalt," and he explained that Jesus accepted his baptism from John the Baptist in order to become a "sinner" for humans and to drown all sins in compliance with God's will (*Luther's Works*, Vol. 51: 315). Jesus was holy and sinless, but he took on human sin and guilt. Grasping this exchange in faith would free one from sin and death and endow one with righteousness. By being baptized one took on Christ who washed away sin.

In that sermon Luther reaffirmed his view that baptism contained water, Word (Matt. 28:19), and God's command or institution. He stated that there were two kinds of word, one spoken with water, and the other commanding an immersion in the water. The character of the administrator of the sacrament did not matter. Through baptism Jesus' innocent blood was poured out spiritually on the recipient. Luther cited 1 John 5:6: "This is the one who comes by water and blood, Jesus Christ, not with water only but with the water and the blood." God endowed water with Jesus' blood.

Ulrich Zwingli was a contemporary of Luther who led the German-speaking Reformed tradition in Zürich, Switzerland. In his 1528 essay "Of Baptism" Zwingli stated that the apostles and Church Fathers ascribed to water a power it lacked, and he contended that nothing external could make anyone pure and righteous (Zwingli 1953: 130). Zwingli defined a sacrament as a soldier's oath, following the old Latin meaning, and he considered it to be a sign (Spinks 2006a: 32). A sacrament was a covenant sign that pledged its recipient to Jesus Christ. Zwingli pointed out that in the New Testament baptism was "a covenant sign which indicated that all those who receive it are willing to amend their lives and to follow Christ. In short, it is an initiation to a new life" (Zwingli 1953: 141).

Zwingli admitted that water could clean the body, but it could not wash away sin. Only God through Christ could remove sin by baptizing inwardly or spiritually. Following Romans chapter six Zwingli argued that persons were baptized into Christ and not in Christ (Zwingli 1953: 150). He referred correctly to the fact that in the Greek text Paul wrote that "as many as were baptized into [*eis*] Christ Jesus, were baptized into [*eis*] his death" (Rom. 6:3). Immersion into the water signified plunging into the death of Christ, and reemergence from the water meant entry into the resurrection of Christ.

Zwingli opposed the Anabaptists' view that only they who could live without sin should be baptized. Their position presumed the doctrine of the perseverance of the saints, as set forth in the Schleitheim Confession of 1527:

Baptism shall be given to all those who have learned repentance and amendment of life, and who believe truly that their sins are taken away by Christ, and to all those who walk in the resurrection of Jesus Christ, and wish to be buried with him in death, so that they may be resurrected with him, and to all those who with this significance request it [baptism] of us and demand it for themselves .... (Lindberg 2000: 133)

The Anabaptists insisted that belief was the essential prerequisite for baptism and, therefore, that infants could not be baptized. Hence, the Anabaptists rebaptized recipients of infant baptism when they grew up and achieved knowledge of the faith. The Anabaptists argued their position from the word order of Matthew 28:19, that is, to "make disciples of all nations, baptizing them ...." Menno Simons, one of the leaders of the Mennonite branch of the Anabaptist movement, interpreted Matthew's words as follows: "Here we have the Lord's commandment concerning baptism, as to when according to the ordinance of God it shall be administered and received; namely, that the Gospel must first be preached, and then those baptized who believe it ...." (White 1992: 169). Since infants were unteachable and could not understand the faith, they should not be baptized. If they were baptized, this would violate the Lord's ordinance.

Against the Anabaptists Zwingli argued that the New Testament approved of only one baptism (Eph. 4:5) and that faith and baptism could not be distinguished. In the New Testament to baptize meant to teach, and baptism included teaching (Zwingli 1953: 174). The Anabaptists' claim that discipleship preceded baptism in Matthew 28:19 neglected the fact that in Greek word order was not fixed. Matthew 28:19 could not be used, therefore, to exclude children from baptism. Infants could be baptized as members of a family wherein the parents were first taught faith (Spinks 2006a: 33).

John Calvin was the leading figure of the French-speaking Reformed movement based in Geneva, Switzerland, and his major work was the *Institutes of the Christian Religion*. In the third or 1559 edition of the *Institutes* he defined baptism as

The sign of the initiation by which we are received into the society of the church, in order that, engrafted in Christ, we may be reckoned among God's children. Now baptism was given to us by God for these ends (which I have taught to be common to all sacraments): first, to serve our faith before him; secondly, to serve our confession before men (*Institutes*, Bk. IV: 1303–1304).

Baptism has brought three things to faith: token or proof of cleansing, mortification and new life in Christ, and union with Christ. Calvin rejected the Latin idea of a sacrament as a pledge or sign, as Zwingli held, and he said that baptism has provided the promise of salvation as purification through the sprinkling of Christ's blood. "Thus, the surest argument to refute the self-deception of those who attribute everything to the power of the water can be sought in the meaning of baptism itself, which draws us away, not only from the visible element which meets our eyes, but from all other means, that it may fasten our minds upon Christ alone" (*Institutes*, Bk. IV: 1305).

Baptism has come from God with the promise that full remission of guilt and punishment for sin have been made. Baptism has provided absolution unlike any other sacrament, and it could not be destroyed by any subsequent sin. "These things, I say he [Christ] performs for our soul within us truly and surely as we see our body outwardly cleansed, submerged, and surrounded with water. For this analogy or similitude is the surest rule of the sacraments: that we should see spiritual things in physical, as if set before our very eyes" (*Institutes*, Bk. IV: 1314). According to Calvin, the term "to baptize" meant to immerse, and immersion was the custom of the early Church. Nevertheless, he thought it was optional whether one were immersed once or three times or sprinkled. Baptism should be administered only by the clergy and not by the laity.

The baptismal theology of the English Reformation was largely shaped by Thomas Cranmer, who served as the Archbishop of Canterbury under King Henry VIII and his son King Edward VI. Cranmer's greatest achievement was his compilation of the *Book of Common Prayer* (BCP) in the 1549 and 1552 editions. Educated at Cambridge University, Cranmer had studied the Bible and Reformation theologies, and he accepted the Reformation doctrine of the justification by faith. For Cranmer justification meant appropriating the righteousness of Christ, so as to be imputed or ascribed righteous for Christ's sake (Null 2006: 122). One acquired imputed righteousness through faith: "And this justification or righteousness, which we so receive by God's mercy and Christ's merits, embraced by faith, is taken, accepted, and allowed of God for our perfect and full justification" (Cranmer 1966: 262).

Baptism has bestowed Jesus' righteousness in the sense that the crucified and risen Christ is present in the water by grace (Bromiley 1956: 57, 59–60). Christ is not in the water as such; rather the Holy Spirit changes the water into a washing away of sin. Baptism has inner and outer aspects in the Holy Spirit and the water, respectively. The baptized become the justified, and with justification remission of sin, saving faith, and love occur simultaneously. Cranmer believed that the freedom of the will was the highest faculty of the human soul and that moral choice was the essence of the Christian faith (Null 2006: 73). Thus, the sacrament readied the human will, making recipients "right-willed," so to speak. Baptism, in particular, brought about a deliverance from sin, movement toward sanctification, and entry into eternal life (Sykes 1990: 134).

Cranmer contended that children belonged to the Kingdom of God and that they could receive regeneration by baptism as an instrument of God's grace (Null 2006: 226, 228). Cranmer believed that a sacrament had to be instituted, commanded, or that it signified the remission of sin in the New Testament (Jeanes 1995: 182). He found in Mark chapter ten the commandment pertaining to infant baptism. When Jesus reacted angrily to the disciples preventing children from coming to him, he said: "'Let the little children come to me; do not stop them; for it is to such as these that the Kingdom of God belongs. Truly I tell you, whoever does not receive the Kingdom of God as a little child will never enter it.' And he took them up in his arms, laid his hands of them, and blessed them" (Mk. 10:14b–16). For Cranmer infant baptism was like Jesus receiving children into his arms. In the Anglican baptismal rite the priest took the child in his arms, reenacting what Jesus did, and declared that the child has been received into Christ's flock, or the congregation, "with the arms of his mercy" (Sykes 1990: 132).

The 1549 edition of the BCP listed the four benefits of baptism as follows: (1) remission of sin, (2) incorporation into the church; (3) bestowal of grace, and (4) regeneration in Christ (Spinks 2006a: 66). Whereas the 1549 edition of the BCP included a blessing of the water in the baptismal font by the priest, the 1552 edition omitted such a blessing (White 1992: 173–174). No blessing of the water was necessary, since Jesus' baptism in the Jordan River had sanctified all water for baptism, as made evident in Luther's flood prayer, cited above (Spinks 2006a: 69). The 1662 edition of the BCP. however, commonly regarded as the canonical version, reinstated the blessing of the water by inserting the following phrase in the prayer before the baptism: "Sanctify this water to the mystical washing away of sin" (Sykes 1990: 137).

The definitive statement on baptism in the Church of England appeared in Article 27 of the 39 Articles:

> Baptism is not only a sign of profession, and mark of difference, whereby Christian men are discerned from others that be not christened, but it is also a sign of Regeneration or New-Birth, whereby, as by an instrument, they that receive Baptism rightly are grafted onto the church; the promises of the forgiveness of sin, and of our adoption to be the Sons of God by the Holy Ghost, are visibly signed and sealed; Faith is confirmed, and Grace is increased by virtue of prayer unto God (BCP 1977: 873).

In the 17th century the Puritans, who were English-speaking Calvinists, pushed for liturgical changes in the Church of England by opposing Roman

Catholic elements in worship services. The Puritans stipulated two conditions for the administration of baptism:

> Baptisme, as it is not unnecessarily to be delayed, so is it not to be administered in any case by any private person, but only by a Minister of God, called to be the Stewart of the Mysteries of God.

> Nor is it to be administered in private places, or privately, but in the place of Publique Worship, and in the face of the Congregation, where the people may most conveniently see and heare; and not in the places where Fonts in the time of Popery were unfitly and superstitiously placed (White 1992: 175).

John Wesley was a priest in the Church of England who inaugurated the Methodist movement in 1739, along with his younger brother Charles, as a means of reforming Anglican life and worship. Wesley admired the BCP, but he agreed with some of the Puritan objections to Catholic elements in the Anglican liturgy (Tucker 2006: 209). Wesley reaffirmed the validity of baptismal regeneration, as taught in the Church of England, as well as the objectivity of divine grace in the sacraments.

In his essay, entitled "On Baptism," Wesley stated that baptism had three requirements: (1) administration by an ordained minister; (2) application of water; and (3) recitation of the Trinity (Outler 1964: 319). These three requirements made baptism a sign and seal of God's covenant. Wesley considered baptism to be a means of grace and a necessity for Christians. The sacrament required water which worked well symbolically. He acknowledged that baptism might be done by washing, dipping, or sprinkling, and he could find no evidence in the New Testament to privilege any of these methods. The Greek term "to baptize" (*baptizein*) did not entail a specific mode of administration.

Wesley pointed out that the basic function of baptism was "the washing away of the guilt of original sin by the application of the merits of Christ's death" (Outler 1964: 321). Both Scripture and early Christianity bore witness to the fact of original sin. In the view of early Christianity, which Wesley considered normative, baptism conferred an everlasting covenant and admission into the church. Just as circumcision was the sign of the covenant for Jews, so baptism became a similar sign for Christians.

Both children and adults may be baptized. The New Testament spoke of children being brought to Jesus (Mk. 10:13–16), and this could only be done by baptism. If infants were circumcised, then they may be baptized. Wesley recognized five benefits of baptism. It (1) washed away original sin; (2) brought recipients into covenant with God; (3) admitted them into the church; (4) made them heirs of the Kingdom of God; and (5) provided spiritual regeneration (Outler 1964: 319, 322–323).

In his sermon on "The New Birth" Wesley clarified that baptism was not the new birth, according to the Church of England (*The Works of John Wesley*, V. 2: 196–197). Water was the outward and visible sign, and regeneration was the inward and spiritual grace. One may be baptized as an infant, but then as an adult take up a life of sin, thereby denying baptism. Hence, adults needed to be born again and experience the process of sanctification (*The Works of John Wesley*, V. 2: 198). Wesley understood sanctification as a gradual, life-long process of moving toward perfect love. He emphasized new birth or conversion as an inward process in contrast to external ceremonial acts.

Whereas John Wesley worked within the Church of England, some in the broad Puritan movement were largely non-Calvinist and known as the Separatists. They believed the Church of England was too Catholic, and they seceded in the 16th century. By the 17th century the Separatists became the Baptists, and they advocated the believer's baptism. The 14th Article of their Confession of Faith stated: "That baptism is the external sign of the remission of sins, of dying and being made alive, and therefore does not belong to infants" (Spinks 2006a: 96). Baptism required a confession of faith, and a total immersion in the water was the normative mode. Baptists believed that the church as a covenanted community mandated a responsible decision for entry, and one had to be of age when one could make a responsible decision. Baptism was not a sacramental means of grace but an ordinance or sign that regeneration had already taken place (Dillenberger and Welch 1988: 101).

The Separatists emigrated to Plymouth, Massachusetts, beginning in 1629, and later Roger Williams founded a Baptist community in Rhode Island. As a result of revivals in New England in the mid-18th century, Baptists began to move into the American South where they continued their evangelical work. They preached to both whites and blacks, and by the 20th century they had become the dominant Protestant denomination in the South. One of the distinctive aspects of Southern Baptists, particularly in rural Louisiana, was outdoor baptism in rivers, lakes, and bayous.

As an example of outdoor believer's baptism, I choose that of St. Paul's Baptist Church, an African-American congregation, in Monroe, Louisiana. Every summer or early fall the congregation gathers at a place called "the old burial ground" at the edge of the Ouachita River (Staten and Roach 1999). The church mothers sew or obtain long, flowing robes with long sleeves to clothe the candidates and to symbolize the bonds of sin. The minister wades into the river to a spot about waist-deep and announces: "We gather here on this old river that drifts into the sea," and he thanks God for "this old river."

He recalls Jesus' baptism in the Jordan River, as portrayed in Matthew 3:13–17, and in the baptismal drama the Ouachita River becomes, in effect, the Jordan River. Deacons escort the candidates into the river to stand in front of the minister. He immerses each one in the name of the Trinity, symbolizing one's burial with Christ, washing away of sin, and raising one up to a new life. When the baptized persons come out of the water, the congregation applauds and sings refrains from their favorite hymns, such as, "Take me to the water; take me to the water; take me to the water to be baptized" (Long 2009: 80). The baptized remove their robes and dress in white Sunday clothes behind curtains erected up the river bank. The discarding of the robes represents removing the bonds of sin, and the reclothing indicates a renewal of life. The worship service ends with the minister and deacons saying a prayer and holding hands at the water's edge.

In current ecumenical discussions an influential document of the Faith and Order Commission of the World Council of Churches defines baptism as "the incorporation into Christ, who is the crucified and risen Lord; it is entry into the New Covenant between God and God's people" (*Baptism, Eucharist, Ministry* 1982: 7). As a gift from God, baptism is administered with water in the name of the Father, Son, and Holy Spirit. From the time of the early church baptism has been a universal Christian practice, as attested by the New Testament and the writings of the Church Fathers. Baptism signifies a new life in Jesus Christ, and it has multiple biblical meanings. Baptism is participation in Christ's death and resurrection, washing away of sin, new birth, reclothing in Christ, renewal by the Holy Spirit, experience of salvation from the flood, exodus from slavery, and liberation into a new humanity without barriers or divisions (*Baptism, Eucharist, Ministry* 1982: 7–8). Baptism is one practice with many images. It is part of a life-long process of spiritual growth which culminates in liberation and regeneration in the glory of God.

In the history of the church the rite of baptism has taken more than one form. Infant baptism emphasizes the corporate faith of the church, as children share the same faith with their parents. Believer's baptism occurs at a later age, when one can make an explicit confession of faith. Whether infant or believer's, baptism is an unrepeatable act (*Baptism, Eucharist, Ministry* 1982: 14). Water signifies the continuity between the old and the new creation and that between humans and the cosmos, as well as a purification of creation and a renewal of human existence (*Baptism, Eucharist, Ministry* 1982: 14).

Summary

The Christian Sacrament of Baptism originated in the baptism of Jesus by John the Baptist, as reported in the Synoptic Gospels. John administered baptism in the apocalyptic tradition of the prophets for repentance and remission of sin. The Acts of the Apostles confirmed that early Christians considered baptism as a ritual washing or cleansing of sin. Paul viewed baptism as a dying and rising with Christ, and he suggested a variety of other meanings. The Gospel of Matthew presented Jesus as the Risen Lord who commanded his followers to make disciples of all nations and to baptize them in the name of the Father, the Son, and the Holy Spirit.

By the second century baptism became a ritual of admission into the church, and it was administered with water and the Trinity. Third century Church Fathers added secondary rites of fasting, anointing, confessing of sins, and exorcism. In the fourth and fifth centuries baptism conferred remission of sin, sanctification, and the seal of the Holy Spirit. Saint Augustine introduced the terms of "visible form" and "invisible grace," the complementarity of water and the Word, and the doctrine of divine agency or *ex opere operato*. He insisted on infant baptism as a remission of original sin, and this became dominant in the Western Church. The Medieval Catholic theologians followed Augustine and developed a systematic sacramental theology based on the duality of form and matter.

In the Protestant Reformation of the 16th century Martin Luther replaced Augustine's *ex opere operato* with the divine promise of eternal life received by faith, and he rejected the dualism of form and matter. Luther considered baptism as a life-long process of dying and rising with Christ, and his model of dying was Noah's flood. The Reformed tradition made baptism a sign or covenant of initiation into the church, and it de-emphasized the sanctity of water. In the English Reformation baptism provided deliverance from sin, incorporation into the church, bestowal of grace, and regeneration in Christ. Anglicans and Methodists performed infant baptism on the model of Jesus' receiving young children. Baptists rejected infant baptism, and they required total immersion and confession of faith as a precondition of baptism. Infant baptism for most Protestants emphasizes the corporate faith of the community and the sharing of faith by children and parents. Both infant and believer's baptism are complementary. They are administered with water and the Trinity and interpreted with multiple biblical meanings of water.

Chapter Five: Natural Sacramentality

Sacramental Universe

In his 1934 Gifford Lectures William Temple, then Archbishop of Canterbury, presented the idea of a sacramental universe to account for a natural or cosmic sacramentality. Temple envisioned God as immanent and transcendent, and he considered the universe to be a historical process of evolution (Temple 1953: 473). Mind was a late-comer in the process, and it emerged when its bearer's conduct was determined by the good and not by causality or means-end connections. Mind evolved from a purely material level to a spiritual dimension.

Science views the universe as a series of levels and "of such sort that the lower is necessary to the actuality of the higher but only finds its own fullness of being when thus used by the higher as its means of self-actualization" (Temple 1953: 474−475). The higher levels are spiritual, and the lower material, but both are real. Mind has emerged from within the living matter of the body, and matter is the necessary condition for the naturalness of life, mind, and spirit. The latter arises from within matter and controls it by means of its spirituality (Temple 1953: 477). The independence of spirit does not contradict or nullify matter. Matter is conditioned by cause and effect processes, and spirit is governed by its responsiveness to the good. Although the universe is a hierarchy of levels, it is a unified system; and spirit is its "highest principle of unity" (Temple 1953: 479).

The entire cosmic system exists by the will of God as the Creator Spirit. The world depends on God for its existence, but God does not depend upon the world. God created the world to be determined by the good, but this cannot be fully explained by the principle of causality. The good is God's own nature. The essence of the world is spiritual and personal; it is the living God. More precisely, the glory of the living God has been revealed in and consists of the death and resurrection of Jesus Christ.

Temple did not frame the relationship of history and eternity or spirit and matter in terms of ground and consequence, cause and effect, thought and expression, purpose and instrument, or means and end. While Temple admitted that these connections functioned in the world, he chose the term sacramental to be more precise (Temple 1953: 481−482). In spite of various theories of the sacraments, a sacrament indicates essentially that "the outward and visible sign is a necessary means for conveyance of the inward and spiritual grace" (Temple 1953: 482). A sacrament requires a material sign to be effective. The meaning of the sacrament is also represented by the *ex opere operato* principle which means "an actual conveyance of the spiritual meaning and power by a material process" (Temple 1953: 484). The sacrament conveys the reality of God to the worshipper. Through the sacrament the love of God seeks entry into the human being. Only God can work a physical, inorganic medium because he created it. Thus, by means of a sacrament God is accessible to matter.

Temple discussed the sacramental principle within the broad Augustinian tradition, but he did not deal with specific sacraments in his lecture. He acknowledged a tendency or pressure among religions to separate the spiritual from the material. If they were separated completely, however, the unity of human life would be broken. "It is the sacramental view of the universe, both of its material and of its spiritual elements, that there is given hope of making humane both politics and economics and of making effectual both faith and love" (Temple 1953: 486).

A sacrament is a spiritual use of matter with a spiritual result. Although a sacrament may involve symbolism and a psychological process, it is more than these. The sacramental vision of the world consists of "spirit first and spirit last, with matter as the effectual expression or symbolic instrument of spirit" (Temple 1953: 492). The sacramental vision affirms the supremacy and freedom of God, the reality of the physical world or God's creation, and the vital significance of matter for spirit. Matter exists in its reality, but it has been created to serve as a vehicle of the spirit. Matter is the sphere of the self-actualization of spirit.

Sacramental Commons

More recently, Roman Catholic ethicist John Hart has recovered Temple's vision of a sacramental universe and proposed that it be located in the sacramental commons (Hart 2006: 13). Hart defines a commons as a shared space whose common goods provide for inhabitants' needs equitably and appropriately. Some examples of a commons are a school and a village, but Hart extends the commons to the entire earth in which diverse species live within integrated and interdependent ecosystems. The sacramental earth commons is a home where needs are balanced and relationships cultivated (Hart 2006: 62–63). The earth commons is the context of natural history and cultural history. Human property and land also belong to the earth commons.

The sacramental commons is a spiritualized form of creation and a place of participation in God as the Creator Spirit. As a sacramental place, it reveals the transcendent and immanent dimensions of the Creator Spirit. Transcendence means that the Spirit is independent, being able to engage several interrelated aspects of reality and not be bound by them. Immanence means that social and spiritual experiences are not separated from the material aspects of life. Transcendence and immanence are integrated by a relational consciousness. The latter means that humans are physical beings who may be drawn into union with the Spirit but still remain connected to various dimensions of reality, such as biological organisms and ecological systems (Hart 2006: xx–xxi).

In the perspective of Hart's theology the universe flows forth from the dynamic imagination of the Creator Spirit, ever since the primordial flaring forth of creation 15 billion years ago. The universe is a self-organizing process in the forms of the scientific laws of biology, physics, and chemistry. The universe is a revelation of spiritual creativity and relatedness. When humans envisage the creation sacramentally, they are motivated to care for it as a commons. In their caring the earth becomes a natural sacrament and a commons for all creatures.

Sacraments are signs of the Creator Spirit drawing people into "grace-filled moments permeated by a heightened awareness of the divine presence" (Hart 2006: xiv). Sacraments may be natural and universal or ritualistic and institutional. The sacramental commons is natural and universal rather than ritualistic and institutional. Hart points out that in the biblical narrative visionaries have encounters with the sacred on journeys or in places outside established religious sites, particularly the Temple (Hart 2006: 5–6). He refers to Moses encountering God in the vision of the burning bush on Mount Sinai (Ex. 3), Elijah speaking with God outside a cave on Mount Sinai (1 Kings 19), and Ezekiel receiving visions by the Chebar River in Babylon (Eze. 1). Hart cites Solomon's Temple dedication prayer, acknowledging that God cannot be confined to a sacred structure: "Even heaven and the highest heaven, cannot contain you, much less this house that I have built" (1 Kings 8:27).

Similarly, Hart finds divine-human encounters in the context of nature portrayed in the New Testament. Jesus faces demonic and angelic spirits in his wilderness temptation (Matt. 4), and he undergoes a transfiguration on a mountaintop (Mk. 9). Paul's conversion takes place on the road to Damascus (Acts 9), and in Athens he declares of God; "In him we live and move and have our being" (Acts 17:28).

Hart believes that God as the Creator Spirit has provided a sufficiency of goods to meet everyone's needs by means of distributive justice. He defines distributive justice as the allocation of sustenance goods equitably and appropriately to all persons according to their needs (Hart 2006: 150). Sustenance goods include land, air, water, and sunlight, all of which are necessary for the production of food, shelter, clothing, and energy. Recognizing those as common goods promotes the common good of the sacramental earth commons.

Hart acknowledges that there are four basic attitudes toward nature within the historic Christian faith, and they are (1) domination, (2) dominion, (3) stewardship, and (4) relational consciousness (Hart 2006: 70, 119). Domination is the excessive use of power to control people, events, and society in order to benefit unjustly the desires of specific groups or species. The attitude of dominion claims a sovereign right to control the earth in satisfaction of human desires. Dominion is the privileged exercise of authority over life or the earth to serve the interests of humanity. Stewardship means that humans take responsibility for the earth as trustees or stewards on behalf of God. Humans care for nature as a trust from God who is the Sovereign owner with the inalienable right of ownership.

Hart indicates that the stewardship model has properly opposed arguments for private property as an absolute right and the appropriation of earth's goods for personal benefits and corporate profits. The attitude of stewardship has promoted responsible care of the earth, but nevertheless it holds a hierarchical authority over nature. "In the hierarchy, humans are closer to God and serve as a bridge between God and nature. Humans mediate God to nature; nature does not mediate God to humans" (Hart 2006: 120).

The fourth is relational consciousness, and this is the approach that Hart prefers. The relational attitude means that humans are a part of a dynamic biotic community, living in egalitarian relationships within ecological systems, where competition and cooperation characterize the interaction of species. In the relational perspective nature mediates God to humans. With a relational consciousness "one appreciates all biokind as mutually connected beings in the cosmos, guides participation in a relational community and is the foundation for relational ethics in which the value and right of both human and nonhuman creation are advocated ...." (Hart 2006: 121)

Hart argues that the Creator Spirit has imparted intrinsic value to nature. "Intrinsic value is a being's inherent worth in itself. It is self-regard or self-worth, whether or not a creature is self-conscious" (Hart 2006: 122). Living beings assert their self-worth when they strive for survival under perilous conditions, and when they seek food, water, and shelter. If a being were unaware, it would still have intrinsic value by virtue of its existence. In contrast, instrumental value is the worth of one being for another. It is a regard by external beings for particular benefits to other beings. Instrumental value is discerned by another being, but intrinsic value is internally active and adhering to an independent being. Both conscious and unconscious beings have instrumental value.

Hart illustrates issues of intrinsic and instrumental value with reference to the plight of the salmon in the Pacific Northwest of the United States. One specific issue deals with four dams in the Columbia-Snake rivers system: Ice Harbor, Lower Monumental, Little Goose, and Lower Granite. As a result of these dams, which block fish migrations, the salmon are nearly extinct (Hart 2006: 98). Building the dams was justified originally as a source of hydroelectric power for irrigation for agriculture and for national security. These dams have severely diminished the river runs of the salmon, preventing them from spawning or laying their eggs.

Hart contends that salmon have intrinsic value within their habitats and instrumental value to bears and humans. "Salmon and all creatures are good, and their natural rights, based on their intrinsic value, are egalitarian rights" (Hart 2006: 111). Hart believes that the four dams, cited above, should be breached in order to affirm the salmon's intrinsic value, natural rights, and species survival.

In the sacramental earth commons humans are not appropriate judges and grantors of intrinsic value. Value exists inherently in beings and independently of humans. Humans must accept and respect intrinsic value beyond themselves. Intrinsic value is autonomous and not anthropocentric; it is there in nature whether or not humans are present. Intrinsic value is not limited to those with self-consciousness and moral agency. Places and flows, such as rivers, have intrinsic value as parts of the divine creation. The entire earth has intrinsic value. Within the whole of nature all beings, including humans, should exist in egalitarian relationships (Hart 2006: 128). All have unique and complementary relationships with one another.

Equality means that rights should be the same for all beings, and egalitarian means that beings have rights that are equivalent (Hart 2006: 129). All aspects of nature have natural rights. Primary natural rights belong to the biotic community, and secondary natural rights pertain to abiotic nature. Natural rights should be recognized in nature in order to promote the common good. Ultimately, all existing beings and species have natural rights as a part of integral being. In the perspective of Christian theology "integral being is the dynamic cosmos as a whole—existing in, engaged with, and sacred because of—divine presence" (Hart 2006: 138). Integral being originates in the Creator Spirit.

Living Water

Hart devotes a separate chapter to the role of water in the sacramental earth commons. Water provides life and nourishment for the earth and its inhabitants, and without water they could not survive on earth. Water is both a spiritual good and a material good, "when people encounter the providential presence of the creating Spirit as they drink the water that sustains their life" (Hart 2006: 79). Water is a common good given by the earth to all humans and biotic communities for their benefit. When water is pure, it can fulfill its life-giving role; but when it is polluted, impure water threatens life and health. Pollution robs water of is sacramental quality. "Water is intended by the Creator to be a sign and mediation of the Spirit's immanence and solicitous care for the living" (Hart 2006: 80).

When water is privatized and used by industries and other commercial enterprises, then it is no longer a common good allocated to all. Hart points out that in the American West water is both polluted and privatized, as agricultural and mining companies purchase land with streams or other bodies of water. For example, in northeastern Montana the reservation lands of the Nakota and Gros Ventre Indian tribes are damaged by soil contamination and water pollution. The reason is that the construction and operation of the Zartman and Lendusky mine required blowing off the tops of sacred mountains to extract gold (Hart 2006: 81). There are debates in the western states about the exploration of coal bed methane, which is purportedly a clean energy source. Such exploration, however, would divert water supplies from local farms and communities, privatize water for commercial use, and raise the salinity levels in water sources.

Hart contends that pure water is a natural right for individuals, families, and communities, as well as for species within the global biotic ecosystem. Local communities should make their own decisions concerning the use, allocation, and distribution of water. Such decisions should not be made by multi-national corporations for the benefit of distant stockholders. People's needs for life and livelihood take precedence over corporate profits. If water were regarded as a commodity and source of profit for a privilege minority, then this common good would be threatened, and people and other species would suffer from disease and dehydration. Consequently, water should be recognized as a natural right, and this right should be codified in national policies and laws and in binding international treaties.

Columbia River Watershed

On January 8, 2001 the Roman Catholic bishops of the Northwestern states and British Columbia, Canada released an international pastoral letter, entitled "The Columbia River Watershed: Caring for Creation and the Common Good" (www.columbiariver.org). John Hart was the project writer and a member of the steering committee (Hart 2006: 248). The bishops presented this letter out of concern for the economic conflicts and ecological conditions of the Columbia River watershed. The watershed comprises 259,000 square miles, and its center consists of the 1,200 miles of the Columbia River. The river originates in British Columbia and flows along the Washington and Oregon state lines and then enters the Pacific Ocean. It is fed by tributaries in Montana, Idaho, Oregon, and Washington.

In their letter the Bishops "call for a thorough, humble and introspective evaluation that seeks to eliminate both economic greed that fails to respect the environment; and ecological elitism that lacks a proper regard for the legitimate rights and property of others." The bishops consider humans to be created in the image of God as stewards of God's creation (Gen. 1:26–27). The watershed belongs to God, and humans are entrusted with responsibility for its care. The watershed has many signs of God's revelatory presence. The watershed is a sacramental commons.

The watershed is also a common home of God's creatures as well as a human community. "People are created in the image and likeness of God and are called to be neighbors to one another. Humans are created as social beings who must exercise a certain responsibility toward our neighbors." Everyone is responsible for promoting the common good of the entire watershed. "The commons belongs to everyone, and yet belongs to no one. We hold this land in trust for our present use, for future generations, and ultimately for God, from whom all things come."

In section one, entitled "The Rivers of Our Moment," the bishops identify glaring contradictions in the watershed, specifically areas of pristine beauty alongside areas of blight and degradation. They see "beautiful farms and deteriorated river banks, degraded forests and landscaped community parks; chemical and radioactive wastes seeping into the rivers ...." Dams, built in the United States for irrigation, energy, and flood control, cause changes to river levels in Canada, flooding farmlands and communities and depriving families of homes, farms, and businesses. Technology has improved the quality of life for people, but at the same time it has produced chemical and waste storage sites that threaten the well-being of the entire region.

The bishops acknowledge that agriculture is a valuable contribution to community life, but owner-operated family farms are declining. Some agricultural operations are dependent on irrigation and energy from dams. Agricultural chemicals are used by farmers to control pests and increase productivity, but these are sources of pollution in land and water. Land and water resources are limited, particularly in arid areas.

Mining has also provided jobs and funded schools, but its residues taint land and water. The watershed has large cleanup sites with environmentally dangerous working conditions. Similarly, forestry provides jobs and supports the economic well-being of the region, but timber harvesting and road construction have increased runoff and sedimentation in the waterways. All of these land-related occupations, particularly farming, fishing, and forestry, are dependent on the flowing waters of the river network.

Section two is entitled "The Rivers Through Our Memory," and it is a reflection on local traditions. Originally, Native Americans called the Columbia Che Wana or The Great River, and they saw it as a continuous flow without political boundaries. They understood nature as a nurturing mother, who provided food for all her creatures, especially the salmon. Native Americans adapted their life styles to the river flows and to the cycles of the seasons. The river was a fundamental source of life for Native Americans.

Beginning in the 16th century, Europeans and Euro-Americans settled in the West, and by the 17th century Captain Robert Gray, an American explorer, renamed the Great River the Columbia. The settlers established fishing, trapping, and canning industries, making claims on the river region and creating new commercial operations in the area. Unregulated fishing and canning practices severely depleted salmon populations and their river runs. Dams on the Columbia-Snake river system diminished the number of species. In 1957 the Dalles Dam was completed, but its backed-up water inundated Celilo Falls, which was a large Indian fishing site. At the same time, climate changes, such as global warming patterns, have altered water temperatures and accelerated declines in salmon populations. With all of these developments the western settlers have defended an ideology of rugged individualism, including a belief in absolute property rights and a narrowly focused view of value as strictly economic. They believed that the West was won by hard work and ingenuity without government assistance.

Against the settlers' attitudes the bishops present the Roman Catholic teaching on human responsibility for creation. As the creator, God has endowed humans with a unique role. "In the physical universe, they alone are consciously able to be caretakers of creation." Only humans can appreciate nature and understand the laws of biology, chemistry, and physics that shape creation. Humans "are called to use these for creation. They are created in the image and likeness of God and are commissioned as stewards of God's created and beautiful universe."

The bishops emphasize that we "neither worship creation nor are worshipped by creation; we relate to creation as its stewards, with the unique responsibilities that God has entrusted to us." Humans are to care for creation out of respect for the Creator and love of neighbor. "The natural world of creation is not itself to be worshipped. It is not an autonomous being, but a revelation of the wondrous power and love of its Creator." Just as the whole universe can be a revelation of God, so can the earth commons be a place of revelation.

The basic element in a natural spirituality is water, and the bishops employ the phrase "living water" to represent that element. "In the Hebrew Scriptures, living water means water that is flowing free and pure; it is contrasted with water from wells or cisterns, which tended to be static and undesirable." The bishops insist that the Columbia River and its tributaries are intended by God to be "living water: bountiful and healthy providers for the common good. The water itself is to be a clear sign of the Creator's presence."

Section three is entitled "The Rivers in Our Vision," and it presents an ideal, figurative watershed for the future in the manner of a spiritual vision. The bishops foresee a place where people will be treated justly and where they will work productively in communities integrated into their environments. Community responsibility will include providing for "the needs of the poor, weak, and vulnerable." They foresee the peoples of the region connected by the web of waters. "In our idealized ecological vision we see the Columbia Watershed Community inhabiting an environment of clean land, clear water, and pure air."

In their vision people will work in factories that recycle resources, use energy efficiently, release clean emissions, and emit no waste material. Forests will be managed wisely, allowing diverse types of trees and vegetation to thrive, and timber harvesting will be done without damaging the land. Fish populations will be abundant as people will understand the interrelatedness of rivers and oceans. Farmers will produce organic crops that preserve water sources and respect local wildlife. Water will be carefully conserved through "innovative irrigation techniques."

Section four is entitled "The Rivers of Our Responsibility," and it is a discussion of the ethics of the common good. "In the concept of the common good, community and individual *needs* take priority over private *wants*. The right to own and use private property is not seen as an absolute individual right; this right must be exercised responsibly for the benefit of the owner and the community as a whole." The bishops maintain that property is a trust from God, and property owners are trustees.

The primary good to be preserved is that of the individual person. Human life is sacred, and the well-being of the community depends upon respect for life. Equally important are the goods of the Columbia River Watershed, as an integrated and carefully nurtured habitat, as well as the presence and health of the salmon and other fish. Fish species are signs of the vitality of the entire region. The common good also includes respect for Native American spirituality, justice for the poor, sustainable economic development, energy conservation with alternative energy sources, respect for racial and ethnic diversity, and correlation of transportation and recreation needs with ecosystem requirements.

Native American Spirituality

The bishops' pastoral letter draws upon Native American culture and spirituality in the Pacific Northwest as a model of natural sacramentality. According to the "Columbia Basin Salmon Policy" of the Confederated Tribes of the Umatilla Indian Reservation (CTUIR) in Oregon, salmon "have been a source of sustenance, a gift of religion, and a foundation of culture for our people since time immemorial. Their existence is vital and linked to ours" (CTUIR 1995: 1). The same document explains that "water is one of our most sacred gifts from the Creator, and is an essential part of our religion. Water is the lifeblood in the veins of the Pacific Northwest. Without good clean flowing water, nothing will survive" (CTUIR 1995: 3).

Salmon are anadromous fish. The term anadromous derives from two Greek terms; *ana* means "up" or "again" and *dramon*, which is an aorist participle of *trexo*, or "I run." Thus, anadromous means "running upriver," and this designates the salmon's migratory journeys to and from the ocean. As anadromous fish, salmon can live in both freshwater and salt water. There are several kinds of anadromous salmon: chinook or king salmon, coho, steelhead, and sockeye. Other anadromous fish are American shad, white sturgeon, lamprey, and smelt.

Of the salmon varieties the chinook are the largest, averaging 22–50 pounds in weight. After spending two to five years in the ocean, they migrate up the Columbia River to the stream where they were born and spawn, after which they die. Their offspring called fry feed and grow in their home streams, and then they begin the process of "smoltification" in preparation for their return to sea water. The smolts are young fish ready to migrate downstream, primarily at high tide and near the shoreline to avoid predators. Smoltification ends when they swim through the estuary where fresh river water mixes with salty ocean water.

Among the Indians of the Pacific Northwest the Coastal Salish have lived in the region for ten millennia, enjoying a prosperous life based upon an abundance of salmon and cedar forests on the shores filled with grouse, deer, elk, and bear. The people are dependent on the fish and the forests, and if these were lost, the people would starve (Crawford 2007: 49).

For generations the Coastal Salish have measured the seasons by the return of the salmon. Twice a year, in the spring and the fall, salmon swim upstream to lay their eggs in the shoals where they had been hatched previously. The Coastal Salish fish for the salmon, catch, cut, dry, and smoke them for storage throughout the winter. Currently, in the Columbia River Watershed salmon harvests are 8% of their size one hundred years ago (Getches 2009: 394). The primary reason for the depleted harvests is the building of the hydropower facilities on the major rivers in the Northwest, thereby destroying spawning migrations, altering water temperatures and velocities, and changing the chemistry of the rivers.

The Coastal Salish believe that they have a reciprocal relationship with the salmon. Human survival depends upon acquiring the spiritual power of the salmon through reverence and respect. Spiritual power resides in other-than-human beings on land, sea, and air, and rituals are the principal means of cultivating that power. John Hart explains that for the Wanapum Indians of the Northwest the salmon are both honored and sacred beings within the creation. The Indians are related spiritually and materially to the salmon. "The Wanapum have a relational consciousness that stimulates their sense of kinship with all life, that is embodied in their unwritten laws, and that is concretized in their ethical actions ... of caring about and being responsible for the ecosystems in which they live" (Hart 2006: 107).

The primary ritual of the Pacific Northwest Indians is the First Salmon Ceremony (Crawford 2007: 25−26). During the month prior to the arrival of the salmon, human activities around the river are restricted, so as not to put any pollutants into the water. The arrival of the fish is celebrated by songs, prayers, and dances. Fishermen catch the first salmon, call it Chief Salmon, lift it onto a canoe, and bring it to the shore. They place it on a cedar platter covered with cedar and fern fronds (Crawford 2007: 28). Chief Salmon is cut in a ritual manner, without dismembering its head and bones, and it is cooked for the people to eat in joy and thanksgiving. Other salmon are caught, cooked over outdoor fires, and eaten by the entire community in a grand feast. Some Indians have suggested that in the communal salmon feast the fish are shared in the same way that bread is shared in the Christian Holy Communion (Hart 2006: 109). The First Salmon Ceremony exemplifies a sacramental commons.

After the feast, the remains of the salmon are carried on a cedar platter, accompanied by drummers and singers, to the shore line. People sing more songs and offer more prayers that honor and thank Chief Salmon for the gift of his life and to ask him to send his brothers and sisters back to his people. Men paddle canoes out to sea, carrying the salmon remains, and return them to the waters for their mythic journey home.

Anglican Commons

The concept of sacramental commons, which informs current Roman Catholic ecological ethics, is an original and important contribution. Unfortunately, the authoritative teaching of sacramental theology in the Catholic Church makes it difficult to establish independent grounds for a natural sacramentality. The Roman Catholic Church maintains that there are seven sacraments, instituted by Jesus Christ, and that they function as a closed system (McKenzie 1971: 165). Consequently, the commons tradition in the Catholic Church does not reside in the sacraments. In contrast, the commons tradition may be found in the social teachings of the Church, particularly in its definition of the common good: "The sum of all those conditions of social life which allow social groups and their individual members relatively thorough and ready access to their own fulfillment" (US Catholic Conference 2000: 45).

A second difficulty involves the role of the magisterium or the hierarchy of bishops in the Catholic Church. As discussed above, John Hart rejects an anthropocentric attitude toward nature that elevates humankind in a hierarchical superiority over nature. Hart affirms a relational model, which makes nature a revelation of God for humanity, and he finds a relational consciousness among Native Americans. In their pastoral letter on the Columbia River Watershed the Catholic bishops appeal to the image of God in Genesis 1:26–27, which places humanity above nature as stewards. The stewardship model of nature also informs current Papal social teaching. In his encyclical *Caritas in Veritate*, issued on June 29, 2009, Pope Benedict XVI states in chapter four, paragraph 50: "Human beings legitimately exercise a responsible stewardship over nature ...." (www.vatican.va) Thus, the concept of hierarchy shapes the Catholic attitude toward nature and is inconsistent with the relational consciousness of Native American spirituality.

A third difficulty is that the Catholic Church defines a sacrament in terms of form and matter, a metaphysical dualism derived from Aristotle and shaped by the Medieval theologians. With reference to baptism the recitation of the Trinity is the form, and the water is the matter. The problem is that form and matter do not represent the multiple meanings of water in the Bible, Christian theology, or even in the religions of the world. The dualism of form and matter is inadequate for a natural sacramentality. Water is the source of all potentialities. It symbolizes the primal substance from which all forms come and to which they return either by their own regression or by a cataclysmic dissolution (Eliade 1959: 130). Water precedes form, as narrated in creation stories, and it dissolves matter, as in flood stories and apocalypses. In his theology of baptism Martin Luther refuted the dualism of form and matter and appealed to Noah's flood as a more profound model. Luther turned Noah's "flood of wrath" into a "flood of grace." Drawing upon Luther's flood prayer, a Lutheran congregation in Washington State has offered a prayer connecting baptismal water with a local watershed:

> Glory to you for oceans and lakes, rivers and creeks.
> Honor to you for cloud and rain, dew and snow.
> Praise to you for Isella Glacier and Railroad Creek, for Lake Chelan and Columbia River,
> Your waters are below us, around us, above us: our life is born in you.
> You are the fountain of resurrection (Stewart 2011: 25).

In light of these difficulties I appeal to a more appropriate resource for a sacramental commons in the Anglican Communion, as represented by William Temple in the early 20th century. In his commentary on Temple's idea of the sacramental universe the Anglican theologian and scientist Arthur Peacocke explains that for Christianity "the world of matter in relation to God, has both the symbolic function of expressing his mind and the instrumental function of being the means whereby he effects his purpose" (Peacocke 1979: 290). The symbolic and instrumental functions characterize the use of physical reality in the sacraments. When viewing these two functions universally, it is possible to understand the physical universe as sacramental.

Beginning in the 16th century, the Anglican Communion took shape around the Book of Common Prayer (BCP), which located the commons tradition in the sacraments and in public worship. Thomas Cranmer compiled the first edition of the prayer book in 1549 and 1552. Affirming Martin Luther's principle of Scripture alone, Cranmer required public reading of the

Bible throughout the church year (Leuenberger 2004: 95). The second edition of the prayer book in 1662 became the "canonical" version; and the theology of this edition was mainly Reformed, but the liturgical structure was Latin-Catholic.

With the primacy of the Bible, as taught by Martin Luther and other reformers, the Anglican Communion recognized two sacraments, Baptism and Holy Communion. Only these had dominical authority and were necessary for faith. Cranmer explained that the sacraments were the instruments for receiving God's grace by effectual persuasion (Null 2006: 232). In his understanding of the Holy Communion, in particular, Cranmer achieved a fundamental new insight. He said that the miracle of the Eucharist was not the changing of the elements on the altar, as in the Roman Catholic Mass, but the changing of the minds and hearts of the people (Null 2006: 242). The Anglican Sacrament of the Holy Communion made the people "right-willed."

The Anglican Communion retained the five so-called non-biblical "sacraments" as sacramentals or sacramental rites. These were not necessary for salvation, but they were means of grace (BCP 1977: 860–861). The Anglican distinction between sacrament and sacramental sharpens John Hart's distinction between ritual-institutional and natural-universal sacraments. From the Anglican perspective Baptism and Holy Communion would be ritual-institutional and the sacramentals natural-universal. The latter applies to the universe and to the multiple symbolic meanings of water in nature. For more than a thousand years of church history there was no consensus on the number of the sacraments within the Roman Catholic Church (White 2000: 181). In the same way there is no limit on the number of sacramentals in nature.

One of the great contributions of the Anglican Communion was the English common law. This differs from the canon law which governs the Roman Catholic Church as a visible, corporate, hierarchical legal system. A centralized legal authority does not fit the egalitarian relatedness of the sacramental earth commons. John Hart's argument that natural rights should be codified does not clarify which legal system is appropriate for the sacramental commons (Hart 2006: 137). Likewise, he states that the purpose of government is to promote the common good and common goods, such as water, but he does not account for the fact that a global government with enforceable authority is absent in the world today (Hart 2006: 149).

The common law is an appropriate legal system for the sacramental commons. Custom and precedent are the primary sources of the common law, and its legitimacy derives from the consent of the people (Berman 2003:

244–246). The common law has evolved throughout time and history by means of judicial decisions which are made by judges using reason. Since decisions or holdings are rational and determined by the normative past through precedent and custom, the evolution of law is known as artificial reason. The reasons judges give for their decisions are called dicta. Custom embodies the consent of the people.

Edward Coke developed the concept of the English common law as that law enforceable through the royal courts, and he considered Roman and Canon law to be foreign and inapplicable to England (Berman 2003: 241–242). Coke regarded the common law as the law of the land and a product of English history. In a series of court cases between 1606 and 1616 Coke, as Chief Justice first of the Court of Common Pleas and then at the King's Bench, proclaimed the supremacy of the common law as an ancient English tradition (Berman 2003: 214).

Coke's successor, Matthew Hale, believed that the continuity of the common law was grounded in the Anglican faith, "a faith that transcended the sharp differences in doctrine and ritual that divided the different branches of Protestant Christianity" (Berman 2003: 249). Hale's historical jurisprudence reflected the Reformation vision of history as an unfolding of divine providence, the divine calling to reform the world and to translate God's will into legal concepts and institutions, and of the community as a divinely-inspired covenant (Berman 2003: 264–265). These perspectives led Hale to emphasize case law, the examination of facts, and the judicial application of precedents in terms of the judge's conscience and the consent of the people.

Summary

William Temple introduced the idea of a sacramental universe to account for the unity of creation and the activity of God in the material world. The principle of sacramentality means a spiritual use of matter for spiritual purposes. In Roman Catholic ecological ethics Temple's concept has been reinterpreted as a sacramental commons. The sacramental commons is natural and universal rather than ritualistic and institutional. Pure running water is a sign of a spiritual presence in nature, and all natural systems have a right to water which should be codified in law.

Roman Catholic bishops in the Pacific Northwest apply the concept of the sacramental commons to the Columbia River Watershed. They appeal to the biblical theme of living water as a revelation of God's presence in nature. The bishops draw upon Native American religion as a resource for natural sacramentality. In the Pacific Northwest the First Salmon Ceremony is an example of a natural sacramental rite. The salmon and pure running water are indispensable to the life and survival of the Indians.

Roman Catholic theology is an inappropriate resource for a sacramental commons. The Catholic Church maintains a closed sacramental system, a hierarchical concept of authority, and a form-matter metaphysical dualism, which do not fit the egalitarian needs for water within natural systems. In contrast, the Anglican Communion bears a sacramental commons within its liturgical tradition. The Anglican sacramental system is open, non-hierarchical, and not reducible to a form-matter dualism. The Anglican tradition has also produced the common law as a legal structure to defend the right to water. The common law is based upon precedent and custom, and it consists of holdings as decisions of artificial reason.

Chapter Six: Water and the Common Law

The Riparian Doctrine

The riparian doctrine was a basic concept in Roman law, and it conferred a right to persons, living on the banks of streams, to divert those waters for personal use, as long as the landowner did not cause damage to those living downstream (Glick 1970: 192). Roman law required that all water users respect the "good neighbor" principle (Scott 2008: 66). Persons whose land or water use suffered damage were entitled to compensation.

Roman law was codified in the *Institutes of Justinian*, or the *Corpis Iuris Civilis*, and promulgated in 533 CE. The Justinian Code decreed that all rivers and harbors were public, but the river banks were subject to "the owners of the adjoining lands, and consequently so too is the ownership of the trees which grow upon it" (Bk. II, tit. I, sec. 4, Moyle, trans. 1913: 35). These were perennial rivers, as opposed to freshets or torrential streams. A riparian right was continuous and permanent, but the landowner had to maintain a level and quality of stream flow (Scott 2008: 63–64).

The Roman riparian doctrine served as a precedent for the English common law. English courts developed the common law, particularly in the 17th and 18th centuries, and the two leading jurists of the 17th century were Edward Coke and Matthew Hale. Coke considered water in relation to land, and he said that land ownership included that of running water and ponds on the land (Lauer 1963: 74). Similarly, Hale stated: "Fresh rivers, of what kind soever do at common right belong to the owners of the soil adjacent" (Lauer 1963: 75). English common law jurists relied upon the principle of Medieval customary law that *aqua currit et debet currere ut currere solebat* or "water flows and should flow as it always used to do" (Teclaff 1996: 362).

During this historical period, running water was used to turn mill wheels, blow air into mines, and smelt iron and lead. Many mills were located on non-tidal streams, frequently near waterfalls, and competition for streams was intense among millers. Thus, water disputes in the 17th and 18th centuries were mainly about diversions among millers competing for the flows (Scott 2008: 72).

Matthew Hale, Lord Chief Justice and historian of the common law, held that any riparian owner had a right to an uninterrupted flow of water.

Speaking from the King's Bench in *Cox v. Matthews*, I Ventris 237, 86 Eng. Rep. 139 (K.B. 1673), as published in the English Reports, Hale held that

> If a man hath a water-course running through his ground, and erects a mill on it, he may bring his action [against a party] for diverting the stream ... and upon the evidence, it will appear, whether the defendant hath ground, through which the stream run before the plaintiff's, and that he [defendant] used to turn the stream as he saw cause, for otherwise he cannot justify it, though the [plaintiff's mill] be newly erected (Maass and Zobel 1960: 126–127).

In the 18th century William Blackstone refined the riparian right to water in his classic statement in Book Two of his *Commentaries on the Law of England*: "For water is a moveable, wandering thing, and must of necessity continue common by the law of nature; so that I can only have a temporary, transient, usufructuary property therein: wherefore if a body of water runs out of my pond into another man's, I have no right to reclaim it" (Blackstone 1979: 18).

According to Blackstone, water cannot be owned; it can only be used. One has a usufructuary right as opposed to a proprietary right. In the same volume he goes on to differentiate between two terms in the common law. Custom is local usage not attached to any person, but prescription is a personal use attached to a person or one's ancestors (Blackstone 1979: 263). In riparian law prescription or prescription easement designated a usufructuary right to water based upon a number of years of use by a non-land owner. For example, a lord granted a stream to a tenant to turn a mill, but after a period of years, the lord could not withdraw the right, and it became effective against other stream owners (Scott 2008: 69).

In the early 19th century English courts defended the natural flow theory of the riparian doctrine. In *Bealey v. Shaw*, 6 East 208, Eng. Rep. 1266 (K.B. 1805) the defendants owned a mill which had diverted water continuously since 1724. In 1787 the plaintiff built a mill on his downstream land. Then the defendants increased the amount of water diverted for their mill, thereby depriving the plaintiff of sufficient water for his mill. At issue was whether the plaintiff had a right to a continuous flow of water for his mill, even though he had only worked it for four years. The court held that the plaintiff had a right to a continuous flow and that even a downstream landowner enjoyed a full and undiminished right to water in an adjacent stream. The court stated the natural flow theory as the "general rule of law," but acknowledged that there could be exceptions to the riparian rule. The exception had to be based upon a grant or prescriptive right of over a span of 20 years. (Maass and Zobel 1960: 131).

In *Wright v. Howard*, 1 Sim and Stu. 190, 57 Eng. Rep. 76 (Ch. 1823) Vice-Chancellor John Leach presented a definitive summary of English riparian law:

> Every proprietor has an equal right to use the water which flows in the stream, and consequently no proprietor can have the right to use the water to the prejudice of any other proprietor. Without the consent of the other proprietors, who may be affected by his operations, no proprietor can either diminish the quantity of water, which would otherwise descend to the proprietors below, nor throw the water back upon the proprietor above. Every proprietor who claims a right [to do either of these] must, in order to maintain his claim, either prove an actual grant or license from the proprietors affected by his operations, or must prove an uninterrupted enjoyment of 20 years ... affording conclusive presumption of a grant (Maass and Zobel 1960: 132).

Wright attributed a right to water flow to all riparian proprietors whether or not they used the water. This case brought out two new principles. One was the natural flow concept, which meant that any use of a stream which changed the quality, quantity, or manner of the flow—except a prescriptive use—was wrongful without consent of the effected riparians, and the second was that wrongful use was legally actionable (Scott 2008: 79). Only riparians who suffered damage could sue for compensation, however, and equality of right excluded priority of right.

In the Industrial Revolution England's waterways had become dumping grounds for wastes. Industries emitted new chemicals, and steam power created thermal pollution. Cities, towns, and villages dumped sewage into rivers. Such pollution on a large scale deprived riparians of clean rivers, and so the courts appealed to the natural flow principle to clean the rivers. Any riparian could sue any polluter without showing who was responsible for the pollution (Scott 2008: 84–85).

With the founding of the United States in the 17th century the American colonists brought with them the common law riparian doctrine, and they settled along the eastern seaboard which contained many flowing rivers and lakes and had abundant rainfall. After the War of Independence and establishment of the country, the eastern states began developing their own water laws. In Connecticut, for example, *Ingraham v. Hutchinson*, 2 Conn. 589, 590 (1818) asserted the natural flow theory on the precedent of the common law:

> By the common law, every person owning land, on the banks of rivers, has a right to the use of the water in its natural stream, without diminution or alteration; that is, he has a right that it should flow, *ubi currere solebat*, and if any person on the river above him, interrupts, or diverts, the course of the water, to his prejudice, action will lie. This will give to every one all of the advantage he can derive from the water,

which does not injure the proprietor of lands on the river below him (Maass and
Zobel 1960: 139).

Massachusetts water law was riparian as well. In *Weston v. Alden*, 8
Mass. 136–137 (1811) the plaintiff, a downstream landowner, sued for
damages on the grounds that the defendant, by employing sluices to irrigate
his own close or enclosed place, had diverted water from an ancient water
course that used to flow through and irrigate the plaintiff's land. The court
ruled against the plaintiff by holding that a "man owning a close on an
ancient brook may lawfully use the water thereof for the purposes of
husbandry, a watering his cattle, or irrigating the close; and ... if the owner
of a close below is damaged thereby, it is *damnun absque injuria* [damage
without legal injury]" (Maass and Zobel 1960: 141). The common law
allowed a landowner to water his garden but not to irrigate non-riparian lands
by means of diverting water from a stream.

The New York Supreme Court case *Palmer v. Mulligan*, 3 Caines 307
(N.Y. 1805) clarified the extent of damages:

> As well, therefore, to secure to individuals the free and undisturbed enjoyment of
> their property, as to the public the benefits which must frequently redound to it from
> such use, the operation of the maxim *sic utere tuo ut alienum non loeldas* [use your
> land without harming your neighbor's} should be limited to such cases only where a
> manifest and serious damage is the result of such use and enjoyment, and where it is
> very clear indeed that the party had no right to use it in that way (Urofsky and
> Finkelman 2008: 185).

The foregoing cases laid the basis for the common law riparian doctrine
in the eastern United States. Legally, the term riparian was shorthand for
"bank-side," "proprietor of adjacent land," or a "person owning lands on the
bank of a river" (Maass and Zobel 1960: 144). Generally, in American cases
the term riparian designated a "bank-side proprietor." Proprietors, whose
lands bordered waterways, received appurtenant rights to use the waters.

In the 19th century the country began to industrialize. The New England
states built textile factories that relied on a moving force of water to turn the
gears in order to rotate the spindles. These factories required large amounts
of water, released from storage reservoirs, to empower the textile machines.
These textile factories did not remove water from streams, however, but
returned it to them for downstream flows (Glennon 2002: 15).

In light of the need for large storage reservoirs the landmark case of
Tyler v. Wilkinson, 24 Fed. Cases 472 (C.C.D.R.I. 1827) came before Joseph
Story, sitting as a judge in the U.S. Circuit Court for the District of Rhode
Island. The plaintiffs were riparians with mills located near a small dam that
was used to store water, so that it would flow more rapidly past their mills,

when it was released. The defendants constructed an upstream dam and diverted water from the Pawtucket River into a trench above the plaintiffs' mills, thereby depriving them of water that would have been stored behind the lower dam.

Justice Story ruled for the plaintiffs, and he reaffirmed that every landowner "has a right to the use of the water flowing over it in its natural current, without diminution or obstruction" (Urofsky and Finkelman 2008: 253). The proprietor does not own the water but only has a right to use it. Consequently, "no proprietor has a right to use the water to the prejudice of another. It is wholly immaterial, whether the party be a proprietor above or below" No one has "a right to diminish the quantity which will, according to the natural current, flow to a proprietor below, or to throw it back upon a proprietor above." There is a "perfect equality of right among all the proprietors of that, which is common to all." "The natural stream, existing by the bounty of Providence for the benefit of the land through which it flows, is an incident annexed, by operation of law, to the land itself."

Story held that riparians could use water in a flowing stream according to reasonable use. This principle was tested by "whether it is to the injury of the other proprietors or not" (Urofsky and Finkelman 2008: 254). Any water use changes the natural flow of the stream, but the measure of the diversion is the extent of tolerable injury to others. The maxim *sic utere tuo ut non allenum laedas* applies.

Story's opinion in *Tyler* departed from the natural flow theory and established the reasonable use standard, which all riparian states invoke today (Getches 2009: 21). In 1828, one year after *Tyler*, James Kent published the first edition of the third volume of his *Commentaries on American Laws*, and he stated the riparian rule as follows: "All that the law requires of the party, by or over whose land a stream passes, is, that he should use the water in a reasonable manner, and so as not to destroy, or render useless, or materially diminish, or affect the application of the water by the proprietors above or below on the stream" (Kent 1873: 441).

In American water law the riparian doctrine was three-fold: (1) no harm could be done to other proprietors; (2) the nature of the use was measured in relation to the size of the owner's stream; and (3) the user's needs had to be taken into account (Webb 1931: 436). Water users could not pollute the stream, and the user had to return any unused portion of the water, if the stream flow were diminished. Riparian rights applied only to those lands that touched the waters, and these rights did not apply to those who lived away from the streams.

At common law a riparian had two uses of water: natural or ordinary and artificial or extraordinary. The former was for necessary, domestic purposes, but the latter was for non-domestic desires, such as mining, manufacturing, or irrigation (Webb 1931: 434–435). Artificial or extraordinary uses were curtailed under common law.

The common law shaped the water laws of the eastern United States, and currently 29 states observe the riparian doctrine: Alabama, Arkansas, Connecticut, Delaware, Florida, Georgia, Illinois, Indiana, Iowa, Kentucky, Maine, Maryland, Massachusetts, Michigan, Minnesota, Missouri, New Hampshire, New Jersey, New York, North Carolina, Ohio, Pennsylvania, Rhode Island, South Carolina, Tennessee, Vermont, Virginia, West Virginia, and Wisconsin.

At the present time, however, riparian rights are altered by statutes due to population growth and urban or suburban development; so the 29 states are not exactly governed by the common law, as such. Permits to use water must be acquired from state agencies. For example, in Massachusetts the 1985 Watershed Management Act requires state permission for any new water withdrawals greater than 100,000 gallons a day, state regulation of stream flow permission, review of rare species, and consideration of other environmental problems (Glennon 2002: 104). Agencies that receive permits are required to detect leaks, calibrate water meters, and use low-flow fixtures.

A city existing next to a watercourse is not a riparian, unless it owns the land on the waterfront. By definition, a watercourse is a natural stream flowing constantly or recurrently on the surface of the earth in a reasonably definite channel. The eastern states require that a stream must flow all year to be classified as a watercourse (Getches 2009: 25). A watercourse includes springs, lakes, and marsh lands. Springs are concentrated flows of water from underground to the surface of the earth, and these are included within the riparian doctrine. A lake is a reasonably permanent body of water essentially at rest in a depression in the surface of the earth. A body of water with aquatic life is a pond. A person who owns land touching a pond or lake is, technically, a "littoral" landowner who also possesses riparian rights.

Riparian rights pertain only to owners' lands within a watershed. A watershed is also called a drainage basin, and it constitutes an area of land that drains into bodies of surface water (Miller 1996: 455). Water that drains into these bodies is surface runoff. At common law any use of water outside a watershed is unreasonable, even if no injury to other riparians occurs (Getches 2009: 53). The reason is that watercourses exist for the benefit of the lands through which the waters flow. Although most eastern and midwestern states observe the watershed limitation, some riparian states permit large-scale water diversions outside watersheds. These states are Georgia, Kansas, Massachusetts, New Hampshire, New York, North Carolina, Oklahoma, Texas, and Vermont. In Massachusetts, for example, The Interbasin Transfer Act requires that any water transferred between basins be approved by the Massachusetts Water Resources Commission. A community requesting a transfer of water must demonstrate a need, having explored all other alternatives including conservation, and the withdrawals must allow reasonable instream flows in the rivers from where the water is diverted (Glennon 2002: 105).

In the states where the watershed exemption is in force, such as Massachusetts, the law shifts from a common law riparianism to a regulated riparianism. Most regulated riparian states exempt from regulation withdrawals of 100,000 gallons a day, and generally they do not deny more water to people, companies, or agencies that need more water (Glennon 2009: 304).

A riparian landowner can store water, as in a reservoir, for reasonable uses without impairing the rights of other riparians. Storage and release procedures, however, must be reasonable, and liability attaches to dam owners if their released water damages other proprietors. A riparian may not unreasonably alter a stream flow, when releasing water from a storage reservoir (Getches 2009: 39).

Normally, riparian rights cannot be lost by non-users, but riparian rights may be lost under certain natural conditions. Avulsion occurs when a stream suddenly and violently changes its channel. An example of avulsion would be the impact of a hurricane on a watercourse. If avulsion moves the water away from a landowner's property, one loses one's riparian rights. Likewise, when water flows unexpectedly into a non-riparian land, the land becomes riparian.

Two related terms are accretion and reliction. Accretion occurs when water banks take on sediment, sand, or alluvium slowly and imperceptibly, so that the addition to the land becomes apparent over time. On the other hand, when water moves away from one side of a stream, this is called reliction. Relictions are lands, formerly covered by water, that become dry after the water recedes. When accretion and reliction take place, the judicial rule is that the property boundary line shifts with the water line, so that a riparian adjacent to the added land gains title to the new land and retains riparian rights (Getches 2009: 71).

Finally, the riparian doctrine confers not only a right to make a reasonable use of water flowing past one's own land but also the rights of access to the water body, fishing, building a wharf into the water body, prevention of erosion in the banks, purity of the water, and the right to claim title to the beds of non-riparian streams and lakes (Getches 2009: 34). Riparian owners are limited by the duty to refrain from harming other riparian owners, by public rights, and by navigability on public waterways.

Prior Appropriation Doctrine

The English common law did not permit irrigation in the manner of diverting water from a watercourse to non-riparian lands. As discussed above, common law allowed only watering one's garden, since irrigation was considered artificial or extraordinary and not an ordinary necessity. Common law maintained the artificial-natural distinction in order to avoid interference with nature (Shiva 2005: 22).

With the settling of the American West the common law riparian doctrine became obsolete in the mountain states west of the 100th meridian. The principal reason was that the settlers found the physical conditions of the West to be different from those in the East. In the West rainfall was neither abundant nor evenly distributed, as compared to the East, and the lands in the West were owned by the federal government which had acquired them from foreign governments and Native American tribes. Since the western settlers did not own the lands, they lacked riparian rights. The settlers were trespassers on government property.

Some of the western settlers were Mormon immigrants to the Utah territory who needed to irrigate that barren land. A centralized system of decision-making facilitated the construction of thousands of canals that supported their cooperative agricultural communities. According to the Mormons, who were members of the Church of the Latter-day Saints, water belonged to the group and not to specific individuals (Glennon 2002: 18).

Many other settlers were miners in the California gold rush of 1848. The miners diverted water, built canals, and constructed sluices to wash out the gold ore. Miners consumed and diverted water from rivers and lakes without returning it to its original watercourse. As trespassers on federal lands, the miners were actually thieves. In 1848 Richard B. Mason, military governor of California, said to a group of miners: "This is public land and the gold is the property of the United States; all of you here are trespassers, but as the Government is benefited by your getting out the gold, I do not intend to interfere" (Glennon 2002: 15). The federal government deferred to the settlers' water usage, because their work was instrumental to mining and agriculture (Getches 2001: 6).

Mining and agricultural irrigation led to a unique customary law which the federal government did not challenge. Unlike the riparian eastern states irrigation in the West became an ordinary and natural necessity. Hence, in the West the common law distinction between artificial and natural, extraordinary and ordinary collapsed (Webb 1931: 435). The western miners and farmers essentially abandoned the common law.

The western water law system became known as the prior appropriation doctrine, and Congress confirmed this standard when it passed the Desert Land Act in 1877 which

> provided that water rights on tracts of desert land should depend upon bona fide prior appropriation; and that all surplus water over and above actual appropriation and necessary use, together with the water of all lakes, rivers, and other sources of water upon the public lands and not navigable, should be held free for appropriation by the public for irrigation, mining, and manufacturing purposes, subject to existing rights (Ranquist 1975: 644).

When settlers made claims to water and diverted it to wherever they needed it, they achieved a priority of appropriation. When they diverted water from a river or stream for irrigation; and they did not replenish the watercourses, as required by the riparian doctrine, their water use became consumptive and extractive. The settlers' change of the nature of water use was grounded in their belief that God had given nature to them for human development (Worster 1985: 89–90).

Several state courts approved the prior appropriation doctrine and acknowledged that the common law was inappropriate for the West. For example, in *Moyer v. Preston*, 6 Wyo. 308, 318, 44 Pac. 845, 847 (1896)/the Wyoming Supreme Court held that the "common law doctrine relating to the rights of a riparian proprietor in the water of a natural stream, and the use thereof, is unsuited to our requirements and necessities, and never obtained in Wyoming" (Maass and Zobel 1960: 110–111).

In *Coffin v. Left Hand Ditch Co.*, 6 Colo. 443, 446–447 (1882) the Colorado Supreme Court held that the prior appropriation doctrine "has existed from the date of the earliest appropriations of water within the boundaries of the state .... We conclude, then, that the common law doctrine ... is inapplicable to Colorado. Imperative necessity, unknown in the countries which gave it birth, compels the recognition of another doctrine in conflict therewith" (Maass and Zobel 1960: 111).

Prior appropriation meant that the first party which claimed water in a watercourse acquired a vested right to the water as private property (Worster 1985: 88). Prior appropriation entailed the following principles: (1) exclusive right to the first appropriation and a conditional right for a later one; (2)

appropriation rights were measured by beneficial uses; (3) water could be used on riparian and non-riparian lands; (4) diversion was permitted regardless of the diminution of a stream; and (5) maintaining the water right depended upon continuous, beneficial use (Gopalakrishnan 1973: 73). The fifth point included the imperative of the water right, namely, use it or lose it. The prior appropriation doctrine promoted a full utilization of water, but it required that a specific volume of water to be diverted be determined by a beneficial use. Undiverted water was considered a waste. Leaving water in a stream did not conserve it but wasted it (Glennon 2002: 17).

Within the western states the prior appropriation doctrine fixed the principle of "first in time, first in right" (Getches 2001: 7). The western states approved claims of the ownership of water within their boundaries, and this practice turned into a free-for-all system. Primary claimants to water comprised a hierarchy of senior water rights holders who received deference from junior water rights holders. In periods of drought senior water rights holders were entitled to their full appropriations. Water rights were determined by the specific dates of the first appropriations.

The rise of the prior appropriation doctrine in the West was due not only to the settlers adaptation to arid geography but also to their belief that the government should encourage economic development and property rights and that nature had only instrumental value for agricultural and industrial exploitation (Glennon 2002: 18). In their drive to replace the common law the western settlers turned rivers into marketable commodities. The American West became a hydraulic civilization, a social order driven by large scale technological manipulation of water in an arid climate (Worster 1985: 7). The western social order was ruled by a technocratic elite in the late 19th century for whom power was shaped by physical control and technical expertise. It became "natural" to alter or destroy a river for maximum economic return.

The social order of the West represented the economic philosophy of possessive individualism (Worster 1985: 92). This concept emerged in 17th century English thought primarily through the writings of Thomas Hobbes and John Locke. According to this point of view, the individual is proprietor of his or her own capacities, owing nothing to society, and existing independently of the wills of other people (Macpherson 1962: 3). Society consists of external relations of exchange among independent proprietors. With possessive individualism property rights confer power to an owner to dispose of property as he or she wishes. This presumes that all property is a commodity that can be given a price and alienated in an exchange. John Locke, in particular, thought of property mainly as land, but he viewed water as an analogy. Locke believed that water and land were so abundant that they could be turned into commodities for the beneficial use of everyone (Gunnemann 2005: 107–108).

Currently, the prior appropriation doctrine is the legal standard in Alaska, Arizona, Colorado, Idaho, Montana, Nevada, New Mexico, Utah, and Wyoming. In these western states the doctrine has three aspects: intent, diversion, and beneficial use (Getches 2009: 92, 127, 129). First, intent requires a public, physical demonstration of appropriation, and having plans alone are regarded as speculation. Second, actual diversion is necessary to complete a water right. Some states have five years as a limit for diversion. Third, the appropriator's right to claim water is determined by beneficial use. There is no right to waste water, but misuse and intent to relinquish water rights constitute abandonment of the right. Non-use must be for an extended period of time, such as ten years in Colorado, for example. Forfeiture is non-use over a span of time set by statute, as in New Mexico which has five years. These principles of prior appropriation are intended to prevent fraud and maintain order.

Under the prior appropriation doctrine trans-basin diversion of water is permitted. In the West water from the Colorado River dams supply Albuquerque, Salt Lake City, San Diego, and Los Angeles. The Central Arizona Project is a concrete-lined canal that takes Colorado River water from the Arizona state line to Phoenix and Tucson, crossing a distance of 330 miles at an altitude of nearly 3000 feet above sea level (Glennon 2009: 108). In Colorado water is diverted from the Colorado River to Denver and cities in eastern Colorado. The Colorado legislature has enacted a statute to protect the western slope's "present appropriations of water and in addition thereto prospective uses of water for irrigation and other beneficial consumptive use purposes" (Getches 2009: 172).

The prior appropriation doctrine also permits the storage of water for beneficial purposes. Generally, states may capture and store water beyond actual appropriation, lest it go to waste. A storage permit must be obtained, and the right to store water is not fulfilled until water is put to a beneficial use (Getches 2009: 202). In cases of conflict involving both diversion and storage senior water rights holders get priority.

Hybrid Water Law

Ten states have a mixture of riparian and prior appropriation doctrines, and they are California, Kansas, Mississippi, Nebraska, North Dakota, Oklahoma, Oregon, South Dakota, Texas, and Washington. These states

originally recognized the riparian doctrine in the English common law, but
they later acknowledged that prior appropriation was more suitable for
allocating water in their climates and terrains.

California was the first hybrid state. In 1850, when California became a
state, the first legislature passed the Act of April 13, 1850, stating that the
"common law of England, so far as it is not repugnant to or inconsistent with
the constitution of the United States, or the conditions and laws of this state,
is the rule of decision in all the courts of this state" (Littleworth and Garner
1995: 30).

At the same time, prior appropriation principles prevailed in the mining
camps on public lands, and the miners' custom of diverting water from
streams for the beneficial use of mining was recognized by the California
Supreme Court in *Irwin v. Phillips*, 5 Cal. 140, 145–147 (1855). Nine years
after the discovery of gold in California in 1848, the California Supreme
Court held in *Hill v. King*, 8 Cal. 336, 378 (1857) that the "right to
appropriate the water from the streams of this state, for mining and other
purposes, has been too long settled to admit of any doubt or discussion at this
time" (Maass and Zobel 1960: 112–113). By 1872 the California legislature
regulated water rights by enacting Civil Code provisions, and Civil Code
section 1410 stated that the "right to use running water flowing in a river or
stream, or down a canyon or ravine may be acquired by appropriation"
(Littleworth and Garner 1995: 30).

Riparian landowners feared losing the upstream water supplies by
appropriation. The conflict between riparians and appropriators was
resolved, however, by the California Supreme Court in *Lux v. Haggin*, 69
Cal. 255 (1886). *Lux* reaffirmed the Act of 1850 which

> adopts the common law of England; not the civil law, nor the *ius commune
> antiquum*, or Roman "law of nature" of some of the civil-law commentaries, nor the
> Mexican law .... And the expression "common law of England" designates the
> English common law as interpreted as well in the English courts as in the courts of
> such of the states of the union as have adopted the English common law (Maass and
> Zobel 1960: 113).

The court explained that the United States held common law water rights
to non-navigable watercourses flowing in the public domain, and that the
United States transferred public domain lands by federal patents and state
grants to private ownership, including riparian water rights (Littleworth and
Garner 1995: 30–31). The *Lux* court also held that the 1872 Civil Code made
riparian rights paramount to non-riparian rights and that a riparian was
entitled to a reasonable volume of water without harming other riparians
(Littleworth and Garner 1995: 31).

In California riparian rights were defended in the courts and prior appropriation rights by the same courts and the legislature through the Civil Code, section 1410–1422 in 1872. Section 1414 of the Civil Code established the "first in time, first in right" principle which is still in force. The Water Commission Act of 1913 endures as the basis of the current California Water Code. All water is the property of the people of the state, and the right to use water can be acquired by law through the state permit system. While riparian rights attach to landowners, water subject to appropriation is limited to the following:

> All water flowing in any natural channel, excepting so far as it has been or is being applied to useful and beneficial purposes upon, or in so far as it is or may be reasonably needed for useful and beneficial purposes upon lands riparian thereto, or otherwise appropriated, is hereby declared to be public water of the state and subject to appropriation in accordance with the provisions of this code. (Water Code, art. 120).

In California only surface water and subterranean streams flowing through known and definite channels, excluding percolating groundwater, can be appropriated (Littleworth and Garner 1995: 43).

All hybrid states impose limits on the exercise of present and future riparian rights, and these limits derive from the reasonable use rule. A riparian cannot oppose an appropriator unless one can prove "undue interference with the riparian's reasonable use of water" (Getches 2009: 213). All hybrid states have also curtailed by statutes the common law principle that non-use does not extinguish riparian rights. These statutes adopt prior appropriation but recognize vested water rights applied to beneficial uses prior to the passage of the statutes. During periods of water shortage, riparians must restrict their uses, while senior appropriators may take their full entitlement (Getches 2009: 217).

In California water in excess of existing, reasonable, and beneficial needs may be appropriated. These are running streams and lakes; water flowing in a natural channel; subterranean streams flowing in known, definite channels; spring waters; and navigable interstate streams (Littleworth and Garner 1995: 43–44).

The two remaining states, Hawaii and Louisiana, have their own unique water laws based upon their respective historical legacies. Hawaiian water law descends from the ancient system of land tenure in premodern Hawaiian society. The basic land unit was the *ahupua'a* which extended from the coast inland, usually along natural boundaries or topographies (Tuggle 1979: 176). Each island was organized radially by many *ahupua'as*. The term *ahupua'a* meant "pig altar" or "pig cairn" (Tuggle 1979: 178). A cairn was a rounded heap of stones. *Ahupua'as* had streams flowing through them for irrigation.

Hawaiian society was divided into chiefs and commoners. The chiefs owned the land and produce in the *ahupua'as*. Chiefs allotted land to the commoners, who supported themselves and the chiefs with their produce. The chiefs had authority because they were closer to the gods genealogically than the commoners. After contact with the westerners, Hawaii achieved a centralized monarchy. The first king was Kamehameha who assumed power in 1810 (Daws 1968: 43). The chiefs were subordinate to the king, but they channeled his authority in the *ahupua'a*. The *ahupua'as* became political subdivisions of the state.

Today Hawaiian water law is an extension of the ancient kingdom. My source is the Hawaiian Supreme Court case *In re: Water Use Permit Applications*, 9 P.3d 409 (Hawaii 2000). The court cites Article XI, section 1 of the Hawaiian Constitution which mandates that

> "for the benefit of present and future generations, the State and its political subdivisions shall protect and conserve ... all natural resources, including ... water ... and shall promote the development and utilization of these resources ... in a manner consistent with their conservation," and further declares that "all public natural resources are held in trust for the benefit of the people" (III. B. 2).

Thus, Hawaiian water law is founded upon the public trust doctrine, which derives from the common law and Roman law. The court discusses the public trust as both duty and responsibility to "maintain the purity and flow of our waters for future generations and to assure that the waters of our land are put to responsible and beneficial uses" (III. B. 3. iii). These latter phrases invoke the riparian and prior appropriation doctrines. Hawaii is, therefore, a public trust oriented hybrid state.

Under the public trust water use permit applications to the Commission on Water Resource Management bear the burden of proof (III. B. f. 1). The criteria for issuing permits are "reasonable and beneficial use" and "consistent with the public interest." Contrary to prior appropriation systems the court does not regard the leaving of water in a stream as a waste (III. B. 6). The court also rejects the surface and groundwater dichotomy, as found in the water laws of many states. The court cites the hydrological unit and defines it as "a surface drainage area or a groundwater basin or a combination of the two" (III. B. iic).

Louisiana water law is based on the French Civil Code which was promulgated in 1804 and implemented by Napoleon. The Louisiana Code is closely related to riparian doctrines, as the following articles illustrate.

> Article 657: The owner of an estate bordering on running water may use it as it runs for the purpose of watering his estate or for other purposes.

Article 658: The owner of an estate through which water runs, whether it originates there or passes from lands above, may make use of it while it runs over his lands. He cannot stop it or give it another direction and is bound to return it to its ordinary channel where it leaves his estate (Getches 2009: 229).

Groundwater Doctrines

The foregoing discussion of riparian, prior appropriation, and hybrid water law doctrines deals primarily with surface water. Many state laws do not clearly account for groundwater in relation to surface water, as they have not kept up with developments in hydrology. Hydrologically, surface water and groundwater comprise an interrelated continuum. The legal gap between surface water and groundwater has persisted since the mid-19th century, when hydrology was in a limited stage of development. In 1850 the Connecticut Supreme Court held in *Roath v. Driscoll*, 20 Conn. 533, 541 (1850) that surface water regulation had to be different from that of groundwater.

Water, whether moving or motionless *in the earth*, is not, in the eye of the law, distinct from the earth. The laws of its existence and progress, while there, are not uniform, and cannot be known or regulated. It rises to great heights and moves collaterally, by influences beyond our apprehension. These influences are so secret, changeable, and uncontrollable [sic], we cannot subject them to the regulations of law, nor build upon them a system of rules, as has been done with streams upon the surface (Glennon and Maddock 1997: 15).

The gap between law and physical reality was articulated at the theoretical level by Classon S. Kinney, a Utah lawyer who published *A Treatise on the Law of Irrigation* in 1894. Kinney believed that an inexhaustible supply of water flowed in "subterranean or underground watercourses" (Glennon 2002: 29). Kinney differentiated between underground water in "unknown" channels and "known" channels, which contain a "subflow" or "underflow." He thought that some groundwater flowed in "known" channels in connection with the rivers or streams, while other groundwater percolated in the ground in "unknown" channels (Glennon 2002: 30). As a western lawyer, he applied the prior appropriation doctrine to surface water and the reasonable use rule to groundwater. To this day most states apply the reasonable use rule to groundwater and the riparian or prior appropriation doctrine to surface water.

In American water law there are four groundwater doctrines employed in various states. The first is the English common law rule of absolute ownership which confers upon landowners the unlimited right to sink domestic wells on their properties and to withdraw water from beneath the surface (Getches 2009: 268). Texas applies this rule to capture groundwater as an absolute right, even if a neighbor's well goes dry. In Texas this is known as the rule of the biggest pump (Glennon 2002: 268). The English rule allows landowners to use the water as they please, even diverting it to other lands or wasting it.

The second groundwater doctrine is the reasonable use rule which allows pumping for any reasonable purpose on one's own land, such as for domestic, irrigation, or industrial uses. There is no limit to the amount of water withdrawn, provided that it be used on the owner's land. This rule is similar to the riparian doctrine, and it is in force in most eastern and some western states.

The third rule is the prior appropriation doctrine in the mountain states. This rule stipulates that parties who begin groundwater pumping first get the best legal rights. The rule protects senior water rights holders. In cases of harm against senior holders liability attaches to junior holders. The prior appropriation rule measures withdrawal of groundwater by beneficial use. For example, Oregon applies prior appropriation to ground and surface waters, but it restricts groundwater pumping when it interferes with surface water (Glennon and Maddock 1997: 25–27).

The fourth standard is the correlative rights doctrine of California, Vermont, and Hawaii. Under this rule groundwater rights are determined by land ownership. Owners of land over a single aquifer are each limited to a reasonable share of the total supply of water as measured by acreage (Getches 2009: 269). In times of shortage landowners must reduce their withdrawals to a fair and just proportion of the water supply.

California recognizes three categories of groundwater: (1) underflow of a surface stream; (2) definite underground stream; and (3) percolating water (Littleworth and Garner 1995: 48). In California the former two types are governed by riparian or prior appropriation rights, but the latter by the correlative rights and reasonable use rule of percolating waters. This principle came out of the California Supreme Court case of *Katz v. Walkinshaw*, 74 P.766, 772 (Cal. 1903), which rejected the common law rule of absolute ownership. According to *Katz*, under the English common law a landowner owns everything beneath the surface, including soil, rocks, and water; but the landowner has no protection against another landowner who digs a deeper well and takes an unlimited amount of water (Littleworth and Garner 1995: 49). Thus, in *Katz* landowners overlying a groundwater basin have equal rights to the water and must share in periods of water shortage. They can pump the basin to use water on their own lands.

Although rights to pump groundwater require state permits, in reality most states allow the pumping of new wells under the reasonable use doctrine, which encourages exploitation. Some of the western states identify critical areas where pumping may be prohibited or curtailed. The criterion is the safe yield standard, which designates a volume of withdrawal that does not exceed discharge (Getches 2009: 289). Phoenix and Tucson have relied heavily upon groundwater pumping to the extent of the drying up of rivers and streams. Consequently, the Arizona legislature passed the 1980 Arizona Groundwater Management Act which has four provisions: (1) it quantifies existing groundwater uses and grandfathers rights to them; (2) it prohibits new groundwater wells, unless they are carefully controlled; (3) it establishes a state agency to administer and supervise all groundwater users; and (4) it imposes water conservation standards on all water users (Glennon 2002: 215). While the act protects existing water rights, it places restrictions on the liberty to pump groundwater.

Nationally, Americans pump 83 billion gallons of groundwater a day, and they get 15% of their water from private wells, while digging 800,000 new wells a year (Glennon 2009: 305). New Mexico allows domestic wells to pump one million gallons of water a year and Arizona three million gallons. Domestic wells are exempt from state regulations, but they consume enormous amounts of water. Ironically, most states recognize no private property ownership rights to groundwater and consider it to be public property (Getches 2009: 273). In light of the extensive private withdrawals of public groundwater it is necessary to explore the status of water under the public trust doctrine.

Summary

The English common law affirms the riparian doctrine of water law on the precedent of classical Roman law. With the riparian standard landowners have the right to use water flowing on or through their lands. Originally, the English courts held the natural flow theory of the riparian doctrine. This legal theory entered the eastern United States, but after *Tyler v. Wilkinson* courts appealed to the reasonable use standard of riparian law. Today 29 eastern and midwestern states follow riparian law.

When the western states were settled the common law became inapplicable to the arid, desert regions of the West. Western miners and agricultural communities needed extensive irrigation, which was impermissible under common law, and a new customary law of prior appropriation emerged. The prior appropriation doctrine established the principle of "first in time, first in right," and it posited the instrumental value of water. Presently, the nine states in the intermountain West and Alaska maintain the prior appropriation doctrine.

Ten of the western states, beginning with California, initially recognized riparian water law, but they incorporated the prior appropriation doctrine for irrigation and formed hybrid systems. Hawaii has a unique hybrid water law system that is heavily influenced by the public trust doctrine, and Louisiana water law is based on the French Civil Code.

Many state laws do not acknowledge the hydrological relation between surface water and groundwater, and they rely upon four different groundwater concepts. Texas applies the common law rule of absolute ownership to groundwater. Many eastern and some western states hold the reasonable use rule, and the mountain states retain the prior appropriation doctrine for groundwater extraction. California, Vermont, and Hawaii use the correlative rights doctrine, which mandates a fair and reasonable sharing of water by landowners.

Chapter Seven: Water and the Public Trust

Historical Precedents

The public trust doctrine is the legal basis for the protection of all freshwater sources. The public trust means that the government holds common water resources in trust for the public and regulates the commons in the public interest (Scanlan 2006: 1336). Invoking the public trust prevents private ownership and over-exploitation of freshwater supplies. Public trust water cannot be defined as property or as a commodity, and, therefore, the public trust doctrine conforms to the sacramental earth commons.

In the western legal tradition the public trust doctrine descends from the *Institutes of Justinian,* as follows: "Thus, the following things are by natural law common to all—the air, running water, the sea, and consequently the sea-shore" (2. 1. 1. Moyle, trans. 1913). No one is "forbidden access to the sea-shore," which "extends to the limit of the highest tide in time of storm or winter" (2. 1. 1–3). The "sea-shore, as of the sea itself, is part of the law of nations ...." (2. 1. 5) Roman law differentiated between navigable and non-navigable waters. The former included commerce and fishing, and the latter pertained to public or private watercourses. Roman law protected the use of navigable waterways for the public benefit (Ingram and Oggins 1992: 517).

In Medieval France the commons were lands, unencumbered by private property rights, jointly owned by the village or community, and they were sustained and protected by customary law (Bloch 1966: 181–183). Within the commons there was a deep feeling that water could not be appropriated by individuals but could be used by everyone. The *Customs of Barcelona*, which appeared about 1070 CE and extended to regions of France, stipulated that the "public highways and byways, running water and springs, meadows, pastures, forests, heaths and rocks ... are not to be held by Lords ... nor are they to be maintained ... in any other way than that their people may always be able to use them" (Bloch 1966: 183).

In Medieval Spain King Alfonso X ordered the codification of Spanish law in *Las Siete Partidas*, which was promulgated in 1265 CE. This body of law acknowledged that water was necessary for human life. In the tradition of the *Institutes of Justinian Las Siete Partidas* provided that water "could be used in common by all persons for certain purposes: drinking, fishing, navigation, docking and repairing of boats, and unloading of merchandise" (Meyer 1996: 117). No permits were needed for these activities.

In Medieval England King John authorized the Magna Carta to be proclaimed throughout the realm in 1215 CE. The Magna Carta promoted the idea of the rule of law not only with abstract principles of justice and equity but also with specific rules (Berman 1983: 293). Section 23 of the Magna Carta offered a precedent for the public trust doctrine (Wilkinson 1988–1989: 429). The section read as follows: "All fish weirs (kidelli) in the Thames and the Medway and throughout England are to be entirely dismantled, save on the sea coasts" (www.archives.gov). Weirs or kidelli were dams or other barriers in watercourses which had nets and similar devices to catch fish (Lauer 1963: 72–73). These constructions interfered with navigation, and so it was necessary to clean all channels and remove obstructions. In 13th century England it was understood that flowing water was common property by natural right and that no one could erect structures that interfered with water flows (Lauer 1963: 66, 69).

The English common law maintained the public trust doctrine. The common law distinguished between "the *jus privatum*, which the Crown could transfer to individuals in fee ownership, and the *jus publicum*, which the Crown held in trust for the public" (Wilkinson 1988–1989: 431). The *jus publicum* granted public rights of use, and these were determined by the coasts and the rivers touched by the ebb and flow of the tide. The public was able to use the beds and banks of navigable rivers for towing, mooring, and anchoring vessels, but in cases of conflict the public right of navigation prevailed juridically.

Non-navigable rivers, in which the tide did not ebb or flow, belonged to the landowners; but navigable rivers with the ebb and flow of the tide were royal rivers, because such rivers were like the sea over which the king had dominion (Lauer 1963: 89). Such rivers were considered branches of the sea. Common law jurists of the 16th and 17th centuries regarded rivers as appendages either of the sea or of adjoining lands (Lauer 1963: 90).

American courts modified the common law to accommodate the fact that the United States had large, inland, navigable rivers that were far away from the ebb and flow of the tide. For example, in *Packer v. Bird* the U.S. Supreme Court acknowledged that the Commonwealth of Pennsylvania never accepted the common law doctrine. "The Supreme Court of that state, in holding that the river Monogehela was a navigable stream, and that its soil up to the low-water mark, and the river itself, were the property of the commonwealth ...." (*Packer v. Bird*, 137 U.S. 661 (1891). This opinion followed Roman law which recognized rivers as navigable, if they were actually used for navigation (Wilkinson 1988–1989: 447).

Since American rivers were navigable beyond the tides, the courts developed new criteria of navigability. In *The Daniel Ball* case the U.S. Supreme Court held that

> Those rivers must be regarded as public navigable rivers in law which are navigable in fact. And they are navigable in fact when they are used, or are susceptible, of being used, in their ordinary condition, as highways for commerce, over which trade and travel are or may be conducted in the customary modes of trade and travel on water (77 U.S. (10 Wall.) 557 (1870). (Ingram and Oggins 1992: 521)

In the United States titles to the beds of navigable waterways passed from the federal government to the states, when they gained statehood; but state titles were neither absolute nor inalienable (Ingram and Oggins 1992: 519). The states were still subordinate to the power of the federal government to regulate commerce on waterways. The Constitution conferred on Congress the right to regulate commerce in The Commerce Clause, which states in pertinent part: "To regulate commerce with foreign Nations, and among several states, and with Indian Tribes" (Art. I, sec. 8). Since commerce was mainly water borne, the clause established federal control of navigable waterways. The states' retention of titles to river beds was subject to the federal "navigation servitude," or the right of the federal government to keep waterways open to navigation (Getches 2009: 237). The states surrendered control of the flows of rivers to the federal government but kept the titles to the river beds.

Early American case law placed lands beneath navigable waterways under the public trust. As an example, the earliest public trust state case was *Arnold v. Mundy*, in which the New Jersey Supreme Court ruled that the state could not sell titles to oyster beds underlying navigable waters, because the state held these in trust for the public good.

> By the law of nature, which is the only true foundation of all social rights ... by the civil law, which formerly governed almost all the civilized world ... [and] by the common law of England ... the navigable rivers where the tide ebbs and flows, the ports, the bays, the coasts of the sea, including both the water and the land under the water, for the purposes of passing and repassing, navigation, fishing, fowling sustenance, and all other uses of the water ... are common to all the people (*Arnold v. Mundy*, 6 N.J.L., 78 (1821). (Ingram and Oggins 1992: 519–520)

Arnold was cited as precedent in two subsequent U.S. Supreme Court cases. One was *Martin v. Waddell*, 41 U.S. (16 Pet.) 367 (1842), which concluded that "shores, rivers, bays, arms of the sea, and the land under them are held as a public trust for the benefit of the whole community" (Ingram and Oggins 1992: 520).

The other and still definitive case in American public trust law was *Illinois Central Railroad Company v. Illinois*, 146 U.S. 387 (1892). The Act of the Legislature of Illinois of April 16, 1869 granted to the Illinois Central Railroad all the right and title "to the submerged lands constituting the bed of Lake Michigan and lying east of the tracks and breakwater of the Illinois Central Railroad Company for the distance of one mile" of Chicago. The grant of land included the central business district of Chicago and "more than one thousand acres of incalculable value, comprising virtually the whole commercial water front of the city" (Sax 1970: 489).

Four years later the legislature revoked the grant, and the railroad company sued the state of Illinois. The railroad company claimed absolute title to the submerged land and complete power to use and dispose of it. The state filed suit for a judicial determination of the title of the submerged land. On appeal the U.S. Supreme Court upheld the revocation and declared that the original grant was invalid.

Justice Stephan J. Field stated the court's holding:

> It is the settled law of this country that the ownership of and dominion and sovereignty over lands covered by tidewaters, within the limits of the several states, belong to the respective states within which they are found, with the consequent right to use or dispose of any portion thereof, when that can be done without substantial impairment of the interest of the public in the waters .... (146 U.S. 435 (1892).

The same doctrine applies to the Great Lakes, which are like the "open sea except in the freshness of their waters and in the absence of the ebb and flow of the tide." They are inland seas whose submerged soil comes under the dominion and sovereignty of the state. Field explained how American law differed from the English common law: "At one time, the existence of tidewaters was deemed essential in determining the admiralty jurisdiction of courts in England. That doctrine is now repudiated in this country as wholly inapplicable to our conditions. In England, the ebb and flow of the tide constitute the legal test of the navigability of waters." In England tidewaters and navigable waters are synonymous. The Great Lakes and rivers of the United States are not touched by the ebb and flow of the tide, but they are navigable for great distances (146 U.S. 436 (1892). In the United States tidewaters and navigable waters are not the same.

Justice Field went on to explain that "the state holds title to the lands under the navigable waters of Lake Michigan, within its limits in the same manner that the state holds title to soils under the tidewater by the common law ...." (146 U.S. 452 (1892). The title is "held in trust for the people of the state, that they may enjoy the navigation of the waters, carry on commerce over them, and have liberty of fishing therein, freed from the obstruction or interference of private parties." The state may grant parcels of land under navigable waters for "wharves, docks, and piers," as long as these do not impair the public interest. The public trust cannot be relinquished by a transfer of property.

> A grant of all the lands under the navigable waters of a state has never been adjudged to be within the legislative power, and any attempted grant of the kind would be held, if not absolutely void on its face, as subject to revocation. The state can no more abdicate its trust over property in which the whole people are interested, like navigable waters and soils under them, so as to leave them entirely under the use and control of private parties ... than it can abdicate its police powers in the administration of government and the preservation of the peace (146 U.S. 453 (1892).

With this holding the court advanced the central concept in public trust litigation: "When a state holds a resource which is available for the free use of the general public, a court will look with considerable skepticism upon *any* governmental conduct which is calculated *either* to reallocate that resource to more restricted uses *or* to subject public uses to the self-interest of private parties" (Sax 1970: 490).

The Supreme Court defined the primary functions of public waterways as those of commerce, navigation, and fishing. Since this case remains the controlling precedent, states hold titles to lands beneath navigable waters as a trust for the citizens of the state (Getches 2009: 242–243).

Islamic Water Law

Outside the western legal tradition Islam has maintained a unique public trust doctrine in its water laws, ever since it arose in the Arabian desert in the seventh century CE. Islam ascribes "the most sacred qualities to water as a life-giving, sustaining and purifying resource" (De Chatel 2002). Water flows from the origin of life on earth, and it is the element from which God created humanity, as the Holy Qur'an testifies:

> It is He Who merged the two seas,
> This one fresh and sweet water,
> That one salty and bitter.
> Between them He erected a barrier, an impassable boundary.
> It is He Who, from water, created man,
> Conferring on him kinship, of blood and of marriage.
> Your Lord is Ever-Powerful (25: 53–54).

The Qur'an emphasizes the central role of water in creation. "Do the unbelievers not realize that the heavens and earth were sewn together, but We ripped them apart, and from water created every living thing?" (21:30). As the primal element of creation, water was present before the heavens and the earth were created: "He it is Who created the heavens and the earth in six days, and His Throne was upon the waters, so as to test you: who among you is the best in works" (11:7).

The waters of rain, rivers, and public fountains symbolize God's benevolence: "From the sky We pour down pure water, therewith to revive a region what was dead, And to give to drink, among what We created, many cattle and humans. And We divided it among them, in order that they remember, but most mankind persist in their denial" (25:48). The Qur'an reminds people that water is a gift of God: "Have you given thought to the water you drink? Was it you who poured it down from the rain-clouds, or was it Us who poured it? If We wish We could turn it into salt water—will you not offer thanks?" (56: 68–70)

Islam came out of the vast, inhospitable Arabian desert which lacked rivers and easily accessible freshwater (Saleh 2010: 21). The average annual rainfall was about four inches a year, barely enough to support small animal herds and some agriculture (Brockopp 2010: 2). The basic social organization was the tribe, and the tribe maintained kinship ties, polytheism, and a common language. Muhammad, the founder of Islam, was born at Mecca in the Quraysh tribe. Beginning at age 40, Muhammad received a series of consecutive revelations from God, commanding him to proclaim a new religion of the one, transcendent God. Since Muhammad's proclamation required that the Arabs forsake the deities of their ancestors, many rejected his message (Saleh 2010: 34). Nevertheless, Muhammad persevered, preaching repentance and the worship of God.

Along with repentance and worship Muhammad emphasized charity as the principal virtue. Water should be given freely to all people on the basis of charity. If one were to refuse water to others, one would sin against God and merit punishment in the Last Judgment at the end of the world. According to the *hadiths*, that is, reports of the sayings of Muhammad or the oral tradition, among the three people God will ignore on the Day of Resurrection, will be "the man who, having water in excess of his needs, refuses it to a traveler ...." (De Chatel 2002)

Islamic law derives from divine revelation to Muhammad and is embodied in the Qur'an. Divine law, or *Shariah*, comprises "the whole body of rules guiding the life of a Muslim in law, ethics, and etiquette ...." (Hodgson 1974: 516) The centrality of water regulation in Islam is reflected in the fact that the root meaning of *Shariah* is "the path to water" or, as in an earlier era, "the law of water" (Abouali 1998: 444).

Shariah contributed four basic principles to water law: (1) water is a gift of God and belongs to the whole community; (2) value added to water by labor in the sense of retaining, distributing, or conserving it may create a qualified right of ownership; (3) a right of appropriation is balanced by a distribution of surplus; and (4) liability attaches to withholding, misusing, polluting, or degrading water (Abouali 1998: 444).

In the *Shariah* water is a common good, according to the principle of solidarity, and it cannot be made the object of a commercial transaction (Stephan 2007: 2). The Islamic idea of the common good corresponds to the public trust doctrine in the western legal tradition. Specific types of water are protected under the Islamic common good: groundwater; natural wells, the great rivers that flow in the public domain, such as the Nile; and the great lakes and seas (Stephan 2007: 2).

Islam affirms two basic human rights. One is the right of thirst, which means "juridically the right to take water to quench one's thirst or to water one's animals" (Caponera 1973: 13). The right of thirst belongs to Muslims and non-Muslims, and it applies to public and private property. This right entails a free use of water for domestic needs, and everyone has the right to water in the public domain. One may satisfy one's thirst on private wells or basins, including watering one's animals, as long as one does not damage the watercourse, ditch, or conduit (Stephan 2007: 3). One may take water from private property with buckets or pitchers to satisfy domestic needs. One may also take water from private property where it is renewed naturally, as in springs.

The Islamic practice of giving water to those who are thirsty represents the virtues of charity and human solidarity (Stephan 2007: 4). This tradition is manifest in the public fountains throughout the Arab world. Before running water was installed in households, inhabitants of Islamic cities fetched their water from fountains, cisterns, or wells (De Chatel 2002). In Medieval Islam woman and young girls would gather at the fountains every day, carrying jugs and pitchers to get water for their families and to socialize with one another.

The second basic human right is that of irrigation, and this may be exercised only in the public domain (Stephan 2007: 5). One may withdraw water from public water sources, provided that one does not damage the community or infringe on the rights of other parties. Irrigation is for the watering of land, trees, and plants; and in times of abundance rainwater may be used by anyone on public lands (Caponera 1973: 15).

Since water cannot be made the object of a commercial transaction in Islamic tradition, water may become private property only under specific conditions: (1) transfer of property from one party to another; (2) inheritance of property; and an (3) intentional occupation of land with a capture of water (Stephan 2007: 6; Abouali 1998: 443). Water that flows out of a well on private property, however, is free to everyone, as is all groundwater.

Islam distinguishes between a public watercourse and a private watercourse. The former, such as the Nile River, is inalienable and cannot be appropriated by private parties (Stephan 2007: 7). There are two kinds of watercourses that flow on private property. One is that of rivers that flow between private properties, and then continue flowing into the public domain. These rivers are public. The other type consists of rivers that flow into channels, which are owned jointly in shares, and these rivers are private property (Abouali 1998: 445).

The Islamic rule is that water follows the earth and cannot be separated from it (Stephan 2007: 8). A landowner who has water flowing on his or her land is free to sell the rights to water. For landowners with small rivers the upper or higher land is irrigated before the lower, and the water quantity should not reach above the ankles (Caponera 1973: 16). This restriction applies only in periods of water scarcity. Joint owners of canals are the only ones who can use the water for irrigation, and construction of other water-works, such as bridges, requires permission from the other owners. A party that digs a well becomes the sole beneficiary and is not required to provide water for the irrigation of other lands. The same rule applies to those who build receptacles to capture rainwater.

Ownership of wells or canals entails ownership of adjacent lands (Caponera 1973: 22). All riparian landowners must clean and maintain their watercourses. Customary law pertaining to water ownership presumes that in periods of scarcity, water becomes real property, while land serves as an accessory (Caponera 1973: 28). The value of land depends upon the irrigation rights attached to it.

These Islamic rights and principles were preserved in customary law, until they were codified in the Mejelle Code of the Ottoman Empire between 1870 and 1876. The code regulates the use of water in articles 1234–1326. The Mejelle Code did not innovate but faithfully preserved the Islamic tradition, emphasizing the rights of the community and allowing all persons to use common water in reasonable ways without causing damage (Stephan 2007: 9). Article 1234 of the Mejelle Code defines water as a non-saleable element to which everyone has a right, and article 1235 states that groundwater belongs to the community (Caponera 1973: 37).

These definitions of water as public and communal refer to flowing waters that are not appropriated. The code recognizes two other water uses: (1) drinking and watering animals and (2) irrigation. Everyone may use public water for irrigation without infringing on third parties. Canals and ditches for irrigation and pumping operations may be constructed, unless they cause flooding, exhaust water flows in a river, or lower water levels so much as to prevent irrigation (Caponera 1973: 38). Uses of privately owned watercourses are restricted to riparian owners, and water rights may be sold as a part of land sales.

After the fall of the Ottoman Empire in 1922, the Mejelle Code was introduced into Palestine and Jordan under the British Mandate and in Lebanon and Syria under the French Mandate (Stephan 2007: 10). The Code remains as basic legislation in Lebanon, and it was the case in Palestine until the establishment of the State of Israel. In Jordan the Mejelle Code is not now stated as a source of water law, but Syria has its own system of water law. Generally, in the Middle East the rights of the state or community come first, but those of individuals or corporations are residual (Abouali 1998: 445). In the post-Ottoman Middle East water is state property in Arab lands, and water uses can be regulated by the Mejelle Code, *Shariah*, and local custom, particularly in rural areas.

Spanish Colonial Water Law

The Spanish legal system began to develop in the fifth century CE after the collapse of the Roman Empire. The Iberian Peninsula absorbed Germanic invaders from the North and Moorish invaders from the South. Each invasion left its own imprint on Spanish law in the early Middle Ages. As discussed above, King Alfonso X ordered the codification of Spanish law in *Las Siete Partidas*, which was completed in 1265. This work affirmed that water was held in common for all people.

With the expansion of the Spanish Empire into the New World another codification of law, known as *Recopilación de Leyes de los Reynas de las Indias*, was published in 1681. After this work appeared the Spanish experiment in the New World lasted for a century and a half, and by 1805 another major compilation came out, entitled *Novísima Recopilación de las Leyes de España*. This work became the fundamental source of Spanish law at the end of the colonial period in the 19th century.

The Spanish legal tradition, as shaped by the *Las Siete Partidas* and *Recopilación*, maintained that flowing surface water and rainwater could be used but not owned by everyone for domestic needs. Groundwater belonged, however, to the owner of the land, on which it rose to the surface, as a form of private property. *Las Siete Partidas* defines private ownership of groundwater as follows:

> Where a man has a spring or well on his property and his neighbor wishes to make one on his property, in order to procure water for his use, the latter may do it, and the former cannot prevent him, notwithstanding the water in the first spring or well may be thereby diminished, unless the person wishing to make the new well has no need of it and acts maliciously, with the intention of doing harm to the other (Meyer 1989: 293).

Since groundwater belonged to land ownership, the landowner needed no permit to use it or limit the volume of use. This was the legacy of Roman law, which privatized groundwater and which the Spanish brought to the American Southwest in the colonial period (Meyer 1989: 292, 294). The landowner had a vested right of ownership of the water itself, possessed in *dominium* or *propriedad perfecta*, but running water could only be used as a usufructuary right or *propriedad imperfect* (Meyer 1989: 294). Thus, one could own groundwater but only use surface water.

Irrigation was a unique category in Spanish water law and not a matter of common usage. Diverting large amounts of water for irrigation was a special function, "because it would not be wise that the benefit of all men be hindered by the interests of some individuals" (Meyer 1996: 117–118). This distinction between water for domestic purposes and water for irrigation appeared in *Las Siete Partidas*, and the distinction continued to be observed in Spanish American water law. Even by the late 20th century Spanish American water law distinguished between water for drinking and bathing and water for industrial and irrigation purposes (Meyer 1996: 118).

The Spaniards brought to the American Southwest a set of arid-land techniques, including technologies for irrigation and institutions for the distribution of water. "These customs and teachings represented, in turn, a prior diffusion of Near Eastern culture introduced into Spain by the Muslims in the early Middle Ages" (Glick 1972: 4). One widespread technique was that of a *qanat* or a series of interconnected, underground wells for the purpose of tapping groundwater and conveying it for irrigation. The Spaniards acquired the idea of the *qanat* from the Arabs who introduced it into Spain during the Muslim occupation, and later they brought the technique to the American Southwest in the Spanish colonial period (Glick 1970: 184).

Both Islamic and Spanish cultures presumed that irrigators received water in proportion to the amount of land irrigated and that they shared maintenance costs in proportion to the amount of water used. In Medieval

Spain the basic social unit was the community of irrigators, or the commons in which members had "rights to irrigate a parcel of land and a right to do so from a specific canal" (Glick 1970: 31). The commons enacted regulations for the just and fair apportionment of water and for the maintenance of the canal system. In Medieval Spain water was public, and the community or commons was the administrative body but not a proprietary agency (Glick 1972: 12). Irrigators used but did not own water.

Historically, Arab cultures have bequeathed two kinds of irrigation systems, the Syrian and the Yemenite. With the Syrian model "the quantity of water available to each user is directly proportional to the amount of land under cultivation," and with the Yemenite model "water distribution is not tied directly to parcel size but is allocated on a fixed, time-released basis, frequently dependent on elite control through the sale of water" (Scarborough 2003: 97). These two types correspond to different systems of land tenure. In the Syrian model water rights are inseparable from the land, and in the Yemenite model water may be sold separately from the land (Glick 1970: 231).

In the Syrian model irrigators at the head of a canal receive the same or proportionate amounts of water as those at the end of the canal. Generally, in the Yemenite model the irrigator at the end of the canal may receive less water due to conveyance loss, evaporation, and seepage, all of which diminish the basic allotment (Scarborough 2003: 99). In periods of drought, when demand exceeds supply, irrigators may shift from the Syrian model to the Yemenite.

Spaniards began to enter the desert regions of the American Southwest in the third decade of the 16th century, but they did not establish permanent settlements until the 17th century. The founding document of the Spanish colonial period was the *Plan de Pitic*, which was written for the town of Hermosillo, which had the assigned date of 1789 in the present-day state of New Mexico. Article 6 of the Plan states that when a new town is established, "its pastures, woodlands, waters, hunting grounds, fishing areas, quarries, fruit trees and other things it produces shall be for the common benefit of Spaniards and Indians" (Meyer 1996: 35). Both Spaniards and Indians were also permitted to share water on royal lands around the town.

Article 19 of the Plan advocates irrigation as the primary means of the future development of the land and of the town. Traditionally, in Mexico the Yemenite model of irrigation was used in the private sector, and the Syrian model operated on community lands (Scarborough 2003: 99). At Hermosillo a special commissioner was appointed to allocate irrigation plots. One could only use the amount of water one needed, and one could not deprive downstream irrigators of water. In case some tried to get more water than they needed, article 19 addressed that situation:

> So that these [settlers] will enjoy with equity and justice the benefits of the water, in proportion to the needs of their respective plantings, the *ayunttamiento* [town council] will name annually an *alcade* or *mandador* for each outlet, whose function it will be to divide the water to the fields in proportion to the needs of each. A list will be drawn up indicating the hours of the day or night a farmer must irrigate his fields (Meyer 1996: 36).

The Spaniards introduced into the American Southwest the *acequia* or irrigation ditch as the principal means of irrigation and distribution of water (Rodríguez 2006: 2). The Spanish term *acequia* drives from the Arabic *as-saquiya*, indicating undeniable evidence of Islamic influence upon Spaniards (Meyer 1996: 20). On arriving in the Upper Río Grande Valley of what is now northern New Mexico, the Spaniards began digging irrigation ditches to divert water from the *Sangre de Christo* Mountains. Water flowed by the force of gravity through the ditches into the farmlands. There were two types of ditches. One was the primary or "mother ditch" (*acequia madre*), and the other consisted of secondary or lateral ditches extending from the "mother ditch" into the fields. The "mother ditch" was dug above the land to be irrigated, so that the water flowed more easily into the laterals. The Spaniards installed wooden headgates to regulate the flow of water from the "mother ditch" into the secondary ditches. The ditches were constructed with logs, brush, or stone. They were so simple that they could be destroyed by flash floods.

On the basis of the Spanish water law tradition the settlers organized *acequia* associations as democratic, communal water sharing groups. Some of the *acequias* were public and some private. The former were adjuncts of municipalities, and the latter had voluntary memberships (Simmons 1972: 140). The private *acequias* elected their own ditch boss or *mayordomo*, who apportioned water, adjudicated disputes, and watched for infractions of regulations (Simmons 1972: 141). In times of water abundance *acequia* members took as much water as they desired, but in periods of scarcity the *mayordomo* rationed water.

Currently, there are about 1000 *acequias* in New Mexico, and since 1895 they have functioned as political subdivisions of the state (Rodríguez 2006: 2–3). While some *acequias* are privately owned by wealthy landowners and some are public, most are voluntary and communal organizations that elect their own *mayordomos* and three commissioners for each group. New Mexico statutes require *mayordomos* and ditch commissioners to distribute water according to "custom, equity, and right" (Crossland 1990: 279).

Acequia associations own their own ditches, ditch works, and headgates but not the waters. These associations do not occupy private lands, subject to eminent domain, but they function as units of communal property that may borrow money and receive state aid (Crossland 1990: 285).

Acequias determine individual water rights, including acreage, points of diversion, places of use, and amounts of water applied to each acre. *Acequia* members use both the Syrian and Yemenite models of irrigation in the Upper Río Grande Valley (Rodríguez 2006: 71). Each irrigator receives a volume of water proportionate to his or her acreage, but all are subject to fixed time releases in periods of water shortage. The Yemenite model is used in the area between Taos and the downstream "mother ditch" on the Río Lucero River, except in periods of abundance, and the Syrian model is used between Taos and the "mother ditch" on the Río Pueblo River (Rodríguez 2006: 4). Depending on weather conditions and water supply, the *mayordomo* must calculate water precisely, according to equity and need, and give priority to animals.

Since 1907, the New Mexico surface water code has been based on the prior appropriation doctrine, and since 1931 the state groundwater code has been based upon prior appropriation as well (Levine 1996: 269). The prior appropriation doctrine mandates that water use be administered in terms of the priority date, when water was first put to beneficial use (Crossland 1990: 278–279). New Mexico law also stipulates that parties appropriate fixed amounts of water for specific purposes and that these appropriations be approved by the State Engineers Office (Levine 1996: 271). Consequently, water rights and adjudications require that *acequias* defend their rights in court, quantify their water usage, and present priority dates.

Acequias practice, however, age-old, immemorial customs of water sharing without assigning priority dates and quantifying amounts of water. The associations contend that Spanish law authorizes equitable allocation, which applies to New Mexico, and that water should be shared according to equity and need (Rodríguez 2006: 5). They believe that the prior appropriation doctrine violates the common good by privileging senior water rights holders and by imposing an all-or-nothing formula on water use. Seniority has never conferred exclusive rights to streams. The *acequia* argument rests upon the fact that New Mexico Water Code (Sec. 72–9–2 (1977) mandates the protection of local community water customs (Tyler 1995: 151). Custom is the repetition of use, which has become compulsory and has acquired the force of law. Some of the age-old *acequia* customs are equitable apportionment, division of surplus water, disposition of return flows, and proportionate distribution in times of drought (Tyler 1995: 165).

New Mexico law requires that *mayordomos* and commissioners meet every spring and decide water allocation. This customary division of water on a river or ditch is called a *reparto* (Rodríguez 2006: 35). Each river has its own *reparto*. Spring is also the season for the cleaning and maintenance of the ditches within each river *reparto*. This practice continues the tradition of Medieval Spain, when cleaning was done in April before the planting of the spring crops (Glick 1970: 48). The cleaning lasted one week, and it involved clearing vegetation and digging out silt and mud. Irrigators used scythes, sickles, or burning the cut-out vegetation.

In New Mexico water allocations follow clear, well-established, consensus principles. The fundamental concept is that no one should go without water. In emergencies, when water is insufficient, it goes first to animals, then to vegetable gardens and orchards. These *acequia* rules reflect the Islamic rights of thirst and irrigation (Rodríguez 2006: 72).

Pueblo Water Customs

As discussed above, the *Plan de Pitic* stipulated that water be shared by both Spaniards and Indians in the American Southwest. Native Americans who live east of the Río Grande River in New Mexico are Pueblos who rely on agriculture, and to the west of the river live the Zuni and Hopi who do dry farming. Seven tributaries flow east from the Río Grande River into the farming region. Pueblos who live near these tributaries have practiced their own communal irrigation techniques for centuries, including methods of rainwater retention, and these techniques were already in place by the time the Spaniards arrived (Simmons 1972: 136). The Spanish organization of the *acequia* under the authority of the *mayordomo* was gradually adopted by the Pueblos, but they differed from the Spaniards by placing prayer sticks on the ditches and by performing ritual dances at spring cleanings (Simmons 1972: 144–145). Otherwise, the secrecy of Pueblo life makes many details of their irrigation systems unknown (Rodríguez 2006: 9–10, 15).

Pueblos have enjoyed water rights consistent with those recognized historically in Spanish law and the Mexican government. In 1848, when the war between Mexico and the United States ended, the Spanish Southwest joined the United States under the Treaty of Guadalupe-Hidalgo. Article III of the treaty states that property rights, including Pueblo rights, should be "inviolably respected" and that heirs and future owners have the same rights, as if their property belonged to American citizens (Tyler 1991: 287–288). In New Mexico and California a new concept, known as "pueblo water rights," had developed under Spanish and Mexican domination. "Under pueblo water rights, the town, or pueblo, holds water rights in trust for the benefit of the entire community" (Glennon 2002: 18). Pueblo water rights are aboriginal, and they encompass both surface flows and groundwater in amounts reasonably required for Indians' needs (Getches 2009: 231–232). Since 2004, New Mexico has permitted Pueblos a future expanded use of water, even though pueblo water rights differ from the statutory prior appropriation doctrine of beneficial use (Getches 2009: 233).

The concept of pueblo water rights has also been influential in California. In 1955 Los Angeles filed suit against the cities of San Fernando, Glendale, Burbank, and others, stating that it had a prior right to all groundwater in the Upper Los Angeles River Basin and that these cities should not pump groundwater without Los Angeles' permission. Los Angeles relied on its pueblo water rights in its suit. In *City of Los Angeles v. City of San Fernando*, 14 Cal. 3d 199 (1975) the California Supreme Court upheld Los Angeles' "pueblo rights," and it reviewed the state's groundwater law (Littleworth and Garner 1995: 54). The court held that extractions of groundwater must not exceed safe yield as well as "any temporary surplus." The court defined safe yield as the "maximum quantity of water which can be withdrawn annually ... without causing an undesirable result" (Littleworth and Garner 1995: 55).

Generally, among Native Americans in the Southwest water is not regarded as private property subject to trading, selling, or purchasing (Meyer 1996: 18). When working with water, Indians do not exploit or exhaust its resources; rather they identify with the ecosystem. Frank Tenorio, Governor of the San Felipe Pueblo, has been quoted as follows: "There has been a lot said about the sacredness of our land which is our body, and the values of our culture which is our soul; but water is the blood of our tribes, and if its life-giving flow is stopped, or it is polluted, all else will die and the many thousands of years of our communal existence will come to an end" (Wilkinson 1988–1989: 430).

The Great Lakes Compact

One example of the application of the public trust doctrine to a water basin is The Great Lakes Compact. Several factors led to the formation of the Compact. Dropping water levels in the Great Lakes had forced heavily-loaded ships to turn back or lighten their loads (Vock 2008). Water levels were extremely low in 2007, as Lake Michigan and Lake Huron dropped about two feet below their long-time average levels, and Lake Superior dropped one foot in only one year (Scanlan 2006: 1335). Lowered water levels have been particularly disturbing in Lake Superior, where a one-inch drop loses 500 billion gallons of water, as well as in Lake Huron, due to the dredging of the Saint Clair River by the U.S. Army Corps of Engineers (Glennon 2009: 98). Repeated dredging of the river has been necessary for freighters' access to the Upper Great Lakes. As an outlet for Lake Huron, the Saint Clair River lets water flow from the Upper Lakes Michigan and Huron into Lake Erie.

Another problem grew out of the attempt by Nestle/Perrier in 2000 to pump water from Meccan Springs in Wisconsin, in order to sell it as bottled water. Although the company was blocked by local opposition from securing a permit, it raised the issue as to whether a private corporation could exploit natural resources beneath state-owned land and market spring water for profit. The FDA defines spring water as underground water that flows to the surface through a bore hole. This rule allows pumping close to the bore hole, resulting in the reduction of the spring's flow (Glennon 2002: 9). Meanwhile, Milwaukee has been selling water to Coca-Cola for the export of bottled water with the company's Dasani brand (Scanlan 2006: 1333, 1335).

Negotiations between the eight Great Lakes states and two Canadian provinces began in 2001. The states are Indiana, Illinois, Michigan, Minnesota, New York, Pennsylvania, Ohio, and Wisconsin. The Canadian provinces are Ontario and Québec. On December 13, 2008 the Great Lakes governors and premiers signed two documents at the Council of Great Lakes Governors' Leadership Summit. One is the Great Lakes-St. Lawrence River Basin Sustainable Water Resources Agreement. This is a good-faith agreement between the states and the provinces which is implemented in Canada through Provincial law. The other is The Great Lakes-St. Lawrence River Basin Water Resources Compact, which is implemented in the United States by the states and congressional approval. The Compact is the subject of the following discussion.

After the signings, the respective state legislatures began the process of ratifying the Compact. Minnesota was the first state to pass the Compact on February 20, 2007; and Michigan was the last state to pass it, when Governor Jennifer Granholm signed it on July 9, 2008. With the support of President George W. Bush the U.S. House and Senate conducted hearings on July 30, 2008, and these led to the passage of the Compact.

While the states were in the process of ratifying the Compact, a controversy erupted during the 2008 presidential campaign. On October 4, 2007 Bill Richardson, Governor of New Mexico, gave an interview to the *Las Vegas Sun*, and he said: "I believe that Western states and Eastern states have not been talking to each other when it comes to proper use of our water resources." He went on to say that "I want a national water policy. We need a dialogue between states to deal with issues like water conservation, water reuse technology, water delivery and water production. States like Wisconsin are awash in water" (Mishak 2007). His latter remark triggered a firestorm in the Great Lakes region, causing people to believe that Richardson's interview pushed legislatures to pass the Compact overwhelmingly (Vock 2008).

Richardson's comments reflected concerns about water scarcity in New Mexico. Two serious observers of the water scene have projected that the major New Mexico cities will go dry between 2012 and 2020 (Barlow and Clarke 2002: 17). Even a resident of New Mexico, who defends the Hispanic *acequia* as an ideal model for periods of water scarcity, foresees her state heading into a severe drought (Rodríguez 2006: 17).

The Great Lakes are the world's largest freshwater preserve, holding 95% of U.S. freshwater and 20% of the world's supply (Fisher 2006: 1085). The Great Lakes provide drinking water to 40 million Americans and Canadians in eight states and two provinces (Glennon 2009: 95). While vast, extending more than 1,500 miles from East to West, the Great Lakes are vulnerable because recharge by annual precipitation cannot keep pace with the depletion caused by the demand for freshwater (Fisher 2006: 1085). Only 1% of Great Lakes water is replenished each year; so the Great Lakes are essentially a non-renewable resource (Glennon 2009: 97).

Section 1a of the Compact invokes the public trust doctrine as follows: "The waters of the Basin are precious public natural resources shared and held in trust by the states ...." The term basin designates the watershed of the Great Lakes and the St. Lawrence River, flowing upstream from Trois-Rivières, Québec to the Atlantic Ocean. The Compact recognizes that the "waters of the Basin are interconnected and part of a single hydrologic system" (1b). Waters comprise both surface water and groundwater. States parties to the Compact "have a shared duty to protect, conserve, restore, improve and manage the renewable but finite waters of the Basin for the use, benefit and enjoyment of all their citizens, including generations to come" (1f). These definitions indicate that the Compact views the Great Lakes not only as a public trust but also as a commons. The Compact affirms that the Great Lakes should remain a public trust and a commons.

Despite the laudable ideals of the Compact, it has serious flaws according to James Olson, a Michigan environmental attorney. I discuss below some of Olson's criticisms, as they pertain to the public trust doctrine. Generally, the Compact bans diversions of water from the basin, unless they are covered by exceptions, such as those of straddling communities, intra-basin transfers, and humanitarian purposes. A major critical issue concerns, however, the definition of diversion as

> a transfer of Water from the Basin into another watershed, or from the watershed of one of the Great Lakes into that of another by any means of transfer, including but not limited to a pipeline, canal, tunnel, aqueduct, channel, modification of the direction of a water course, a tanker ship, tanker truck or rail tanker *but does not apply to Water that is used in the Basin as a Great Lakes watershed to manufacture or produce a Product that is then transferred out of the Basin or Watershed* (my emphases).

The principal defect in the Compact is, therefore, the exemption of a product from the definition of a diversion (Olson 2006: 1109). The Compact defines a product as "something produced in the Basin by human or mechanical effort or through agricultural processes and used in manufacturing, commercial or other processes or intended for intermediate or end use consumption." The remainder of the paragraph clarifies that "packaging of a Product shall be considered to be part of the Product," but water "used primarily to transport materials, in or out of the Basin, is not a Product or part of a Product."

Thus, the Compact prohibits diversions of water from the basin, according to section 4. 8, but it does not ban the diversion of water for the manufacturing or packaging of a product. Further, a diversion subject to the prohibition must be in a container larger than 5.7 gallons, as specified in the Bulk Water Transfer" clause (4. 12. 10):

> A Proposal to Withdraw Water and to remove it from the Basin in any container greater than 5.7 gallons shall be treated under this Compact in the same manner as a Proposal for a Diversion. Each Party shall have the discretion, within its jurisdiction, to determine the treatment of Proposals to Withdraw Water and to remove it from the Basin in any container of 5.7 gallons or less.

Since the Compact prohibits bulk water transfers in containers larger than 5.7 gallons, it implies necessarily approval of the transfer of water packaged in containers of fewer than 5.7 gallons (Olson 2006: 1109). This is known as the "bottled water exemption," which permits the export of water for commercial purposes.

Another problem concerns the "multiple use" language of section 1. 3. 1 (c):

> The Waters of the Basin can concurrently serve multiple uses. Such multiple uses include municipal, public, industrial, commercial, agriculture, mining, navigation, energy development and production, recreation, the subsistence, economic and cultural activities of native peoples, Water quality maintenance, and the maintenance of fish and wildlife habitat and a balanced ecosystem. And, other

purposes are encouraged, recognizing that *such uses are interdependent and must be balanced ....* (my emphases)

Balancing multiple uses undermines the public trust doctrine and common law property rights (Olson 2006: 1135). All the Great Lakes states follow the riparian doctrine of the common law, according to which landowners are entitled to a reasonable use of water on their lands, as long as the use does not unreasonably harm other riparians' uses. Technically, where the body of water is a lake, landowners' rights are called littoral. The multiple use clause separates water use from property ownership and brings together various functions that must be balanced. This shifts water rights from property ownership to equality of any use (Olson 2006: 1135). Bottled water advocates could contend that water severed from property may become products for commercial use.

Out of respect for the public trust and the common law, states parties to the Compact should create an explicit hierarchy or prioritization of lawful uses. In the common law domestic needs get priority as opposed to mining, commercial and industrial uses, and so forth. When water is placed under the public trust, it cannot be disposed of, alienated, or transferred for private commercial purposes, unless there is explicit legislative authority and the purpose is primarily a public one (Olson 2006: 1130). Explicit public trust standards of decision-making are not fully represented in the Compact.

The Compact creates the Great Lakes-St. Lawrence River Basin Water Resources Council as the supervisory agency of the state parties (2. 1). One task of the council is to assist states parties to develop water conservation and efficiency programs (4. 2). These include ensuring improvement of the waters and dependent natural resources; protecting and restoring hydrologic and ecosystem integrity of the Basin; retaining quantity of surface water and groundwater; ensuring sustainable water uses; promoting efficiency of use and reducing water loss (4. 2. 1 (a-e). While these goals are good, the list omits an explicit requirement that any water use is unlawful, if it diminishes the flow of a stream and the level of a lake (Olson 2006: 1132). Ecosystems depend on instream flows and lake levels, and maintaining flows and levels is an integral function of the common law riparian doctrine.

The implication of the foregoing criticism is that the Compact fails to represent the public trust adequately. Even though the Compact has become law, it should be amended by the state legislatures. The primary amendment would be the repeal of the bottled water exemption. Such an amendment would reduce the likelihood that some corporations could claim that the Compact discriminates against commerce by banning bulk transfers of water, as in tankers and pipelines, while permitting bottled water exports (Scanlan

2006: 1345–1346). The amendment should be narrowly tailored to prohibit any diversion of water for sale as a commercial product.

The Compact permits water diversions for humanitarian purposes. Section 4. 13. 2) allows diversions "to use in a non-commercial project on a short-term basis for firefighting, humanitarian, or emergency response purposes." Taking water from the Great Lakes to put out a fire would be a short-term admissible diversion. The Compact does not explain what constitutes a humanitarian purpose, however, whether for short-term or long-term uses. Humanitarian uses bear upon the general issue of the right to water. If there is a right to water, then the Compact does not violate that right, if water is withdrawn from the lakes and transported to distant lands to satisfy the people's right to water (Yabur 2006: 1329). This raises further questions. What is the right to water, and what is its content? Is the right to water a universal duty, or is it limited by practical constraints? Roman law teaches that one has a right only if the object of the right is "practically possible or reasonably available" (Yabur 2006: 1330).

Summary

The public trust doctrine protects all freshwater sources within the sacramental earth commons. This doctrine originated in classical Roman law and evolved in Medieval French, Spanish, and English law. In the English common law the Crown held all public waterways as a trust for the people, and it granted public rights to use water in rivers and coasts touched by the ebb and flow of the tides. American courts modified the common law standard by holding that the large inland lakes and rivers, far away from the tides, had public uses, such as navigation. American water law rejected the common law identification of the tidewaters and navigable waters, and it promoted commerce, navigation, and fishing on public waterways.

Islam has a public trust in its concept of the common good which prohibits making water a commercial commodity. The Islamic public trust protects groundwater, natural wells, rivers flowing in the public domain, and the great lakes and seas. Islam defends the absolute right of thirst and the qualified right of irrigation.

Spanish water law developed a synthesis of Roman and Islamic principles. It placed surface water under the public trust, but it privatized groundwater. The Spaniards brought to the American Southwest an Islamicized irrigation system called the *acequia*, which included water sharing associations based on equity and need. The concept of pueblo water rights also appeared in the Southwest, and it meant that the town held water rights as a trust for all the people. Pueblo water rights encompass both surface water and groundwater.

Eight Great Lakes states and two Canadian provinces established the Great Lakes Compact which placed these large bodies of freshwater under the public trust and made them a commons. At its inception, however, the Compact was flawed by an inclusion of a bottled water exemption, violation of riparian law, and a failure to protect water levels of the lakes.

Chapter Eight: The Right to Water

International Human Rights Law

In the aftermath of World War Two and the Holocaust the United Nations General Assembly adopted the Universal Declaration of Human Rights on December 10, 1948. The preamble of this Declaration began with the following recognition: "the inherent dignity and ... equal and inalienable rights of all members of the human family" as "the foundation of freedom, justice and peace in the world" (www.un.org). After the preamble Article 1 states: "All human beings are born free and equal in dignity and rights. They are endowed with reason and conscience and should act towards one another in a spirit of brotherhood." These assertions of the Declaration reflected modern Roman Catholic social teaching (Browning 2006: 163).

Article 25(1) of the Declaration stipulates that everyone "has the right to a standard of living adequate for the health and well-being of himself and of his family, including food, housing ...." In current commentary it is understood that this right cannot be realized without a minimum amount of water (International Experts' Meeting, UNESCO 2009: 2). The right to water is, therefore, implied in these rights to a standard of living, health, and well-being, which come under the category of welfare rights (McCaffrey 1993: 8). A minimum amount of water is also necessary to prevent death from dehydration, reduce the risk of water related diseases, and provide for cooking and sanitation (Gleick 1998: 491).

Work on human rights continued at the United Nations, and the General Assembly adopted two covenants that elaborated on the rights contained in the Universal Declaration. One was the International Covenant on Civil and Political Rights, which went into force on March 23, 1976. Article 6(1) states that every "human being has the inherent right to life," that this "right shall be protected by law," and that no "one shall be arbitrarily deprived of his life." Fulfillment of this right also requires access to water (International Experts' Meeting, UNESCO 2009: 2).

The second was the International Covenant on Economic, Social and Cultural Rights which went into force on January 3, 1976. Article 11(1) asserts that "States Parties to the present Covenant recognize the right of everyone to an adequate standard of living for himself and his family, including adequate food ...." Similarly, Article 12(1) says that "States

Parties to the present Covenant recognize the rights of everyone to the enjoyment of the highest attainable standard of physical and mental health." Altogether, these Covenant rights support a right to water as inferred in the basic Covenant rights (Gleick 1998: 492).

These two covenants are treaties, and they are binding on all states parties. The United States is a party to the International Covenant on Civil and Political Rights, but not to the International Covenant on Economic, Social and Cultural Rights. The Universal Declaration and two Covenants comprise the International Bill of Human Rights, and as a body of international law they declare that every human being has inherent dignity and that no one should deny any one's inherent dignity (Perry 2005: 102).

On December 18, 1979 the United Nations General Assembly adopted the Convention on the Elimination of All Forms of Discrimination against Women, and it went into force as an international treaty on September 3, 1981. This convention established an international bill of human rights for women and the means of action for women to enjoy basic rights. Article 14(2) prohibits discrimination against women in rural areas, and on the basis of equality with men allows women to participate in and benefit from several rights. Article 14. 2(h) asserts the right of access to water explicitly: "to enjoy adequate living conditions, particularly in relation to housing, sanitation, electricity and water supply ...."

The Convention on the Rights of the Child of 1989 mandates the right to water in Article 24(1): "States Parties recognize the right of the child to the enjoyment of the highest attainable standard of health and to facilities for the treatment of illness and rehabilitation of health." Article 24(2) provides that "States Parties shall pursue full implementation of this right and, in particular, shall take appropriate measures ...." These include in 24. 2(d) "foods and clean drinking water, taking into consideration the dangers and risks of environmental pollution ...."

The Convention of the Rights of Persons with Disabilities of 2006 declares in 50 articles a series of rights for disabled persons. Article 28 requires an adequate standard of living and social protection, and 28(1) asserts that "States Parties recognize the rights of persons with disabilities to an adequate standard of living for themselves and their families, including adequate food, clothing and housing, and to the continuous improvement of living conditions ...." Article 28(2) clarifies the first section by recognizing "the right of persons with disabilities to social protection and to the enjoyment of that right without discrimination." This is followed by 28. 2(a) "to ensure equal access to persons with disabilities to clean water services ...."

On September 13, 2007 the United Nations General Assembly adopted The Declaration on the Rights of Indigenous People as a means of protecting indigenous people with the international human rights regime. This Declaration includes the "right of indigenous families and communities to retain shared responsibility for the upbringing, training, education and well-being of their children, consistent with the rights of the child." As discussed above, the Convention on the Rights of the Child guarantees clean drinking water in Article 24.

Article 24(2) ensures that indigenous people "have an equal right to the enjoyment of the highest attainable standard of physical and mental health. States shall take the necessary steps with a view of achieving progressively the full realization of this right." Article 25 specifies that indigenous people "have the right to maintain and strengthen their distinctive spiritual relationship with their ... waters and coastal areas and other resources ...." The provisions of Articles 24 and 25 imply the right to water.

Content of the Right to Water

Although international human rights law has established the right to water, either explicitly or implicitly, in the Declaration, two Covenants, and Conventions of the United Nations, it has not clarified the content of that right. A definitive statement has appeared, however, in Comment 15 on the International Covenant on Economic, Social and Cultural Rights. The Committee on Economic, Social and Cultural Rights, which is the official monitoring agency for the respective international covenants, presented Comment 15 in 2002 as a general exposition of the right to water. Comment 15 clarifies normative content for customary international law.

In the introduction Comment 15 acknowledges that water is "a limited natural resource and a public good fundamental for life and health. The human right to water is indispensable for leading a life in human dignity. It is a prerequisite for the realization of other human rights" (I. 1). These rights are stated in the International Covenant of Economic, Social and Cultural Rights.

"The human right to water entitles everyone to sufficient, safe, acceptable, physically accessible and affordable water for personal and domestic uses" (I. 2). The Covenant indicates several rights pertaining to an adequate standard of living, such as "adequate food, clothing and housing." "The right to water clearly falls within the category of guarantees essential for securing an adequate standard of living" (I. 3). "The right to water is also inextricably related to the right to the highest attainable standard of health ...." (I. 3)

Water is required not only for personal and domestic uses but also for agriculture and environmental hygiene. Water is important for the right to make a living through work and the right to enjoy certain aspects of cultural life. "Nevertheless, priority in the allocation of water must be given to the right to water for personal and domestic uses. Priority should also be given to the water resources required to prevent starvation and disease ...." (I. 6)

The second section of Comment 15 discusses the normative content of the right to water, and this means that the "right to water contains both freedoms and entitlements. The freedoms include the right to maintain access to existing water supplies necessary for the right to water ...." (II. 10) This prohibits separating people from and contaminating their water sources. The "entitlements include the right to a system of water supply and management that provides equality of opportunity for people to enjoy the right to water" (II. 10). Water sufficiency should not be defined quantitatively or technically, but rather water should be regarded as "a social and cultural good, and not primarily as an economic good" (II. 12).

Water adequacy should be measured by three factors: availability, quality, and accessibility. Accessibility has four aspects: physical, economic, non-discriminatory, and informational.

With respect to availability the "water supply for each person must be sufficient and continuous for personal and domestic uses" (II. 12. a). With respect to quality the "water required for each personal or domestic use must be safe, therefore free from micro-organisms, chemical substances and radiological hazards that constitute a threat to a person's health" (II. 12. b). With respect to accessibility water and "water facilities and services have to be accessible to everyone without discrimination, within the jurisdiction of the State party" (II. 12. c).

Physical accessibility means that water and "adequate water facilities and services, must be within safe physical reach for all sections of the population" (II. 12. c. i). Economic accessibility means that water and "water facilities and services, must be affordable" (II. 12. c. ii). Non-discriminatory accessibility means that water, water facilities and services must be "accessible to all, including the most vulnerable or marginal sections of the population ...." (II. 12. c. iii). Informational accessibility means "the right to seek, receive and impart information concerning water issues" (II. 12. c. iv).

Section three of Comment 15 deals with obligations of States parties to the Covenant. Two general obligations are imposed. First, "States parties have immediate obligations in relation to the right to water, such as the

guarantee that the right will be exercised without discrimination of any kind
...." (III. 17) Second, "States parties have a constant and continuing duty
under the Covenant to move as expeditiously and effectively as possible
towards the full realization of the right to water" (III. 18).

The phrase "immediate obligations" goes beyond the standard of
"progressive implementation" of the Covenant on Economic, Social and
Cultural Rights. The standard of "progressive implementation" has been
criticized on the grounds that it makes States' obligations relative to their
development and that it offers no guidelines (Chapman and Russell 2002:
4–5). The standard lacks a time frame and, in effect, allows a loophole, so
that states can neglect their legal obligations. The standard of "progressive
implementation" is also present in The Declaration on the Rights of
Indigenous People in Article 24. 2, as cited above. Thus, international human
rights law needs a consistent standard, and that of "immediate obligations" is
stronger and more suitable.

Comment 15 imposes three compelling obligations, namely, those to
respect, protect, and fulfill the right to water (III. 20). "The obligation to
respect requires that States parties refrain from interfering directly or
indirectly with the enjoyment of the right to water" (III. 21). These include
prohibitions against diminishing or polluting water supplies or destroying
water sources or services during armed conflict. Under The Protocols to
Geneva Conventions of 1977 adversaries are forbidden "to cause
widespread, long-term and severe damage to the natural environment and
thereby to prejudice the health or survival of the population" (Flynn 2007:
19).

"The obligation to protect requires States parties to prevent third parties
from interfering in any way with the enjoyment of the right to water" (III.
23). An example of a third party is a corporation that controls or manages
water supplies in pursuit of profits and limits access to water for the poor or
marginalized sections of the population. Comment 15 mandates
"independent monitoring, genuine public participation and imposition of
penalties for non-compliance" (III. 24).

"The obligation to fulfill can be disaggregated into the obligations to
facilitate, promote and provide" (III. 25). States parties must take positive
steps to assist their citizens in enjoying the right, protect water supplies,
minimize waste, and help people fulfill their right to water, when they are
unable to do so. The obligation to fulfill also means that States parties should
establish national water policies, preferably through legislatures, that contain
a strategy to respect, protect, and fulfill the right to water. Water services
must be free or low-cost. "Any payment for water services has to be based on

the principle of equity, ensuring that these services, whether privately or publicly provided, are affordable for all, including socially disadvantaged groups" (III. 27).

Section four of Comment 15 discusses violations of the right to water. The failure of States parties to act in good faith is the principal violation, but it is necessary to distinguish between the inability and unwillingness to comply. A State which is unwilling to devote all of its resources to realize the right to water violates the Covenant. A State whose limited resources make it unable to realize the right "has the burden of justifying that every effort has nevertheless been made to use all available resources at its disposal in order to satisfy, as a matter of priority, the obligations outlined above" (IV. 41).

Some examples of violations are unjustifiable exclusion of people from water services, disproportionate increases in water costs, and reduction or pollution of water supplies. Other examples are the failure to enact laws protecting water sources, to regulate water providers, and to maintain an adequate distribution system.

Section five of Comment 15 stipulates that all States parties implement at their national levels legislative measures of Covenant obligations (V. 45). Not only must States establish national water policies in conformity with human rights law but also install institutional accountability mechanisms. Policies must be non-discriminatory and participatory. Individuals and groups have the right to share in decision-making processes and to receive information on water, water services, the environment, and agencies or corporations involved in the water sector.

"Any persons or groups who have been denied their right to water should have access to effective judicial or other appropriate remedies at both national and international levels ...." (V. 55) This provision strengthens the Covenant on Economic, Social and Cultural Rights which does not describe legal remedies (Yabur 2006: 1327). Victims of violations are entitled to restitution, compensation, and guarantee of non-repetition. There should be legal remedies for victims and assistance in obtaining legal remedies. "Where such action is based on a person's failure to pay for water their capacity to pay must be taken into account. Under no circumstances shall an individual be deprived of the minimum essential level of water" (V. 56).

The sixth and last section of Comment 15 addresses duties of entities other than States parties, and the section consists of only one paragraph. It encourages the various United Nations agencies and other international organizations, such as the World Trade Organization, to cooperate with States parties to the Covenant. "The international financial institutions, notably the International Monetary Fund and World Bank, should take into account the right to water in their lending policies, credit agreements, structural adjustment programs, and other development projects ... so that the enjoyment of the right to water is promoted" (VI. 60).

Priority in financial assistance, distribution, and management of water resources should be given to the most vulnerable or marginalized people. As discussed in the introduction to this study, the International Monetary Fund and World Bank have made privatization a condition of their loan programs toward poor countries. These organizations regard water as a commodity to be traded on the global market outside state ownership and government regulation. Privatization and commodification impede the realization of the right to water.

Charters and Treaties

Several regional agreements and conferences, convened over a span of many years, have produced accords supporting the right to water. On July 17–20, 1979 the African States members of The Organization of African Unity assembled in Monrovia, Liberia to begin deliberations on an African Charter on Human and People's Rights. The final draft of 68 articles was adopted by the Assembly of Heads of State and Government in June, 1981 in Nairobi, Kenya. Article 16(1) stipulates that every individual shall have the right to enjoy the best attainable state of physical and mental health. Article 24 provides that a "people shall have the right to a general satisfactory environment favorable to their development." A "satisfactory environment" is "unattainable without access to water and sanitation" (International Experts' Meeting, UNESCO 2009: 3).

On July 8, 2001 800 delegates from 35 countries assembled at the Water for People and Nature Summit in Vancouver, Canada, and they endorsed The Treaty Initiative to Share and Protect the Global Water Commons. I cite the pertinent parts of the treaty as follows:

We proclaim these truths to be universal and indivisible:

That the intrinsic value of the Earth's fresh water precedes its utility and commercial value and therefore must be respected and safeguarded by all political, commercial, and social institutions,

That the Earth's fresh water belongs to the Earth and all species, and therefore must not be treated as a private commodity to be bought, sold, and traded for profit,
That the global fresh water supply is a shared legacy, a public trust, and a fundamental human right .... (Barlow and Clarke 2002: xvii)

Maude Barlow, the primary author of the Vancouver Treaty reaffirmed its central theses in her address to the United Nations General Assembly on April 22, 2009. She emphasized that

> We need to assert once and for all that access to clean, affordable water is a fundamental human right that must be codified in nation-state law and as a full covenant at the United Nations.
>
> A United Nations right to water covenant would set the framework for water as a social and cultural asset and would establish the indispensable groundwork for a just system of distribution. It would serve as a common, coherent body of rules for all nations and clarify the right to clean, affordable water for all regardless of income. A UN right to water covenant would establish once and for all that no one anywhere should be allowed to die or forced to watch a beloved child die from dirty water supply simply because they are poor (www.canadians.org).

On May 23, 2004 the League of Arab States adopted the Arab Charter on Human Rights in Tunis, Tunisia for the protection of civil, cultural, economic, political, and social rights. Article 39(a) mandates that "States parties recognize the right of everyone to the enjoyment of the highest attainable standard of physical and mental health ...." The right to health entails a provision "of basic nutrition and safe drinking water for all" (39(b). 5).

Finally, The Zaragosa International Exhibition concluded on September 14, 2008 at Zaragosa, Spain and presented a comprehensive international water policy. The Zaragosa Expo determined among many principles that "access to drinking water and sanitation is a human right that must be guaranteed by all public authorities" (www.expozaragoza2008.es). The conference linked the right to water to the United Nations Millennium Development Goals.

Church Programs

The World Council of Churches affirms the right to water through its Ecumenical Water Network. The network consists of Christian churches, movements, and individuals who, according to the network website, have come together

> To protect and realize people's access to water around the world
> Making a common Christian witness be heard in the debate on water issues
> Promoting community-based initiatives and solutions to overcome the water crisis
> Protecting water as a gift of God and
> Advocating for water as a human right at the local, regional, and international level
> (www. oikoumene.org).

On May 21–25, 2007 The Ecumenical Water Network convened a conference in Enttebe, Uganda. Church leaders, theologians, and water experts from 19 African countries affirmed "that access to water is a fundamental human right ... and that water must not be treated as a commodity, but as an essential good for the present and future generations" (www.oikoumene.org). The final statement of the conference emphasized the obligations of governments and multi-national institutions to respect the right to water by prioritizing "the just and sustainable provision of water to the poor and the most excluded and to make water and sanitation a strong component of national budgets and other financial allocations ...."

For the Roman Catholic Church water is a right to life issue. On March 22, 2003 Renato R. Martino, President of the Pontifical Council for Justice and Peace, released from the Vatican a definitive statement entitled "Water, An Essential Element for Life" (www.vatican.va). He made his presentation during the Third World Water Forum, which convened in Kyoto, Japan on March 16–23, 2003. His position paper sharply countered the conclusion of the Third World Water Forum.

The leading question of the forum was whether water should be regarded as a human right or as an economic good, but the proponents of the latter idea dominated the forum proceedings (Cain 2004: 189). The agenda emphasized privatization and globalization, and the ministerial statement viewed access to clean water and adequate sanitation as a basic need but not a human right (Cain 2004: 190). Some representatives proposed building more dams, improving investments, and opening markets to private capital. Others called for public-private partnerships and large-scale centralized infrastructures (Cain 2004: 191–192).

The Roman Catholic Church recognizes that the current water crisis is not one of absolute scarcity but rather one of distribution and resources. The Roman Catholic position is based on two ethical norms, namely, respect for life and the dignity of the person. "The first priority of every country and the international community for sustainable water policy should be to provide access to safe water to those who are deprived of such access at present."

These two norms are implemented through a central Catholic principle known as the universal destination of the goods of creation. Water is a common good of humanity, and it is for the use of every human being and all peoples. As a common good, access to water has priority for those in poverty and who live in areas with fewer resources.

Within the present-day context of globalization people should become active advocates of safe water policies. This imperative is governed by two additional guidelines. One is that of solidarity, which means a commitment "to the common good, to the good of all and of each individual. It presupposes the effort for a more just social order and requires a preferential attention to the situation of the poor." The other is that of subsidiarity, which means that decisions and management responsibilities pertaining to water should take place at the lowest appropriate level of society. Governments should not do what local communities can do.

The Vatican statement acknowledges, as a major achievement, a network of "universally recognized human rights." Although access to water is a basic precondition to these rights, the right to "clean drinking water" is affirmed in the Convention on the Rights of the Child and in other documents. "Sufficient and safe drinking water is a precondition for the realization of other human rights." The statement supports "a growing movement to formally adopt a human right to water," because the "dignity of the human person mandates its acknowledgement." The question remains "as to how such a right to water would be realized and enforced at the local, national and international levels." The statement concludes that "a right to adequate and safe drinking water should be interpreted in a manner fully consistent with human dignity and not … by viewing water primarily as an economic good."

Pope Benedict XVI has also declared in his encyclical *Caritas in Veritate* (2. 23) "food and access to water as universal rights of all human beings, without distinction or discrimination" (www.vatican.va. 2009). Benedict appealed to the Catholic norms of respect for life and the inviolable dignity of the human person. These norms also rest upon the principles of the universal destination of the goods of creation, solidarity, and subsidiarity.

The Protestant and Catholic churches of Brazil and Switzerland have joined together to produce a water policy entitled "Ecumenical Declaration on Water as a Human Right and a Public Good" (www.sek-feps.ch. 2005). This policy statement coincided with the beginning of the UN's "Water for Life" international decade for action. These churches acknowledge that water is a basic precondition for life and that it is a gift of God for the enjoyment of life.

Water is a human right derived from the "right to adequate food" in the Universal Declaration of Human Rights (art. 25) and the International Covenant on Economic, Social and Cultural Rights (art. 11). The increasing scarcity of water due to high per capita consumption, population growth, waste, life style, and destruction of forests, land, and water reserves requires urgent and specific attention to water.

These churches demand that the human right to water be recognized at local and international levels without delay. Water should be regarded as a public good, which means that states must guarantee access to water to all of their populations. This includes setting affordable prices, making the technical and financial resources available, and involving local communities or councils in making decisions about water policies. States must establish legal priorities for water, favoring drinking water for humans and animals first and then water for crops. Globally, the right to water should be regulated through an international covenant to be adopted by the UN.

The churches pledge to support this declaration in their congregations, institutions, and ecumenical groups. They commit themselves to motivate public opinion, mobilize political forces, and stimulate their congregations to oppose the tendency toward privatization. These churches resolve to lobby their respective governments to pass laws declaring water as a human right and a public good.

Clarifying the Right to Water

The cumulative weight of international human rights law, charters, treaties, and church policies cited above supports a right to water implicitly, explicitly, and fundamentally. Such a right requires a sufficient supply of safe drinking water to sustain life, and it correlates with the obligation of the state to provide it (McCaffrey 1993: 12). As stated in Comment 15 on the Covenant on Economic, Social and Cultural Rights, states bear an "immediate obligation" to ensure safe drinking water for their citizens. The term "immediate obligation" has been interpreted to mean "due diligence," a concept based on the common law which guarantees that a state uses its administrative infrastructure with vigilance (McCaffrey 1993: 13–14).

The issue of immediate obligation raises the question as to the quantity of water necessary to fulfill the right. Acknowledging that water resources in the earth are finite, Peter Gleick, President of the Pacific Institute, has recommended a minimum of 50 liters of water per person per day for drinking, cooking, bathing, and sanitation (Gleick 1998: 496). Five liters would be devoted to drinking, ten to food preparation, 15 to bathing, and 20 to sanitation. These four factors represent vital human needs, and a right to water means that governments must supply enough water to meet these needs. If water systems are managed by cooperative agencies, they must be subordinate to government regulations and public scrutiny.

More recently, Gleick has discussed further the implications of a right to water. The right cannot mean a right to an unlimited amount of water, due to finite resources, and it need not be free. He has said that "water should be paid for, even basic water requirements, but that when a basic water requirement cannot be paid for by individuals—for reasons, of poverty, emergency, or circumstance—it is still the responsibility of local communities, local governments, or national governments to provide that basic water requirement through subsidies or outright entitlement" (Gleick, www.pacinst.org. 2007). Gleick has formulated the right to water as follows: "All human beings have an inherent right to have access to water in quantities and of a quality necessary to meet their basic needs. This right shall be protected by law" (Gleick 1998: 501; www.pacinst.org. 2007).

The Water, Engineering and Development Centre of Loughborough University has prepared a report for the World Health Organization for water in an emergency situation. All people should "have safe and equitable access to sufficient quantity of water for drinking, cooking and personal and domestic hygiene" and that public water facilities should be "sufficiently close to households to enable use of the minimum water requirements." Generally, for short-term survival in an emergency 30 liters of water per person per day are necessary for drinking and cooking (http://wedc.lboro.ac.uk. 2009). For non-emergency situations 100 liters per person per day are recommended.

International human rights law imposes the obligation upon states to ensure the right to water for their populations. It is not clear, however, how the right to water applies to people living in occupied territories, such as the Palestinians. An older but still valid study has pointed out that Israelis and Palestinians rely on the Jordan River, Mountain Aquifer, and Gaza Aquifer as their primary water sources (Abouali 1998: 420). The first two sources are transboundary, but the latter is Palestinian. Israel controls all the water resources, and the Israeli legal-military structure infringes on Palestinian property rights in four ways. First, Israel has appropriated large amounts of water for consumption in Israel and in the settlements. Second, it prevents the registration of private water rights. Third, it limits Palestinian access to work by physical seizure, limiting the digging of new wells for pumping, and by digging deep bore holes for settlements that cause nearly all Palestinian wells to dry up or salinate. Fourth, Israeli overconsumption of water has caused substantial and sustained damage to the Gaza Aquifer, Mountain Aquifer, and Lake Tiberias (Abouali 1998: 472–473).

The International Covenant on Economic, Social and Cultural Rights is the leading international human rights instrument in this area; but the Covenant says nothing about territories under occupation, and Israel is a party to the Covenant. Israel contests the application of the Covenant to occupied territories, and it contends that the Covenant applies only to states (Abouali 1998: 498).

Israeli occupation violates Covenantal obligations. For example Article 1 guarantees that "all people may, for their own ends, freely dispose of their natural wealth and resources .... In no case may a people be deprived of their own means of subsistence." This article represents the principle of natural sovereignty over natural resources and is a customary norm of international law (Abouali 1998: 505). This right allows the Palestinian people as a whole to manage and develop their own water resources, a right denied by Israeli occupation.

Article 11(1) guarantees a right to an adequate standard of living, including housing. An adequate house must contain facilities for health and nutrition, with access to drinking water, sanitation, washing facilities, refuse disposal, and site drainage. Many West Bank villages are not connected to a central water system. Thus, in the absence of piped- water Palestinians must rely on rain-fed cisterns, springs, and open-air irrigation canals, but these carry risks of contamination (Abouali 1998: 527).

The World Council of Churches has released several reports calling attention to the plight of the Palestinians. One report, entitled "No water for the neighbors," discusses the tiny Bedouin community of Umm Al Kher in the South Hebron Hills of the West Bank. The village is not connected to any water supply network, and the Israeli army refuses to issue permits for the residents to dig wells (www.oikoumene.org. 2009). The community has to buy water from Mekorot, the national Israeli water company which charges five shekels, or about $1.30 per cubic meter. The cost prohibits shepherds from irrigating their crops. The only other source of water supply is a pipe about the size of a garden hose which runs from the pump in the settlement. "Demolitions of storage facilities and denial of access to aquifers, along with bans on digging wells, mean that up to 200,000 Palestinians in rural communities have no access to running water at all." In contrast, Israeli settlers, with their irrigation systems, lush gardens, and swimming pools, enjoy all the water they want.

Another report, entitled "Taking water to the Jordan," deals with the Jordan Valley encampment of Ein Al Hilweh, where the 25 families living in tents must get their water from a source an hour's drive away (www.oikoumene.org. 2010). Sometimes the Israeli army prevents them from driving on the road, or it may fine the Bedouin several hundred shekels for making the trip. "Around 9,600 Israelis now live in the illegal settlements that blanket much of the Jordan Valley." Settlers live in well-built homes with running water, and they frequently harass the Bedouin. The settlers grow a variety of fruits and vegetables for export to Europe. "Experts estimate that with their artificial irrigation systems, these settlements use over half of all water consumed in the West Bank."

The sewage from Palestinian towns is not treated, because Israel does not allow Palestinians to build new treatment plants. In some cases the Israeli army destroys water infrastructures built by Palestinians, including rainwater collecting systems. Even where water sources are not damaged, water taps remain dry for several weeks or months at a time.

In October, 2009 Amnesty International released a comprehensive report on the water crises in the Occupied Palestinian Territory, entitled "Troubled Waters—Palestinians Denied Fair Access to Water." The report begins with a quotation of a resident of Susya, a Palestinian village in the South Hebron Hills:

> Water is life; without water we can't live; not us, not the animals, or the plants. Before we had some water, but after the army destroyed everything we have to bring water from far away; it's very difficult and expensive. They make our life very difficult, to make us leave. The soldiers first destroyed our homes and the shelters with our flocks, uprooted all our trees, and then they wrecked our water cisterns. These were old cisterns, from the time of our ancestors. Isn't this a crime? Water is precious. We struggle every day because we don't have water (www.amnesty.org. 2009: 1).

The report documents in detail that the Israeli army destroyed rain-harvesting water cisterns, ancient caves and shelters housing people, water-heating solar panels, homes and water facilities in Susya and several other villages between 1999 and 2001. The official Israeli reason for the destruction was that the structures lacked building permits, but the army refused to grant those permits. The basic Israeli motivation was to seize Palestinian land and water supplies on behalf of Israeli settlers, so that they may enjoy their irrigated vineyards, herb farms, lawns, and swimming pools. The more than 450,000 settlers, living in the West Bank in violation of international law, use as much or more water than the Palestinian population of 2.3 million.

The average Palestinian water consumption is about 70 liters per person per day, a rate well below the 100 liters per person per day recommended by the World Health Organization, while the Israeli consumption is about 300 liters per person per day. In some rural Palestinian villages residents get between 70 and 20 liters per person per day (www.amnesty.org. 2009: 4). Israel uses more than 80% of water in the Mountain Aquifer and all the surface water in the Jordan River. The Mountain Aquifer flows beneath Israel and the West Bank, and it is recharged by rainfall and snowmelt. These are the only water sources available to the Palestinians, but the Israeli army prevents Palestinian access to all the Jordan River water. In the Gaza Strip the only water source is the Coastal Aquifer; but 90–95% of its water is contaminated due to sewage and sea water infiltration, making it unfit to drink. Israel does not permit the transfer of water from the West Bank to Gaza. The Coastal Aquifer yields an estimated 450 million cubic meters in Israel yearly, but only 55 million cubic meters per year in Gaza. Consequently, Palestinians must purchase water from Israel, which is extracted from the Mountain Aquifer, and they receive it by tankers at a high price.

When the United Nations partitioned the land into Palestine and Israel under Mandate Palestine, Resolution 181 of November 29, 1947 provided: "Access for both States and for the City of Jerusalem on a non-discriminatory basis to water and power facilities" (4. D. 2. a). The Israeli Water Law of 1959 denies, however, the sharing of surface water and groundwater, and it is defined as "a framework for the control and protection of Israel's water resources" (www.amnesty.org. 2009: 22). All water resources in Israel are public property, and landowners have no right to any water flowing through or under their lands. Everyone may use water, as long as the use does not cause salinization or water depletion. Water use comes under the jurisdiction of the Ministry of Agriculture and its Water Commission.

Israel has expropriated large areas of Palestinian land under an old Ottoman land law. This law defines the *miri* class of property use and provides that land not cultivated for three years may be sold at auction (www.amnesty.org. 2009: 41). Buyers may cultivate the land for ten years, after which they achieve rights of ownership. Israeli military actions and policies prevent Palestinians from cultivating the land due to a lack of water, but the military grants ample water supplies to settlers.

The report concludes that Israel maintains "policies which are manifestly incompatible with pre-existing domestic or international legal obligations in relation to the right to water" (www.amnesty.org. 2009: 95). Israel also violates the Hague Regulations' prohibition of an occupying power from changing the property and natural resources of the occupied territory and to administer water resources according to the rule of usufruct and not to benefit the occupying power. The report summarizes Israeli illegal actions and policies, including diversion of the Jordan River and its tributaries, imposition of quotas and restrictive allocations of water extracted from aquifers, and restriction on the construction of new water facilities.

The report calls upon Israel to stop its illegal actions and policies, observe the standard of equitable and reasonable utilization in international law, cease extracting water from aquifers in excess of their yearly sustainable yield, and guarantee "a sufficient, safe and regular supply of water" to the Palestinians for their personal, domestic, agricultural, and economic needs. Palestinians have rights to "an adequate standard of living, water, food, adequate housing, health and work" (www.amnesty.org. 2009: 95–96).

On July 26, 2010 the United Nations General Assembly recognized "the right to safe and clean drinking water and sanitation as a human right that is essential for the full enjoyment of life and all human rights." This resolution calls upon states and international organizations to "provide financial resources, capacity-building and technology transfer, through international assistance and cooperation, in particular to developing countries, in order to scale up efforts to provide safe, clean, accessible and affordable drinking water and sanitation for all" (www.un.org. 2010).

The resolution received 122 votes in favor, zero against, and 41 abstentions. Among the countries abstaining were Australia, Austria, Greece, Israel, Japan, Sweden, United Kingdom and the United States. Several African countries also abstained, including Botswana, Ethiopia, and Kenya. China, Egypt, France, Germany, Iran, Pakistan, the Russian Federation, South Africa, United Arab Emirates, Zimbabwe, and others voted in support of the resolution (www.un.org/news. July 28, 2010).

An official with the Ecumenical Water Network of the World Council of Churches commented: "Although the resolution is not legally binding, it is a crucial milestone in the recognition of the human rights to water and sanitation" (Ecumenical Water Newsletter, No. 3, 2010). Similarly, Maude Barlow stated: "Our network of allies have been fighting for over 10 years towards achieving a legally binding recognition of the human right to water at the United Nations. While the resolution is nonbinding, it is a crucial first step to providing clean water and sanitation to all." She portrayed the final vote "as an amazing and surprising victory for water justice" (www.ipsnews.net. July 28, 2010).

The representative of Bolivia introduced the resolution and observed that "the human right to water had not been formally recognized, despite references to it in various international instruments" (www.un.org/news. July 28, 2010). He added that the lack of access to water killed more children annually than AIDS, malaria, and measles combined and that the lack of sanitation effected 2.6 billion people or about 40% of the global population.

The Observer for Palestine pointed out that water and sanitation were the key issues in the Israeli-Palestinian situation. "Israel's ongoing violations of the Palestinian people's access to water hampered their enjoyment of other rights ... Palestinians were only allowed 10 per cent of their own water."

The representative of the United Kingdom said her delegation abstained because "there was no sufficient legal basis for declaring or recognizing water or sanitation as freestanding human rights, nor was there evidence that they existed in customary law." She expressed regret that the resolution had been initiated without developing a consensus.

Although the United States had called for the vote, its representative announced that the American delegation would abstain. He said the resolution did not achieve a consensus or support the ongoing work of the Human Rights Council in Geneva. He contended that the "resolution described the right to water and sanitation in a way that is not reflected in existing international law, as there is no right to water and sanitation in an international legal sense as described by this resolution" (www.ipsnews.net. July 28, 2010).

In response to the American abstention Peter Gleick wrote that the United States has a "flawed position" on economic and social rights, including the right to water. It is a position characterized by bad logic and a narrow and inconsistent interpretation of human rights law" (www.huffingtonpost.com. August 4, 2010). He noted that the 2002 Comment 15 on the Covenant on Economic, Social and Cultural Rights, along with other works, clearly support an implicit and explicit right to water. He cited the 2007 statement of the United Nations Human Rights Council that "the open debate as to whether the human right to access to safe drinking water is a stand-alone right or is derived from other human rights should not impair the recognition of access to safe drinking water as a human right."

Gleick objected to "the endless bureaucratic shuffling of this topic from one council to another, from one committee to another ...." The United States and other abstaining nations should stop their delaying tactics and read and interpret economic and social rights laws to ensure the right to water. He charged that abstention was an admission that no right to water existed. He challenged the abstainers to declare: "We accept that there is a human right to safe drinking water and sanitation. We're happy to say so, and work out the fine details later."

Amnesty International released a statement after the vote, affirming that there is "no legal reason why countries could not support the resolution; the right to water is already part of international law and there is also a strong legal basis for the right to sanitation." The statement continued: "Women who risk their lives when they go to public toilets at night and people whose children die due to lack of clean water should be able to hold their leaders to account over clean water and sanitation" (www.amnesty.org. July 29, 2010).

On September 24, 2010 the United Nations Human Rights Council in Geneva adopted the following resolution: "Affirms that the human right to safe drinking water and sanitation is derived from the right to an adequate standard of living and inextricably related to the right to the highest attainable standard of physical and mental health, as well as the right to life and human dignity" (www.pacinst.org. November 12, 2010). According to the UN Independent Expert on the right to water and sanitation, Catarina De Albuquerque, "this means that for the UN the right to water and sanitation is contained in existing human rights treaties and is therefore legally binding." She went on to say that the "right to water and sanitation is a human right, equal to all other human rights, which implies that it is justiciable and enforceable" (www.ohchr.org. October 1, 2010).

Peter Gleick offered four reasons why adopting a right to water and sanitation was a good idea: (1) it will encourage governments and the international community to meet basic water needs for their populations; (2) it enhances the possibility of clarifying specific national and international obligations; (3) it will shine a spotlight on the deplorable state of water management in many parts of the world; and (4) it will help prioritize policy objectives and guarantee water for all people. He added that it is necessary now to develop the mechanism "to achieve progressively the full realization of these rights"(www.pacinst.org. November 12, 2010).

The UN delegation from the United States declared that it was "proud to take this significant step of joining consensus on the important resolution regarding the right to safe drinking water and sanitation which is to be progressively realized" (www.oikoumene.org. October 6, 2010). The Ecumenical Water Network of the World Council of Churches also commented: "This is a solid base for churches and other supporters of the right to water worldwide to hold their governments accountable for its implementation."

The idea of progressive realization, cited by two commentators above, contradicts the standard of immediate obligation in Comment 15 on the International Covenant on Economic, Social and Cultural Rights. The text of the Human Rights Council resolution says that the right to water is derivative of existing human rights law. As a definitive policy, however, the United Nations ought to adopt a resolution stating that the right to water is fundamental, not only derivative, that it is a binding precondition for other rights, and that it applies to all people, whether they live in states or occupied territories. The right to water is both free-standing and a precondition of life and human dignity.

Summary

The International Bill of Human Rights supports the right to water as implied in the rights to a standard of living, health, and well-being. United Nations conventions include explicit affirmations of the right to water. Comment 15 on the Covenant on Economic, Social and Cultural Rights is the definitive document declaring that all State parties to the Covenant are under the immediate obligation to respect, protect, and fulfill the right to water. The Vancouver Treaty of 2001 affirms that the earth is a commons, that water has intrinsic value, and that all have a fundamental right of access to clean, affordable, and accessible water. Ecumenical church policies share the same perspective.

A precise clarification of the quantity of water to satisfy the right is not yet established. Current estimates range between 100 and 50 liters of water per person per day. Since water is a finite resource in the earth, the right to water cannot be unlimited.

The right to water applies to all people living in states and occupied territories. Current reports indicate that Israeli occupation of Palestinian territory violates the Palestinians' right to water, that Israeli settlements are illegal under international law, and that Palestinians are deprived of a sufficient amount of water to support their right to a standard of living, health, and well-being.

In July, 2010 the United Nations General Assembly adopted a non-binding resolution on the right to water and sanitation. In September, 2010 the UN Human Rights Council clarified that the right to water and sanitation exists in international human rights law and is legally binding. This resolution makes the right derivative and enforced by progressive realization in contradiction to the standard in Comment 15 on the Covenant on Economic, Social and Cultural Rights. Altogether, the UN treaties, conventions, and resolutions alternate between a fundamental right enforced by immediate obligation and a derivative right enforced by progressive realization. The contention of this study is that the right to water is fundamental and free-standing; it is the prerequisite to the realization of other basic human rights and is enforceable by immediate obligation.

Conclusion

Irrigation Associations

Many years ago Lynn White, Jr., a University of California historian, published a provocative article that helped give rise to the contemporary environmental movement. He pointed out that all cultures modify their environments, but that the most decisive event in modern history was the convergence of science and technology for the obtaining of power over nature. That union, accomplished largely in the 19th century, combined knowledge and action to control nature (White 1967: 1204).

The achievement of power over nature grew out of Medieval Western civilization, and by 1000 CE westerners "began to apply water power to industrial processes other than milling grains." Even earlier in northern Europe peasants had introduced a new kind of agricultural technology. By the seventh century CE, "Northern peasants were using an entirely new kind of plow, equipped with a vertical knife to cut the line of the furrow, a horizontal share to slice under the sod, and a mold board to turn it over" (White 1967: 1205). This type of plow differed from that used in the Ancient Near East and Mediterranean countries, where farmers worked a scratch plow, drawn by two oxen, which merely scratched the soil but did not turn over the sod. These farmers did cross-plowing in square fields, and they were subsistence farmers.

In the northern European countries peasants needed eight oxen not two, and they "attacked the land with such violence that cross-plowing was not needed ...." Since no peasant could afford eight oxen, peasants pooled their resources to form "plow-teams" to cut into strips of land in proportion to individual contributions. Allocations of parcels of land were based no longer on single family needs but on "the capacity of a power machine to till the earth." This agricultural technique not only changed the function of farming but also the human relation to nature. Formerly humans cooperated with nature, but with this new technology they became exploiters of nature.

Such ruthlessness toward nature presupposed the triumph of Christianity over paganism. Only in a Christian-oriented society could peasants attack the earth. The reason was that the creation story in the Bible introduced linear time, replacing the endless cycles of nature, and it elevated humankind above nature as the pinnacle of creation. The biblically-sanctioned human dominance in creation made humanity indifferent to nature. This religiously-driven dominance has led to our present environmental degradation. The crisis cannot be resolved by more science and technology but by a new human understanding of nature (White 1967: 1206). White proposed the spirituality of Saint Francis of Assisi as an alternative approach to nature.

White's perceptive insights can be illustrated by a few observations on the creation story. The pivotal concept is the image of God: "Then God said, 'Let us make humankind in our image, according to our likeness, and let them have dominion over the fish of the sea ....'" (Gen. 1:26ab) The use of the plural exemplifies, in my judgment, a plural of majesty. As discussed above in chapter five, there are different interpretations of dominance, such as dominion, and so forth; but all views presume a hierarchy of humanity over nature. Within the biblical narrative humankind is created from the ground. God "breathed into his nostrils the breath of life, and the man became a living being" (Gen. 2:7). God planted a garden filled with trees, and through the garden four rivers flowed. "The Lord God took the man and put him in the garden of Eden to till it and keep it" (Gen. 2:15). This implies the use of tools to cultivate the garden; and, therefore, technology is consistent with creation.

In my opinion, White's tracing of human power over nature to the creation story is entirely correct. His illustration of peasants' cutting into the earth with steel plows in northern Europe is also pertinent. Peasants had to use plows with knives in the sticky soil and wet climate of northern Europe. In contrast, scratch plows were more appropriate in the sandy soils and arid climate of the Ancient Near East and Mediterranean countries.

While agreeing with White, I appeal, however, to a different agricultural technique which historically has deployed an alternative human-nature relationship, namely, irrigation. Beginning in the first civilized cultures of the Ancient Near East, irrigation supported agriculture, food surplus, and community life. Irrigation systems demanded cohesion, organization, and cooperation in order to function (Meyer 1996: 12). These characteristics promoted the common good among humans and encouraged cooperation with nature.

The earliest reference to irrigation occurred in the third millennium in Sumerian communities in southern Mesopotamia. "By the mid-third millennium, there was a reference by one of the rulers of Lagash to his having diverted Tigris water southward into portions of Sumer previously watered only by the Euphrates" (McC, Adams 1974: 3). In the late third and early second millennia there were references to large-scale canal and dam constructions. The people also made dykes and sluices, and they dug ditches to channel water into fields of about two or three acres.

The Code of Hammurabi of 1790 BCE mandated maintenance and repair of canals and dykes throughout the year. Each riparian owner had the duty neither to flood his neighbor's land nor to deprive him of water by excessive diversion of a stream (Driver and Miles 1952: 152). Anyone who owned a plot of land had to keep dykes and stream banks in proper repair. If through neglect, the water flowing through one's land flooded another riparian's land, one had to replace the corn crop that was destroyed (Driver and Miles 1952: 152–153). If one did not make compensation for the damage one committed, one's goods were sold; and the neighbors, whose crops were destroyed, divided up the proceeds. Liability attached to leaving one's gates open, thereby causing water to flood the neighbor's land and damage crops, fences, or ditches. Compensation was proportionate. After damaging an entire crop, one had to repay an equivalent amount of corn; but with less damage one had to pay a year's rent or one third of the estimated crop destruction (Driver and Miles 1952: 154).

In retrospect, three irrigation systems came out of the Ancient Near East. These systems were diffused throughout the Mediterranean world, mainly under Roman authority, and perfected in Islam as it advanced into North Africa and the Iberian Peninsula (Glick 1970: 176). From Spain these systems were taken into the New World and introduced into the Hispano-American Southwest in conjunction with Native American techniques. Between 1000 and 1300 CE, or the classical Pueblo period, Indians developed methods of irrigation in what is now Southwestern Colorado, Northwestern New Mexico, Central and Southern Arizona (Meyer 1996: 12).

The oldest method was the building of dams to raise water from a stream and divert it into irrigation canals. Dams for storage of water came later. One well-known early diversion dam was the Marib Dam of Yemen, which had a probable construction date in the fifth century BCE (Glick 1970: 176–177). The Marib Dam diverted water from the Wadi Dhana into two canal distribution systems. The purpose of the diversion dams was to slow water flows, particularly during flash floods, and to raise the water levels for diversion.

The second type was the Persian wheel, or *noria*, which consisted of a wheel with buckets that lifted water out of a stream. These wheels were moved by animals or men. The animal-driven Persian wheel was introduced into the Iberian Peninsula in the eighth century CE, and it continued to be used into the 20th century (Glick 1970: 178). Some wheels were small, some large, depending on the width and depth of the stream.

The third method was the *qanat*, and it consisted of a series of interconnected, underground wells that tapped and diverted groundwater (Glick 1970: 182). The history of the *qanat* was closely related to that of the Persian wheel, and it was first used in western Persia, northern Mesopotamia, and eastern Turkey about 2,500 years ago. Unlike surface canals, *qanats* prevented evaporation and precluded the construction of water-lifting devices. The Romans dug and installed *qanats* in Europe and North Africa, and they were succeeded by the Arabs who used them widely in Spain.

These traditional irrigation systems were local, ecological, and cooperative. They were sanctioned by local customs and not imposed by a centralized political authority. Irrigation associations were autonomous and decentralized. The irrigation traditions of the Ancient Near East, Roman Empire, and Islam converged in Medieval Spain, where they exhibited three working principles: (1) proportionate allocation of water, as measured by the size of the land irrigated; (2) responsibility of individual irrigators to the entire community, as with the maintenance of the canal that bordered one's property; and (3) collective responsibility for administering and supervising irrigation (Glick 1970: 187). These irrigation communities were self-governing and self-regulating, and they maintained their practices and social controls on the basis of customary law. Irrigators did not attack or dominate nature, but rather they worked with nature to sustain human life and protect ecological systems.

International Watercourse Management

Historically, nations have attempted to resolve international water conflicts through treaties. A water treaty appeared for the first time in 2500 BCE, when the two Sumerian city-states of Lagash and Umma negotiated an agreement ending a water dispute along the Tigris River in Mesopotamia (UNESCO Water Newsletter No. 189 2007). Urlama, King of Lagash from 2450 to 2400 BCE, had diverted water from the Gu'edena region to boundary canals, thereby drying up boundary ditches to deprive Umma of water His son Umma II shut off the water supply to Girsu, a city in Umma (Gleick 2004: 236).

More than 3600 international water treaties were made between 805 and 1984 CE. In the 20th century only seven minor conflicts erupted between nations over water, and during that century more than 145 treaties were signed (UNESCO Water Newsletter No. 189 2007).

According to the Transboundary Freshwater Dispute Database at Oregon State University, there are 263 rivers that cross or demarcate international political boundaries (www.transboundarywater.orst.edu. 2007). Europe has the highest number with 69, followed by Africa with 59, Asia 57, North America 40, and South America with 38. These numbers are not fixed, since political boundaries change due to war, national unification, or dissolution of countries. The 263 international river basins account for nearly one half of the earth's land surface, providing about 60% of global freshwater flows, and they are home to approximately 40% of the world's population. A combined total of 145 countries have territory within international basins. Thirty three nations have more than 95% of their territories within the hydrological boundaries of one or more international basins. For example, the Danube River has 17 riparian states, and the Congo, Niger, Nile, Rhine, and Zambesi Rivers are each shared by more than nine countries.

As a matter of law, uses of international lakes and rivers are divided into navigation and non-navigation purposes. In the early 19th century rules of navigation began to emerge to facilitate the transportation of goods and materials during the Industrial Revolution in Europe. The major European powers concluded in 1815 the Act of the Congress of Vienna, and this treaty established "the principle of freedom of navigation for all riparian states on the rivers they share, on a reciprocal basis, as well as its priority over other uses" (Salman 2007: 626). Subsequent treaties extended the freedom of navigation to non-riparian states and approved rivers for hydropower and irrigation in light of the growing populations. After World War Two and the division of Europe into eastern and western zones, the freedom of navigation was restricted to riparian states on shared rivers.

In the post-war period of the 20th century, when larger populations relied on rivers and lakes increasingly for non-navigational uses, the principle of limited territorial sovereignty emerged to shape modern international water law. This principle asserts "that every riparian state has a right to use the waters of the international river" but has a "corresponding duty to ensure that such use does not harm other riparians" (Salman 2007: 627). This principle posits the equality of all riparians in the uses of the waters of international rivers.

Two scholarly non-governmental organizations have made major contributions to the law of international watercourses by recommending rules and resolutions. One is the Institute of International Law (IIL), and the other is the International Law Association (ILA). Founded in 1873 both organizations aim to codify existing international laws, but their rules and resolutions are not binding. Their rules and resolutions are sources of customary international law. In contrast, treaties and conventions become binding when the states sign and ratify them.

The IIL has emphasized the duty not to cause harm, and its proposals took shape as the Madrid Declaration on the International Watercourses for Purposes other than Navigation. This declaration prohibited unilateral changes and harmful alterations of international river basins, and it advocated joint water commissions (www.transboundarywaters.orst.edu.) The Madrid Declaration acknowledged that riparian states on a common stream shared a permanent physical dependence on one another, and it established two rules: (1) no state could use the waters of a frontier stream in a way that interfered with their use by another state and (2) that the essential nature of a stream crossing two or more states could not be altered by an excessive use of water (Teclaff 1996: 366).

On the basis of the Madrid Declaration the ILA adopted in 1966 the Helsinki Rules on the Uses of the Waters of International Rivers. These rules apply to the waters of an international drainage basin, which is defined in Article II as "a geographical area extending over two or more States determined by the watershed limits of the system of waters, including surface and underground waters, flowing into a common terminus" (Report of the Committee on the Uses of the Waters of International Rivers 1967). This was the first statement on transboundary groundwater by an international legal instrument (Salman 2007: 629). In keeping with the emphasis of the ILA these rules established "a reasonable and equitable share in the beneficial uses of the waters of an international drainage basin" for a basin state (art. IV). A basin state is a state whose territory includes a portion of an international drainage basin.

In order to assess a reasonable and equitable share the Helsinki Rules list relevant factors to be considered in making a judgment: (1) the geography of the basin, particularly the extent of the drainage area in each basin state; (2) hydrology of the basin: (3) climate; (4) past utilization of the waters of the basin; (5) economic and social needs of each basin state: (6) population dependent on the basin waters; (7) comparative costs of satisfying alternative economic and social needs; (8) availability of other resources; (9) avoidance of waste in the utilization of the waters; (10) practicability of compensation as a means of adjusting conflicts; and (11) degree to which a state's needs may be satisfied without causing "substantial injury" to a co-riparian state.

The Helsinki Rules made reasonable and equitable use fundamental to international water law, placed the no-harm rule in the list of factors instead of making it independent, and made navigational and non-navigational uses equal (Salman 2007: 629–630). The rules prohibited pollution in chapter three, and they provided procedures for the prevention and settlement of disputes. While not binding, these rules became an authoritative instrument of customary international law.

On December 8, 1970 the United Nations asked the International Law Commission (ILC), a UN body of legal experts nominated by states and elected by the UN General Assembly, to codify the articles on international water law. The outcome was the Adoption on May 21, 1997 of the United Nations Convention on the Law of the Non-Navigational Uses of International Watercourses, or more simply the UN Watercourse Convention (http://untreaty.un.org/ilc/texts/instruments/english/conventions/8_3_1997.pd f). Although 103 countries approved the convention, as of this writing the law is not in force due to an inadequate number of state signatories.

Article 5 of the UN Convention reaffirms the Helsinki standard of water usage in an "equitable and reasonable manner," but it adds "participation" in the sense that it "includes both the right to utilize the watercourse and the duty to cooperate in the protection and development thereof." This convention lists a series of factors for the determination of reasonable and equitable use, and they are essentially the same as those in the Helsinki Rules. Watercourse states shall cooperate with one another and consider all of the relevant factors in reaching a conclusion on the basis of the whole. Even though the no-harm rule is stated in the last of the list of relevant factors, Article 7(1) stipulates that watercourse "States shall, in utilizing an international watercourse in their territories, take all appropriate measures to prevent the causing of significant harm to other watercourse States." Nevertheless, reasonable and equitable utilization remains the fundamental rule. Article 10(2) provides that in "the event of a conflict between uses of an international watercourse, it shall be resolved … with special regard being given to the requirements of vital human needs." The convention does not define, however, vital human needs.

This UN Convention requires states to protect and preserve ecosystems of watercourses (art. 20), to reduce and control pollution that may cause significant harm to the environment, human health and safety of other states (art. 21. 2), to "prevent the introduction of species, alien or new, into an international watercourse" that may harm its ecosystem (art. 22); and states shall prevent or mitigate damaging conditions resulting from "flood or ice conditions, water-borne diseases, siltation, erosion, salt-water intrusion, drought or desertification" (art. 27). This convention prohibits discrimination against those who suffer significant transboundary harm, and it advocates access to judicial relief or "a right to claim compensation" (art. 32).

In 1997 the ILA began to revise the Helsinki Rules, and this revision produced the Berlin Rules of 2004. These rules take into account developments in environmental, human rights, and humanitarian law. Whereas the previous work of the ILA dealt only with international rivers, the Berlin Rules apply to the management of both national and international rivers. Whereas the Helsinki Rules and the UN Convention assigned priority to a reasonable and equitable utilization, the Berlin Rules add the no harm rule in Chapter III, Article 12: "Basin States shall in their respective territories manage the waters of an international drainage basin in an equitable and reasonable manner having due regard for the obligation not to cause significant harm to other basin states" (www.internationalwaterlaw.org. 2009). Thus, The Berlin Rules make reasonable and equitable utilization and no harm co-equal principles. This duality goes beyond the Helsinki Rules and the UN Convention, which make reasonable and equitable use fundamental.

Unlike the Helsinki Rules the Berlin Rules define vital human needs as "waters used for immediate human survival, including drinking, cooking, and sanitary needs, as well as water needed for the immediate sustenance of a household" (I. 3. 20). Article 21 clarifies waters as both surface and groundwater, but it excludes marine waters. Vital human needs have priority in determining reasonable and equitable use. The Berlin Rules go beyond their predecessors by asserting the right of access to water. "Every individual has a right of access to sufficient, safe, acceptable, physically accessible, and affordable water to meet that individual's vital human needs" (III. 17. 1). States shall implement the right of access to water by progressive realization, nondiscrimination, and prevention of third parties from interfering with the enjoyment of the right. The Berlin Rules also innovate by presenting several articles on environmental integrity and protection. These rules even reaffirm the freedom of navigation, in that "each riparian State is entitled to freedom of navigation on the entire watercourse to which they are riparian on a basis of equality and nondiscrimination" (IX. 43. 1).

While the Berlin Rules offer several new principles, three criticisms have been offered (Salman 2007: 637–638). First, the rules apply to both national and international waters, making the latter applicable to the former. The difficulty is that the world community has not yet established a treaty to regulate international watercourses, and therefore the international principles should not be applied to domestic waters. Second, the Berlin Rules incorporate both established and emerging rules and designate both by the word "shall," but they do not differentiate between the two. Established rules are legally binding, but emerging principles are not. Third, the Berlin Rules downgrade the established fundamental principle of equitable and reasonable utilization and equate it with the non-harm principle. Historically, the rule of equitable and reasonable utilization has been applied to transboundary waters, but the no-harm principle to environmental protection. Hence, the legal status is unclear and confusing.

On December 11, 2008 the United Nations General Assembly adopted the Resolution on the Law of Transboundary Aquifers. The International Hydrological Programme (IHP) of UNESCO assisted, but the UN International Law Commission (UNILC) prepared the articles. The IHP had inventoried 273 transboundary aquifers, some of which were shared by two or more countries (UNESCO Water Newsletter No. 212 2009). The law recognizes that "each aquifer State has sovereignty over the portion of a transboundary aquifer or aquifer system located within its territory. It shall exercise its sovereignty in accordance with international law and the present draft articles" (art. 3). The governing principle is that of "equitable and reasonable utilization," as determined by the following relevant factors: (1) population dependent on aquifer or aquifer system; (2) social, economic and other needs, present and future of aquifer states: (3) natural characteristics of aquifer states; (4) contribution to formation and recharge of aquifer or aquifer system; (5) existing and potential use of aquifer or aquifer system; (6) actual and potential effects of aquifer use: (7) availability of alternatives to existing and planned aquifer utilization; (8) development, protection, conservation of the aquifer and the costs of those measures; and (9) role of aquifer in related ecosystems. All of these factors shall be considered in determining an "equitable and reasonable utilization," but special attention shall be devoted to "vital human needs" (art. 5. 2). These needs are not defined, however.

Aquifer States are obliged "to prevent the causing of significant harm to other aquifer States or other States in whose territory a discharge zone is located" (art. 6. 1). Aquifer States are encouraged "to enter into bilateral or regional agreements" (art. 9), and States "shall take all appropriate measures to protect and preserve ecosystems ... including measures to ensure that the quality and quantity of water retained in an aquifer ... are sufficient to protect and preserve such ecosystem" (art. 10).

As with the Berlin Rules, the Law of Transboundary Aquifers uses the word "shall" to apply the principles of equitable and reasonable utilization and no-harm to aquifers. Unlike the Berlin Rules, however, the law neither defines vital human needs nor asserts a right of access to water. The law applies only to states and not to occupied territories.

Reserved Water Rights

An important variation on the right to water, as developed in America law, is the doctrine of federal reserved water rights. This concept has come from *Winters v. United States*, 207 U.S. 564 (1908), and it has been known as the Winters doctrine. The case involved the fact that on May 1, 1888 the federal government set aside and reserved land in the territory of Montana as the permanent home of the Gros Ventre and Assiniboin Indian tribes, and it designated the land as the Fort Belknap Indian Reservation. The court also designated the Milk River as the northern boundary, and its waters provided irrigation for the tribes.

In 1900, after Montana had become a state on February 22, 1889, several non-Indians built dams and reservoirs on the Milk River and its tributaries to divert water through ditches, canals, and other waterways, thus depriving the Indians of the use of the water. On appeal from the Ninth Circuit Court of Appeals the U.S. Supreme Court held that the "power of the government to reserve the waters and exempt them from appropriation under the state laws is not denied, and could not be. That the government did reserve them we have decided, and for a use which would be necessarily continued through years" (*Winters v. U.S.*, 207 U.S. 577 (1908).

The Winters doctrine protects water on all Indian reservations in sufficient quantities to fulfill the purposes of the reservations. The doctrine came out of a prior appropriation state and has remained in conflict with those states holding the prior appropriation doctrine (Ranquist 1975: 641, 647). The Winters and prior appropriation doctrines are mutually exclusive to each other. Essentially, *Winters* rejected the principle of "first in time, first in right" (Pelcyger 1977: 20).

For 55 years after the *Winters* decision debates continued in the West, particularly between Arizona and California over the appropriations of the Colorado River water. One issue involved the fact that on March 3, 1865 Congress established the Colorado River Reservation, on behalf of five Indian tribes, and asserted their rights to use mainstream river water. Arizona argued that the federal government lacked the power to reserve water in Arizona, after it had become a state. The U.S. Supreme Court resolved those disputes in 1963.

> The Court in Winters concluded that the Government, when it created that Indian Reservation, intended to deal fairly with the Indians by reserving for them the waters without which their lands would have been useless. Winters has been followed by this Court as recently as 1939 in United States v. Powell .... We follow it now and agree that the United States did reserve the water rights for the Indians effective as of the time the Indian Reservations were created. This means ... that

these water rights ... are "present perfected rights" and as such are entitled to priority under the Act (*Arizona v. California,* 376 U.S. 600 (1963).

In this case the Supreme Court not only reaffirmed the Winters doctrine but also extended it beyond Indian reservations to federal enclaves. The Court ruled that

the reservation of water rights for Indian Reservations was equally applicable to other federal establishments such as National Recreation Areas and National Forests. We agree ... that the United States intended to reserve water sufficient for the future requirements of the Lake Mead National Recreation Area, the Havasu Lake National Wildlife Refuge, the Imperial National Wildlife Refuge, and the Gila National Forest (376 U.S. 601 (1963).

Eight years after *Arizona* the Supreme Court reaffirmed the Winters doctrine once again. Writing for a unanimous court, Justice William Douglas stated that

It is clear from our cases that the United States often has reserved water rights based on withdrawals from the public domain. As we said in *Arizona v. California* ..., the Federal Government had the authority, both before and after a state is admitted into the union, "to reserve waters for the use and benefit of Federally reserved lands." The federally reserved lands include any federal enclave (*United States v. District Court for Eagle County,* 401 U.S. 522–523 (1971).

After the Eagle County case, courts could assert a federal reserved water right, if (1) the land at issue is a federal enclave or reservation; (2) the land is withdrawn from the public domain; and (3) the situation involved in the creation of an enclave or reservation reveals an intent to reserve water (Ranquist 1975: 651). An enclave is a land wherein the federal government exercises exclusive jurisdiction and legislative authority.

According to the Winters doctrine, sufficient water is reserved for the purposes of reservation lands, and reserved water is not subject to appropriation and disposal by private parties. All water reservations are treated equally. With reference to Indians, in particular, a federal reserved water right is a private right held in trust for the benefit of Indians (Ranquist 1975: 655). Water rights are appurtenant to reserved lands. Unlike the prior appropriation doctrine, however, reserved water rights cannot be lost by non-use. The Winters doctrine protects Indian water rights for present and future needs of the Indians. Western states have resisted such protection on the grounds that present and future needs are not quantified (Ranquist 1975: 656). Western states are concerned that insufficient water is left for them, after the federal reservation.

Originally, the amount of water reserved for Indian reservations was determined primarily by irrigation. The U.S. Supreme Court held that "the water was intended to satisfy the future as well as the present needs of Indian Reservations and ruled that enough water was reserved to irrigate all the practically irrigable acreage on the reservations" (*Arizona v. California*, 376 U.S. 601 (1963). The court said that the term "irrigable acreage" was fair, feasible, and reasonable.

While agriculture was a primary purpose, there were other purposes as well. Reservations were intended to be places where Indians could maintain their way of life, including hunting and fishing, and enjoy viable, permanent, secure, and self-sustaining homelands (Pelcyger 1977: 25). Since the Indian way of life depended upon hunting, fishing, and other methods of gathering food, the Winters doctrine defined these activities as both on-and off-reservation rights (Pelcyger 1977: 26). These activities were just as necessary as agriculture to fulfill the purposes of the reservations. Reservations were also places where Indians could make their own laws and live by them.

The Winters doctrine applies to national parks and monuments for recreation, protection and conservation of fish, wildlife, and to national forests for recreation and protection of timber. Even military bases come under the Winters doctrine. All of these areas have been removed from the public domain and granted water rights sufficient for the purposes of the reservations. Generally, wildlife, fishing, and recreation have not been recognized as beneficial by western states (Ranquist 1975: 679). Beneficial use is the standard of the prior appropriation doctrine.

Under the Winters doctrine Indian Tribes are entitled to the quantity and quality of stream flows necessary for the preservation and maintenance of the on-and off-reservation fisheries. (Pelcyger 1977: 24). This allows the flushing out of gravel and maintaining stream temperatures to facilitate the migration and spawning of fish. The doctrine also prohibits clear cutting of forests, strip mining, and the discharge of effluent into streams. Polluting and silting streams can destroy protected water sources. Thus, the Winters doctrine supports the environmental integrity of federal reservations.

By the Proclamation of January 17, 1952 President Harry S. Truman withdrew from the public domain a 40-acre tract of land surrounding Devil's Hole, a deep limestone cavern in Nevada, making it a detached component of the Death Valley National Monument. Below the opening of the cavern is a pool of water 65 feet long, ten feet wide, and at least 200 feet deep. The pool is the habitat to a peculiar species of desert fish called pupfish. President Truman reserved Devil's Hole as a national monument on federal land and as an object of historical or scientific interests.

The Cappaert family owned a 12,000 acre ranch on land nearby, and in 1968 they began pumping groundwater two and one half miles from Devil's

Hole. They were the first to appropriate groundwater, and therefore under the Nevada prior appropriation water law they claimed to get primary water rights. The groundwater they pumped came out of an aquifer which also supplied water to Devil's Hole. Between March and October of 1968 the Cappaerts' groundwater pumping lowered the water level in Devil's Hole and exposed a rock shelf, reducing the spawning area of the pupfish and threatening its survival.

In April, 1970 the Cappaerts applied for a permit from the state to change the water use in several of their wells. The State Engineer approved the permit, and he stated that there was no recorded federal water right with respect to Devil's Hole, and that the Cappaerts' pumping would not unreasonably lower the water table or adversely effect existing water rights. The National Park Service objected to the Engineer's decision but did not appeal.

The federal government filed for an injunction in the U.S. District Court of Nevada, prohibiting groundwater pumping from six specific wells and from locations near Devil's Hole. The federal government claimed that the establishing of Devil's Hole as part of Death Valley National Monument "reserved the unappropriated waters appurtenant to the land to the extent necessary for the requirements and purposes of the reservation." The government also alleged that "the Cappaerts had no protected water rights as of the date of the reservation" and that their pumping from specific wells lowered the water level of Devil's Hole. The Ninth Circuit Court of Appeals upheld the injunction.

The U.S. Supreme Court granted certiorari and agreed with the Court of Appeals. The Supreme Court reaffirmed the federal reserved water rights doctrine and applied it to groundwater for the first time. "Thus, since the implied-reservation-of-water-rights doctrine is based on the necessity of water for the purpose of the federal reservation, we hold that the United States can protect its water from subsequent diversion, whether the diversion is of surface or groundwater" (*Cappaert v. United States*, 426 U.S. 143 (1976). Chief Justice Warren Burger, writing for the majority, stated that the Cappaerts' pumping depleted federal water supplies, because groundwater and surface water are physically interrelated as integral parts of the hydrologic cycle."

In *Cappaert* Chief Justice Burger held: "Federal reserved water rights are not dependent upon state law or state procedures, and they need not be adjudicated only in state courts; federal courts have jurisdiction under 28 U.S.C. § 1345 to adjudicate water rights claims of the United States" (426 U.S. 145 (1976). The securing of federal reserved water rights is the task of the National Park Service, Forest Service, Fish and Wildlife Service, Bureau of Land Management, and Indian Tribes. Relevant federal laws are the National Environmental Policy Act of 1969, the Clean Water Act of 1972, and the Endangered Species Act of 1973, along with case laws of federal court decisions.

Of these environmental laws the Endangered Species Act has been the most commonly used instrument to protect rivers (Postel and Richter 2003: 98). The Act empowers the Department of Interior to identify a species as endangered and to prohibit any federal agency from acting so as to threaten its continued existence. While the Act has been influential, it has three major disadvantages: (1) it protects individual species but not the entire ecosystem; (2) it is reactive not proactive, as it is triggered only when a conservation group sues the government; and (3) its impact is too late, because by the time a species is endangered its habitat has been severely degraded (Postel and Richter 2003: 99).

The Clean Water Act has a clearer and broader purpose: "To restore and maintain the chemical, physical, and biological integrity of the Nation's Waters" (U.S. Code, title 33 §1251). Section 401 of the Act requires that a city must obtain a water quality certification from the state for any proposed water diversion project in navigable waters and that the project will not violate water quality standards. The Clean Water Act mandates that the states enact comprehensive water quality standards in all intrastate waters. These standards consist of three parts: (1) designation of the uses of a waterway; (2) specific criteria to protect those uses; and (3) prohibition of any degradation of existing water uses (Ransel 1995: 262).

The U.S. Supreme Court has clarified the proper scope of Section 401 in *PUD No. 1 of Jefferson County v Washington Department of Ecology*, 119 U.S. 1900 (1994). The Court held that states may impose reasonable water quality criteria and that water quantity is an integral part of water quality. Without a sufficient instream flow volume the designated uses and the anti-degradation standards cannot be protected (Ransel 1995: 267). Thus, the Clean Water Act pertains to water quantity.

The Jefferson County case has far-reaching implications for water policy. States may act to protect the physical and biological integrity of their waters, based on specific numerical and chemical criteria, and their authority applies both to point and non-point discharges into waterways (Ransel 1995: 268–269). This means, for example, that states can control grazing and timber cutting, as well as any discharge of pollutants or pollution.

States may also act to maintain water quality and quantity where federally permitted dams diminish river flows. For example, the Hell's

Canyon Dam Complex in Idaho has blocked upstream migration of salmon. This migration is a designated use, but it is lost from hydropower development. The state can require, in a relicensing application, a company to make changes in order to recover a pre-existing use of a stream flow (Ransel 1995: 271). This is an important provision in the irrigated, arid western states where low water flows frequently impair designated uses and facilitate the buildup of pollutants.

The quantity of federal reserved water rights means the volume of water necessary to fulfill the primary purpose of the reservation. Federal reserved water rights do not depend on a beneficial use, as in the prior appropriation doctrine, and leaving water undeveloped is not considered a waste. Non-quantifiable water uses in federal reservations are not illegal. In *Avondale Irrigation District v. North Idaho Properties*, 577 P.22 9, 19 (Idaho 1978) the Idaho Supreme Court ruled that "a claim to the entire flow, if it is necessary, cannot be faulted for uncertainty" and "is sufficient quantification for the reserved rights claimed" (Silk et al. 2000: 311).

On the basis of the foregoing discussion I propose that the concept of reserved water rights be extended globally to cover groundwater, large bodies of surface water, and the oceans or parts of them. The mechanism would be a binding United Nations Covenant. The oceans stretch across 70% of the earth, and they contain remarkable biological diversity. The oceans are imperiled, however, by destructive fishing practices, pollution, commercial aquaculture, climate change, and acidification (www.worldwatch.org. 2007). Rising concentrations of carbon dioxide are increasing the acidity of oceans (Gleick 2010: 689). In order to protect the oceans a global ecosystem approach should be initiated.

> Paramount to the application of this approach is the establishment of networks of fully protected marine reserves—in essence "national parks" of the sea. These provide protection of whole ecosystems and enable biodiversity to both recover and to flourish. They also benefit fisheries by allowing for spillover of fish and larvae or eggs from the reserve into adjacent fishing grounds (www.worldwatch.org. 2007).

Creating "national parks" of the seas is the same as granting reserved water rights under international authority. This proposal follows classical Roman law in which the sea is subject to the law of nations (*Institutes of Justinian*, II, I, 1. Moyle, trans. 1913). Currently, the older law of nations is replaced by world law which includes international law and functions as a common law among nations (Berman 2005: 71–72). World law includes nations, people, their ethical principles, and religious traditions.

Since World War Two, a body of world law has emerged, comprising international agreements, treaties, and conventions, as well as customary international law created by voluntary transnational organizations (Berman 2005: 72). An example of the latter would be policy statements on the right to water produced by the churches and human rights organizations, such as Amnesty International. World law comprises shared values and non-governmental organizations existing outside sovereign states. An example of the impact of world law is the modification of Part XI of the Law of the Sea Treaty in 1994, which prevented public exploitation of shared resources of the sea bed (Christenson 1997: 734). In this particular case world law opposed a monopoly of states from extracting natural resources for the production of wealth.

Expanding the Public Trust

Implied in the Winters doctrine is the concept of the public trust. The federal government holds the reserved waters as a trust for the Indian Tribes. In American water law one of the most far-reaching applications of the public trust doctrine was the Mono Lake case, handed down on February 17, 1983 by the California Supreme Court in *National Audubon Society*. Mono Lake is a saline body of water in eastern California. The lake contains no fish; but is supports a large population of brine shrimp which feeds vast numbers of nesting gulls, and its islands serve as havens for migrating birds. Mono Lake gets some water from rain and snow on its surface, but most of its water comes from snowmelt in the Sierra Nevada Mountains, which five freshwater streams carry to the lake.

In 1940 the Division of Water Resources, the forerunner of the current California Water Board, granted The Department of Water and Power of the City of Los Angeles (DWP) a permit to appropriate water from the five tributaries to Mono Lake. DWP constructed a diversion tunnel to transport water into the Los Angeles aquaduct, and in 1970 DWP completed the second diversion tunnel that appropriated virtually all of the waters in the five tributary streams to Mono Lake.

As a result of these diversions, the water level of Mono Lake dropped. The surface area receded by one third, and the two main islands became a peninsula. The latter formed a water-bridge, allowing predator coyotes to attack bird nests, while the migrating birds abandoned the islands. The water diversion increased the salinity in the lake, and consequently the brine shrimp population decreased. Since the lake began to recede, the exposed lake bed, consisting of fine silt, dried out and became airborne, threatening the mucous membranes and respiratory systems of humans and animals.

The National Audubon Society filed suit to prevent the diversion of Mono Lake water on the grounds that the shores, bed, and water of the lake were protected by the public trust doctrine. The Court pointed out that the case brought the public trust doctrine into conflict with the prior appropriation doctrine in California water law. The California Supreme Court ruled, however, in favor of the National Audubon Society, and it summarized its holding as follows:

> In our opinion, the core of the public trust doctrine is the stated authority as sovereign to exercise a continuous supervision and control over navigable waters of the state and the lands underlying these waters. This authority applies to the water tributary to Mono Lake and bans DWP or any other party from claiming a vested right to divert waters once it becomes clear that such diversions harm the interests protected by the public trust (*National Audubon Society v. Superior Court*, 33 Cal. 3d 419 (1983).

The Court went on to clarify three aspects of the public trust doctrine. First, the doctrine has evolved beyond its traditional triad of uses—namely navigation, commerce, and fishing—into the protection of recreational and ecological values. Mono Lake is not only a navigable waterway or "fishery" but also a place of great beauty and ecological functions for wildlife.

Second, unlike the English common law, which limited the public trust to tidal waters and tide lands, in American law the public trust extends to all navigable lakes and streams. As a navigable waterway, Mono Lake deserves protection in its bed, shores, and water. The tributaries, from which Los Angeles diverts water, are not navigable streams. This fact leads to the following question: Are the tributaries protected by the public trust? The Court answers yes and draws upon precedent in state case law that diversions of water from non-navigable streams that harm navigable waters violate the public trust.

Third, the Court reviewed the duties and powers of the state as trustee, and it affirmed the state's sovereign power to supervise the public trust. The Court acknowledged that previous cases in California had approved the precedent of *Illinois Central Railroad Company v. Illinois*, 146 U.S. 387 (1892), discussed above in chapter seven. The California Supreme Court concluded that the public trust doctrine affirmed "the duty of the state to protect the people's common heritage of streams, lakes, marshlands, and tide lands, surrendering that right of protection only in rare cases, when the abandonment of that right is consistent with the public trust."

The National Audubon Society case served as a precedent for the Hawaiian Supreme Court in *In re: Water Use Permit Applications*, 9 P.3d 409 (Hawaii 2000). In the latter case the Hawaiian Supreme Court also acknowledged, following *Illinois Central Railroad Company*, that traditionally the public trust doctrine protected the public rights of navigation, commerce, and fishing (III. B. 3. B. i). The Hawaiian Court even acknowledged that the California Supreme Court went beyond the traditional three-fold rights of the public trust to that of resource protection in the Mono Lake case:

> One of the most important public uses of the tidelands—a use encompassed within the tidelands trust—is the preservation of these lands in their natural state, so that they may serve as ecological units for scientific study, as open space, and as environments which provide food and habitat for birds and marine life, and which favorably affect the scenery and climate of the area.

In agreement with the California Supreme Court the Hawaiian Supreme Court "has likewise acknowledged resource protection, with its numerous derivative public uses, benefits, and values as an important underlying purpose of the reserved water resources trust." The Court went on to hold "that the maintenance of waters in their natural state constitutes a distinct case under the water resource trust." This assertion refuted the prior appropriation doctrinal idea that waters in their natural, undeveloped state were a waste. The Court explained that the public trust "is an affirmation of the duty of the state to protect the people's common heritage of streams, lakes, marshlands and tidelands, surrendering that right of protection only in rare cases when the abandonment of that right is consistent with the purposes of the trust."

While the Hawaiian Supreme Court essentially agreed with the holding of the Mono Lake case, it indicated three unique differences from the California Supreme Court. First, the Mono Lake case dealt with the diversion of water for the domestic uses of Los Angeles, but the Hawaiian case did not claim offstream public needs. Second, the California case advanced the public trust against the prior appropriation water rights system that linked non-consumptive water with waste. Instead, the Hawaiian Court declared the natural state of undeveloped waters a beneficial use. Third, unlike California water law the Hawaiian Court reaffirmed the state's constitutional duty (XII. 7) "to protect traditional and customary Native Hawaiian rights" (III. B. 3. B. ii). Thus, the Hawaiian Supreme Court has gone beyond the California Supreme Court in affording more public trust protection and sustaining customary law in Native Hawaiian tradition

Nevertheless, despite these differences, the Hawaiian Supreme Court found in the Mono Lake case the fundamental and abiding principles of the public trust doctrine. First, "the state has both the authority and duty to preserve the rights of present and future generations in the waters of the state."

Second, the state bears an "affirmative duty to take the public trust into account in the planning and allocating of water resources and to protect public trust uses whenever feasible." This means that the public has an interest in the development of water resources, but such uses must be for reasonable and beneficial purposes. The uses may be instream or offstream, but they must promote the best social and economic interests of the people of the state.

Third, in periods of water scarcity the state must balance competing uses, weighing public and private purposes on a case-by-case basis. Judicial balancing begins with "a presumption in favor of public use, access, and enjoyment." Public values are superior to private uses. Since the public trust is a state constitutional principle, the ultimate authority of interpretation and defense lies in the courts.

Within the context of emerging world water law the public trust doctrine converges with the concept of reserved water rights. In order to protect imperiled waters globally, they need to be placed under reserved water rights on the basis of the public trust. One example of the convergence of reserved water rights and the public trust exists in South Africa. Post-apartheid South Africa's National Water Act, passed in 1998, defines water as a common good subject to the public trust. The public trust doctrine is integrated with the natural flow theory of the common law and with ecosystem preservation values. The law establishes a system of water allocation known as the Reserve, which consists of two parts. The first part is "a non-negotiable allocation to meet the basic water needs of all South Africans for drinking, cooking, sanitation and other essential purposes," and the second is "an allocation of water to support ecosystem functions ...." (Postel and Richter 2003: 85) The Act ensures that the "quantity, quality and reliability of water required to maintain the ecological functions on which humans depend shall be reserved so that the human use of water does not individually or cumulatively compromise the long term sustainability of aquatic and associated ecosystems" (Postel and Richter 2003: 85).

Water that constitutes the Reserve has priority over all other uses, and only this water is guaranteed as a right (Postel and Richter 2003: 86). Uses of water outside the Reserve, as for irrigation or industrial purposes, have a lesser priority and must receive authorizations. South Africa's National Water Act offers an exemplary synthesis of federal reserved water rights, the public trust doctrine, and the right to water. Maintaining these three concepts is a fundamental human obligation in the world today.

A Recapitulation

Since ancient times, irrigation associations have practiced proportionate allocations of water, responsibility of individual irrigators to their respective communities, and self-governing policies based upon customary or codified law. These communities share water in cooperation with nature. A contemporary example of an egalitarian water sharing community is the Hispanic *acequia* in northern New Mexico. The *acequia* serves as a model of water sharing in an age of impending scarcity and international conflict.

Historically, nations have tried to resolve water disputes in terms of treaties or agreements. Beginning in the early 20th century, the international legal community formulated rules to manage international watercourses. The Madrid Declaration set forth two rules, namely, that one state could not use water in a manner that would interfere with water use in another state and that a natural watercourse could not be altered by an excessive use of water. The Helsinki Rules established the principle of equitable and reasonable utilization as the fundamental standard of international water law. The Law of the Non-Navigational Uses of International Watercourses and the Law of Transboundary Aquifers maintained the fundamental Helsinki principle, but the Berlin Rules balanced that with the obligation to do no harm to other states. Harm may be quantitative or qualitative.

American courts have established precedents to guide water usage domestically and internationally. The Winters doctrine of federal reserved water rights reverses the prior appropriation doctrine and sets aside sufficient water resources for the purposes of the reservation. The state Supreme Courts of California and Hawaii have extended the public trust doctrine beyond the traditional triad of navigation, commerce, and fishing to the protection of ecosystems and recreational needs. The Hawaii Supreme Court, in particular, affirmed the public trust as a constitutional principle, and it incorporated indigenous religious traditions into the public trust.

The idea of "vital human needs," which the Berlin Rules specify, must include adequate amounts of water to satisfy personal needs for drinking, cooking, bathing, and sanitation. As discussed in chapter eight, at least 50 liters of water per person per day are required, according to the Pacific Institute. The phrase "vital human needs" should also include natural habitats and ecosystems on which human life depends. Humans share with all other natural species a vast hydrological cycle which includes interrelated flows of surface water and groundwater.

Water is the basis of life on earth. In an evolutionary perspective, life arose in the sea, evolved on land, and then moved to the sky. While the sea was necessary for the inception and diversity of life, it did not produce large brains until species became terrestrial and adapted to land challenges (Rolston 1999: 3, 8). Nevertheless, terrestrial life needs water to survive. Within the planetary hydrological cycle water is distributed equitably but not uniformly to all species. The natural allocation of water does not discriminate between needs of microbes, plants, mammals, and humans (Shiva 2005: 107). This non-discriminatory allocation represents a water democracy in the earth, and it functions as an ecological basis for egalitarian human water sharing.

Water quality and water quantity are equally necessary to satisfy human and environmental needs. Currently, water quality is threatened by contamination, widespread lack of proper waste disposal, pollution by agriculture, industry, and mining. These water quality problems must be resolved on a global scale in three ways: (1) prevention of pollution, (2) treatment of polluted water, and (3) restoration of ecosystems (Palaniappan et al. www.pacinst.org. 2010).

At the same time, poor water quality creates deficiencies of water quantity. Polluted water that cannot be used for domestic or agricultural needs reduces the quantity of water in specific regions of the world. The poorer the water quality the more energy is required for treatment, but treated water becomes less clean and less available for human uses. Surfaces on the earth that are covered by highways, parking lots, buildings, and other constructions prevent water from percolating down to aquifers. Consequently, base flows of streams diminish, and the volume of contaminated surface water increases (Palaniappan et al.www.pacinst.org. 2010).

As discussed in chapter five, the concept of sacramental commons offers an appropriate worldview for dealing with water quantity and water quality issues on a global scale. Viewing the earth as a sacramental commons mandates a reasonable and equitable sharing of water supplies and avoidance of environmental harm in accord with international law. The increasing acidity of the oceans due to rising concentrations of carbon dioxide necessitates placing them under international reserved water rights. Similarly, all freshwater systems and indigenous religious traditions should be protected by the public trust. The legal basis of these protections would be customary international law or world law with its non-governmental associations and religious traditions.

In the global sacramental commons water has intrinsic value, as distinguished from its instrumental value, for all biotic and abiotic systems. Widespread problems of water scarcity, as documented in the introduction, make a purely utilitarian approach to water unsustainable. The intrinsic value of water obligates humans to leave enough water in streams, lakes, and aquifers for their ecological well-being. In contrast to the prior appropriation doctrine undeveloped water is not a waste, and non-use does not mitigate the right to water. Water is a common good and a benefit. Constructions of dams and other water diversion systems, as well as excessive groundwater pumping, should be restrained or curtailed in some locations. Instead conservation and efficiency of utilization should be encouraged under local community supervision. Each body of water has its own unique flow or level that must be preserved for its own sake.

Viewing the earth sacramentally inspires reverence and awe toward bodies of water and motivates humanity to take care of them as symbols of the sacred. The right to water, reserved water rights, and the public trust are sanctioned by a natural sacramentality. In the words of a natural resource lawyer the public trust is based on "a belief that our rivers and canyons are more than commodities, that they have a trace of the sacred" (Wilkinson 1988–1989: 471–472). With a natural sacramentality water is revered but not worshipped.

A natural sacramentality is supported by visions of water in the religions of the world. It is present in the Hindu adoration of rivers as goddesses, in the respect for rivers as symbols of the ultimate unity of nature in Taoism, and in the primordial quality of water in Shinto, Hawaiian religion, and in the Native American traditions. In Judaism and Islam water is a gift of God that belongs to all (Civic 1998: 440–441). According to these religions, sharing water is a sacred duty and denying water to anyone is an offense against God.

In the Old Testament or Hebrew Bible water has many meanings and symbolic representations. It is present before the creation of the world in the dark, primordial ocean (Gen. 1:2) out of which rivers flow in Eden (Gen. 2: 10–14). By the word of God water gets the power to fertilize life (Gen. 1:20a) and the power to destroy life (Gen. 6:17). In the preaching of the prophets pure running water comes from God who is the fountain of living waters (Jer. 2:13). Water flows symbolize justice and righteousness (Am. 5:24), and water renews the creation at the end of time (Isa. 35:6–7). At the end water will be available abundantly to all and at all times (Zech. 14:8). In the New Testament Jesus is the source of living water that gives eternal life (Jhn. 4:14; 7: 37–39).

In Christianity the Sacrament of Baptism has multiple symbolic meanings. It cleanses from sin, brings a seal of the Holy Spirit, bestows a new humanity, and confers equality within the church as the Body of Christ. Baptism reenacts the decisive episodes in the biblical narrative, specifically,

Noah's flood, the Exodus, John the Baptist's apocalyptic preaching, and dying and rising with Christ. These multiple meanings testify that water is an ultimate element that dissolves form and matter, brings forth life, and flows with a primal splendor. As the primary sacrament of the church, baptism transfigures the world in a sacramental vision, making the waters of the cosmos sparkle with the primal beauty of the sacred.

Bibliography

Abouali, Gamal. 1999. "Natural Resources Under Occupation: The Status of Palestinian Water Under International Law." *Pace International Law Review* 10: 411–574.

African Charter on Human and People's Rights. 1979. www.achpr.org. Accessed May 9, 2010.

Aitken, Bill. 1992. *Seven Sacred Rivers.* New Delhi: Penguin Books.

Allen, James P. 2003. "From Coffin Texts Spell." In *The Context of Scripture, Vol. 1,* 40. Ed. by William W. Hallo. Leiden: Brill.

Amnesty International. 2007. "Human Rights at Risk in La Parota Dam Project." www.amnesty.org. Accessed September 7, 2007.

_____. 2009. *Troubled Waters—Palestinians Denied Fair Access to Water.* www.amnesty.org. Accessed October 27, 2010.

_____. "States urged to Support Rights to Water and Sanitation." www.amnesty.org. July 29, 2010. Accessed August 13, 2010.

Arab Charter on Human Rights. 2004. www.arableagueonline.org. Accessed May 9, 2010.

Arizona v. California, 373 U.S. 546 (1963).

Aquinas, Saint Thomas. *Summa Theologica.* Trans. by The Fathers of the English Dominican Province. New York: Benziger Brothers, 1947–1948.

Augustine, Saint. *Confessions and Enchiridion.* Trans. by Albert C. Outler. The Library of Christian Classics. Philadelphia: The Westminster Press, 1955.

_____. *Tractates on the Gospel of John.* Trans. by John W. Rettig. The Fathers of the Church, Vol. 79. Washington, D.C.: The Catholic University of America Press, 1988.

Barlow, Maude. 2007. *Blue Covenant.* New York: The New Press.

_____. "Remarks to the United Nations General Assembly, April 22, 2009." www.canadians.org. Accessed February 4, 2010.

_____. "UN Declares Water and Sanitation a Basic Human Right." 2010, July 28. www.ipsnews.net. Accessed August 10, 2010.

Barlow, Maude and Clarke, Tony. 2002. *Blue Gold.* New York: The New Press.

Barr, James. 1998. "Was Everything that God Created Really Good?" In *God in the Fray,* 55–65. Ed. by T. Linafelt and T. Beal. Minneapolis: Fortress Press.

Barry, Michelle and Hughes, James M. 2008. "Talking Dirty—The Politics of Clean Water and Sanitation." *The New England Journal of Medicine* 359: 784–787.

Basham, A. L. 1967. *The Wonder That Was India.* London: Sidgwick & Jackson.

Beckwith, Martha. 1923. "Polynesian Analogues to the Celtic Otherworld and Fairy Mistress Themes." In *Vassar Medieval Studies,* 29–55. Ed. by Christabel F. Fiske. New Haven: Yale University Press.

_____. 1970. *Hawaiian Mythology.* Honolulu: University of Hawaii Press.

Beegle, Dewey M. 1972. *Moses, The Servant of Yahweh.* Grand Rapids: William B. Eerdmans.

Benedict XVI, Pope. *Caritas in Veritate*, 2009, June 29. www.vatican.va. Accessed February 2, 2010.

Berlin Rules on Water Resources. 2004. www.internationalwaterlaw.org. Accessed January 10, 2011.

Berman, Harold J. 2003. *Law and Revolution, II*. Cambridge: Harvard University Press.

_____. 2005. "Faith and Law in a Multicultural World." In *Religion in Global Civil Society*, 69–89. Ed. by Mark Juergensmeyer. New York: Oxford University Press.

Bix, Herbert P. 2000. *Hirohito and the Making of Modern Japan*. New York: Harper Collins.

Blackstone, William. 1979. *Commentaries on the Laws of England, Vol. II. Of the Rights of Things*. Chicago: The University of Chicago Press.

Bleeker, C. J. 1963. *The Sacred Bridge*. Leiden: Brill.

Blenkinsopp, Joseph. 1983. *A History of Prophecy in Israel*. Philadelphia: The Westminster Press.

Bloch, Marc. 1966. *French Rural History*. Trans. by Janet Soneheimer. Berkeley: University of California Press.

Bolt, Peter G. 2003. *Jesus' Defeat of Death*. Cambridge: Cambridge University Press.

Book of Common Prayer. Kingsport, TN: Kingsport Press, 1977.

Bord, Janet and Colin. 1985. *Sacred Waters*. London: Granada.

Bottero, Jean. 1980. "La Mythologie de la Mort en Mesopotamie Ancienne." In *Death in Mesopotamia*, 25–52. Ed. by B. Alster. Copenhagen: Akadensisk Forlag.

_____. 1983. "Les Morts et L'ou-Delá dans les rituels en accadien." *Zeitschrift für Assyriologie und Vorderasiatische Archeologie* 73: 191–196.

Boyce, Mary. 1990. *Textual Sources for the Study of Zoroastrianism*. Chicago: The University of Chicago Press.

Brockopp, Jonathan E. 2010. "Introduction." In *The Cambridge Companion to Muhammad*, 1–18. Ed. by Jonathan E. Brockopp. Cambridge: Cambridge University Press.

Bromiley, G. W. 1956. *Thomas Cranmer Theologian*. New York: Oxford University Press.

Brown, Raymond E. 1966. *The Gospel According to John*. The Anchor Bible. Garden City, NY: Doubleday.

Browning, Don S. 2006. "The United Nations Convention on the Rights of the Child: Should it be Ratified and Why?" *Emory International Law Review* 20: 157–183.

Burkert, Walter. 1985. *Greek Religion*. Trans. by John Raffan. Cambridge: Harvard University Press.

Cain, Nicholas L. 2004. "3rd World Water Forum in Kyoto: Disappointment and Possibility." In *The World's Water 2004–2005*, 189–197. Ed. by Peter H. Gleick. Washington, D.C.: Island Press.

Calvin, John. *Institutes of the Christian Religion*. Trans. by Ford L. Battles. The Library of Christian Classics. Philadelphia: The Westminster Press, 1960.

Caponera, Dante A. 1973. *Water Laws in Moslem Countries*. Rome: Food and Agricultural Organization of the United Nations.

Cappaert v. United States, 426 U.S. 128 (1976).

Chapman, Audrey R. and Russell, Sage. 2002. "Introduction." In *Core Obligations*, 185–215. Ed. by Audrey R. Chapman and Sage Russell. Antwerp: Intersentia.

Christenson, Gordon A. 1997. "World Civil Society and the International Rule of Law." *Human Rights Quarterly* 19: 724–737.

Civic, Melanne A. 1998. "A Comparative Analysis of the Israeli and Arab Water Traditions and Insights for Modern Water Sharing Agreements." *Denver Journal of International Law and Policy* 26: 437–452.

Collins, Adela Y. 1995. "The Origin of Christian Baptism." In *Living Water, Sealing Spirit*, 35–57. Ed. by Maxwell E. Johnson. Collegeville, MN: Liturgical Press.

Columbia River Watershed: Caring for Creation and the Common Good. 2001, January 8. An International Pastoral Letter by the Catholic Bishops of the Region. www.columbiariver.org. Accessed October 17, 2010.

Committee for Economic, Social and Cultural Rights General Comment 15: The Right to Water. www.cesr.org. Accessed April 29, 2008.

Confederated Tribes of the Umatilla Indian Reservation. Columbia Basin Salmon Policy. 1995.

Convention on the Elimination of All Forms of Discrimination against Women. www.un.org/womenwatch. Accessed May 9, 2010.

Convention on the Law of the Non-navigational Uses of International Watercourses 1997. http://untreaty.un.org/ilc/texts/instruments/english/conventions/8_3_1997.pdf. Accessed May 23, 2008.

Convention on the Rights of the Child (1989). www.unicef.org. Accessed April 9, 2008.

Convention on the Rights of Persons with Disabilities. www.un.org/disabilities. Accessed May 9, 2010.

Cranmer, Thomas. "Certain Sermons, or Homilies." In *English Reformers*, 262–286. Ed. by T. H. L. Parker. The Library of Christian Classics. Philadelphia: The Westminster Press, 1966.

Crawford, Suzanne J. 2007. *Native American Religious Traditions*. Upper Saddle River, NJ: Prentice-Hall.

Crossan, John Dominic. 2007. *God and Empire*. San Francisco: HarperCollins.

Crossland, Charlotte B. "Acequia Rights in Law and Tradition." *Journal of the Southwest* 32: 278–287.

Cyril of Jerusalem. *The Catechetical Lectures*. In *Cyril of Jerusalem and Nemesius of Emesa*, 64–192. Ed. by William Telfer. The Library of Christian Classics. Philadelphia: The Westminster Press, 1955.

Davidson, H. R. Ellis. 1988. *Myths and Symbols in Pagan Europe*. Syracuse: Syracuse University Press.

Davies, Jon. 1999. *Death, Burial and Rebirth in the Religions of Antiquity*. London: Routledge.

Daws, Gavan. 1968. *Shoal of Time*. Honolulu: University of Hawaii Pres.

De Chatel, Francesca. 2002. "Drops of Faith: Water in Islam." www.islamonline.net. Accessed June 26, 2009.

Deutsch, Eliot and van Buitenen, J. A. B. 1971. *A Source Book of Advaita Vedanta*. Honolulu: University of Hawaii Press.

Dillenberger, John and Welch, Claude. 1988. *Protestant Christianity*. New York: Macmillan.

Dinzelbacher, Peter and Kleinschmidt, Harald. 1984. "Seelenbrücke und Brüchenbau im Mittelalterlichen England." *Numen* 21: 242–287.

Dionysius of Halicarnassus. *The Roman Antiquities*. Trans. by Earnest Cary. The Loeb Classical Library. Cambridge: Harvard University Press, 1960.

Dodd, C. H. 1968. *The Interpretation of the Fourth Gospel*. Cambridge: Cambridge University Press.

Dresner, Samuel H. 1994. *Rachel*. Minneapolis: Fortress Press.

Driver, G. R. and Miles, John C. 1952. *The Babylonian Laws, Vol. I*. Oxford: Clarendon Press.

Earhart, Byron. H. 1974. "The Ancient Mythology." In *Religion in the Japanese Experience: Sources and Interpretations*, 14–19. Ed. by H. Byron Earhart. Encino, CA: Dickenson.

Ecumenical Declaration on Water as a Human Right and a Public Good. 2005. Institute for Theology and Ethics ITE, Berne. www.sek-feps.ch. Accessed August 16, 2010.

Ecumenical Water Network Newsletter No. 3. 2010, August. "UN Resolution Recognizes Right to Water and Sanitation." www.oikoumene.org. Accessed August 10, 2010.

Ecumenical Water Network. 2010, October 6. "EWN Welcomes Affirmation of Right to Water and Sanitation." www.oikoumene.org. Accessed November 19, 2010.

Eliade, Mircea. 1959. *The Sacred and the Profane*. Trans. by Willard Trask. New York: Harcourt, Brace & World.

_____. 1973. *Australian Religions*. Ithaca: Cornell University Press.

Emerson, Nathaniel B. 1909. *Unwritten Literature of Hawaii*. Washington: Government Printing Office.

Faith and Order Paper No. 111. 1982. *Baptism, Eucharist & Ministry*. Geneva: World Council of Churches.

Finn, Thomas M. 1989. "Ritual Process and the Survival of Early Christianity: A Study of the Apostolic Tradition of Hippolytus." *Journal of Ritual Studies* 3: 69–89.

"First Apology of Justin, the Martyr." In *Early Christian Fathers*, 242–289. Trans. by Edward Rochie Hardy. The Library of Christian Classics. Philadelphia: The Westminster Press, 1953.

Fisher, Keith R. 2006. "Foreword." *Michigan State Law Review* 2006 Special: 1085–1101.

Flood, Josephine. 1988. *Archaeology of the Dreamtime*. Honolulu: University of Hawaii Press.

Flynn, Eileen P. 2007. *How Just is the War on Terror?* Mahwah, NJ: Paulist Press.

Foster, Benjamin R. 2003. "The Birth Legend of Sargon of Akkad." In *The Context of Scripture*, Vol. I, 461. Ed. by William W. Hallo. Leiden: Brill.

_____. 2003. "Epic of Creation." In *The Context of Scripture*, Vol. I, 390–402. Ed. by William W. Hallo. Leiden: Brill.

_____. 2003. "Gilgamesh." In *The Context of Scripture*, Vol. I, 458–460. Ed. by William W. Hallo. Leiden: Brill.

Gardiner, Alan. 1950. "The Baptism of Pharaoh." *The Journal of Egyptian Archaeology* 36: 3–12.

Genthe, Hans J. 1996. *Martin Luther, Sein Leben und Denken*. Göttingen: Vandenhoeck & Ruprecht.

Getches, David H. 2001. "The Metamorphosis of Western Water Policy." *Stanford Environmental Law Journal* 20: 4–71.

_____. 2009. *Water Law*, 4th ed. St. Paul, MN: West.

Geyer, John B. 2004. *Mythology and Lament*. Aldershot: Ashgate.

Gibson, McGuire. 1974. "Violation of Fallow and Engineered Disaster in Mesopotamian Civilization." In *Irrigation's Impact on Society*, 7–19. Ed. by Theodore Downing and McGuire Gibson. Tucson: The University of Arizona Press.

Gilday, Edmund T. 1993. "Dancing With Spirit(s)." *History of Religions* 32: 273–300.

Gleick, Peter H. 1996. "Basic Water Requirements for Human Activities." *Water International* 21: 83–92.

_____. 1998. "The Human Right to Water." *Water Policy* 1: 487–503.

_____. 2004. "Water Conflict Chronology." In *The World's Water 2004–2005*, 236–238. Ed. by Peter H. Gleick. Washington, D.C.: Island Press.

_____. 2007. "The Human Right to Water." www.pacinst.org. Accessed August 13, 2010.

_____. 2009. "China and Water." In *The World's Water 2008–2009*, 79–100. Ed. by Peter H. Gleick. Washington, D.C.: Island Press.

_____. 2010. *Bottled and Sold*. Washington, D.C.: Island Press.

_____. 2010, May 7. "Climate Change and the Integrity of Science." *Science* 328: 689–690.

_____. 2010, August 4. "The Human Right to Water (and Sanitation)." www.huffingtonpost.com. Accessed August 10, 2010.

_____. 2010, October 26. "A Long Time Coming: The Human Right to Water." www.huffingtonpost.com. Accessed November 12, 2010.

_____. 2010, December 1. "Not Going Away: America's Energy Security, Jobs and Climate Challenges." Testimony for the Select Committee on Energy Independence & Global Warming Hearing. www.pacinst.org. Accessed December 6, 2010.

Glennon, Robert. 2002. *Water Follies*. Washington, D.C.: Island Press.

_____. 2009. *Unquenchable*. Washington, D.C.: Island Press.

Glennon, Robert and Maddock, Thomas. 1997. "The Concept of Capture." *Proceedings of the Rocky Mountain Mineral Law Annual Institute* 43: 1–89.

Gopalakrishnan, Chennat. 1973. "The Doctrine of Prior Appropriation and Its Impact on Water Development." *The American Journal of Economics and Sociology* 32: 61–72.

Grayston, Kenneth. 1952. "The Darkness of the Cosmic Sea." *Theology* 55: 122–127.

Great Lakes—St. Lawrence River Basin Water Resources Compact. www.cglg.org. Accessed June 2, 2009.

Gunnemann, Jon P. 2005. "Property and Sacred Ordering in Global Civil Society." In *Religion in Global Civil Society*, 91–113. Ed. by Mark Juergensmeyer. New York: Oxford University Press.

Hart, John. 2006. *Sacramental Commons*. Lanham, MD: Rowman & Littlefield.

Hawkes, Jacquetta. 1973. *The First Great Civilizations*. New York: Alfred A. Knopf.

"Helping water flow freely in Asia." 2010, December 16. World Council of Churches. www.wcc-coe.org. Accessed December 17, 2010.

Helsinki Rules on the Uses of the Waters of International Rivers. 1967. Report of the Committee on the Uses of the Waters of International Rivers. London: International Law Association.

Heschel, Abraham J. 1962. *The Prophets*. New York: Harper & Row.

Hippolytus. *Apostolic Tradition. A Text for Students.* Trans. by Geoffrey J. Cuming. Bramcote Notts: Grove Books, 1976.

Hodgson, Marshall G. S. 1974. *The Venture of Islam, Vol. I, The Classical Age of Islam.* Chicago: The University of Chicago Press.

Hori, Ichiro. 1968. *Folk Religion in Japan.* Ed. by Joseph M. Kitagawa and Alan Miller. Chicago: The University of Chicago Press.

Hugh of Saint Victor. *On the Sacraments of the Christian Faith.* Trans. by Roy J. Defferrari. Cambridge, MA: The Medieval Academy of America, 1951.

Hughes, Richard A. 1993. "The Symbolism of the Bridge." *Szondiana* 13: 46–58.

_____. 2009–2010. "Pro-Justice Ethics, Water Scarcity, Human Rights." *Journal of Law and Religion* 25: 521–540.

Husain, Shadid. 2003. "The Indus Delta Goes Thirsty." www.islamonline.net. Accessed June 26, 2009.

Husser, Jean-Marie. 1999. *Dreams and Dream Narratives in the Biblical World.* Trans. by Jill Munro. Sheffield: Sheffield Academic Press.

Hutton, Ronald. 1991. *The Pagan Religions of the Ancient British Isles.* Oxford: Basil Blackwell.

Hymns of the RgVeda. Trans. by Ralph T. H. Griffith. Ed. by J. L. Shastri. Delhi: Motilal Banarsidass, 1973.

Illinois Central Railroad. Company. v. Illinois, 146 U.S. 387 (1892).

Imhof, Aviva and Lanza, Guy R. 2010. "Greenwashing Hydropower." *World Watch* 23: 8–14.

In re: Water Use Permit Applications, 9 P.3d 409 (Hawaii 2000).

Ingram, Helen and Oggins, Cy R. 1992. "The Public Trust Doctrine and Community Values in Water." *Natural Resources Journal* 32: 515–537.

Institutes of Justinian. Trans. by J. B. Moyle. Oxford: Clarendon Press, 1913.

International Covenant on Civil and Political Rights. 1976. www.hrweb.org. Accessed July 8, 2007.

International Covenant on Economic, Social and Cultural Rights. 1976. www.unhchr.ch. Accessed April 1, 2008.

Irenaeus. "Selections from the Work *Against Heresies.*" In *Early Christian Fathers,* 358–397. Trans. by Edward Rochie Hardy. The Library of Christian Classics. Philadelphia: The Westminster Press, 1953.

Jacobsen, Thorkild. 1960. "The Waters of Ur." *Iraq* 22: 174–185.

Jeanes, Gordon. 1995. "A Reformation Treatise on the Sacraments." *Journal of Theological Studies* 46: 149–190.

Johnson, Steven R. 1993. "Baptism in the Pauline and Matthean Communities." A paper presented at the Annual Meeting of the Pacific Coast Region of the Society of Biblical Literature.

Justice, Christopher. 1997. *Dying the Good Death.* Albany: SUNY Press.

Keel, Othmar. 1985. *Symbolism of the Biblical World.* Trans. by Timothy J. Hallett. New York: Crossroad.

Kelly, J. N. D. 1960. *Early Christian Doctrines.* New York: Harper & Row.

Kent, James. 1873. *Commentaries on American Law, Vol. III.* Ed. by O. W. Holmes, Jr. Boston: Little, Brown.

Knauth, Robin J. DeWitt. 2000. "Many Waters." In *Eerdmans Dictionary of the Bible*, 854. Ed. by David Noel Freedman. Grand Rapids: William B. Eerdmans.

_____. 2000. "Rainbow." In *Eerdmans Dictionary of the Bible*, 1107–1108. Ed. by David Noel Freedman. Grand Rapids: William B. Eerdmans.

Knight, G. A. Frank. 1953. "Bridge." *Hastings Encyclopedia of Religion and Ethics*, Vol. II, 848–857.

Knipe, Rita. 1989. *The Water of Life*. Honolulu: University of Hawaii Press.

LaFleur, William R. 1992. *Liquid Life*. Princeton: Princeton University Press.

"A landmark decision to make the right to water and sanitation legally binding." www.ohchr.org. Accessed December 16, 2010.

Lauer, T. E. 1963. "The Common Law Background of the Riparian Doctrine." *Missouri Law Review* 28: 60–107.

Law of Transboundary Aquifers. 2008. www.untreaty.un.org. Accessed February 15, 2010.

Lee, Michelle V. 2006. *Paul, the Stoics, and the Body of Christ*. New York: Cambridge University Press.

Lesko, Leonard H. 1989. "Egyptian Religion." In *Religions of Antiquity*, 34–61. Ed. by Robert M. Seltzer. New York: Macmillan.

Leuenberger, Samuel. 2004. *Archbishop Cranmer's Immortal Bequest*. Eugene, OR: Wipf and Stock.

Levenson, Jon D. 2006. *Resurrection and the Restoration of Israel*. New Haven: Yale University Press.

Levine, Frances. 1990. "Dividing the Water." *Journal of the Southwest* 32: 268–277.

Lichtheim, Miriam. 2003. "The Great Hymn to Osiris." In *The Context of Scripture*, Vol. I, 41–43. Ed. by William W. Hallo. Leiden: Brill.

Carter Lindberg, ed. *The European Reformation Sourcebook*. 2000. Malden, MA: Blackwell.

Littleworth, Arthur L. and Garner, Eric L. 1995. *California Water*. Point Arena, CA: Solano Press.

Long, Thomas G. 2009. *Accompany Them with Singing*. Louisville: Westminster John Knox Press.

Luckert, Karl W. 1977. *Navajo Mountain and Rainbow Bridge*. Flagstaff. AZ: Museum of Northern Arizona.

Luther, Martin. "The Holy and Blessed Sacrament of Baptism." In *Luther's Works*, Vol. 35, 29–41. Trans. by Charles Jacobs. Philadelphia: Fortress Press.

_____. *The Babylonian Captivity of the Church*. In *Luther's Works*, Vol. 36, 3–126. Trans. by A. T. W. Steinhauser. Philadelphia: Fortress Press.

_____. "Sermon at the Baptism of Bernard von Anhalt." In *Luther's Works*, Vol. 51, 315–329. Trans. by John W. Doberstein. Philadelphia: Fortress Press.

_____. "The Order of Baptism Newly Revised." In *Luther's Works*, Vol. 53, 106–109. Trans. by Paul Z. Strodach. Philadelphia: Fortress Press.

Maass, Arthur and Zobel, Hiller B. 1960. "Anglo-American Water Law." *Public Policy* 10: 109–156.

Macpherson, C. B. 1962. *The Political Theory of Possessive Individualism*. Oxford: Clarendon Press.

Magna Carta. www.archives.gov. Accessed March 31, 2010.

Marika, Wandjuk. 1980. "Foreword." In *Australia Dreaming*, 5. Ed. by Jennifer Isaacs. Sydney: Landsdowne Press.

Martino, Renato R. 2003. "Water, An Essential Element for Life." Pontifical Council for Justice and Peace. www.vatican.va. Accessed October 6, 2006.

McC. Adams, Robert. 1974. "Historic Patterns of Mesopotamian Irrigation Agriculture." In *Irrigation's Impact on Society*, 1–5. Ed. by Theodore Downing and McGuire Gibson. Tucson: The University of Arizona Press.

McCaffrey, Stephen C. 1992–1993. "A Human Right to Water." *Georgetown International Environmental Law Review* 5: 1–24.

McKenzie, John L. 1971. *The Roman Catholic Church*. Garden City, NY: Image Books.

Meeks, Wayne A. 1983. *The First Urban Christians*. New Haven: Yale University Press.

Meyer, Michael C. 1989. "The Living Legacy of Hispanic Groundwater Law in the Contemporary Southwest." *Journal of the Southwest* 31: 287–299.

_____. 1996. *Water in the Hispanic Southwest*. Tucson: The University of Arizona Press.

Meyers, Carol L. and Meyers, Eric A. 1993. *Zechariah 9–14*. The Anchor Bible. New York: Doubleday.

Milgrom, Jacob. 1991. *Leviticus 1–16*. The Anchor Bible. New York: Doubleday.

Miller, Daniel. 1985. "Ideology and the Harappan Civilization." *Journal of Anthropological Archaeology* 4: 34–71.

Miller, G. Tyler, Jr. 1996. *Living in the Environment*, 9th ed. Belmont, CA: Wadsworth.

Mintz, Eric D. and Guerrant, Richard L. 2009. "A Lion in Our Village—The Unconscionable Tragedy of Cholera in Africa." *The New England Journal of Medicine* 360: 1060–1063.

Mishak, Michael J. 2007, October 4. "Sharing water is Key to Richardson's Plan." *Las Vegas Sun*. www.lasvegassun.com. Accessed June 20, 2010.

Mitchell, Nathan. 1995. "Baptism in the *Didache*." In *The Didache in Context*, 226–255. Ed. by Clayton N. Jefford. Leiden: Brill.

Molé, M. 1960. "Daena, le pont Cinvat et l'initiation dans le Mazdéisme." *Revue de l'histoire des religions* 157: 155–185.

Muffs, Yochanan. 1992. *Love & Joy*. New York: The Jewish Theological Seminary of America.

Nakamura, Hajime. 1977. *Gotama Buddha*. Los Angeles: Buddhist Books International.

National Audubon Society v. The Superior Court of Alpine County, 33 Cal. 3d 419 Supreme Court of California.

National Conference of Catholic Bishops. 2000. *Economic Justice for All*. Washington, D.C.: US Catholic Conference.

Needham, Joseph. 1969. *Science and Civilization in China*, Vol. 2. Cambridge: Cambridge University Press.

Nigosian, S. A. 2008. *World Religions*, 4th ed. Boston: Bedford/St Martins.

"No water for the neighbors." 2009, December 3. World Council of Churches. www.oikoumene.org. Accessed December 30, 2009.

Null, Ashley. 2006. *Thomas Cranmer's Doctrine of Repentance*. New York: Oxford University Press.

Olson, James M. 2006. "Navigating the Great Lakes Compact." *Michigan State Law Review* 2006 Special: 1103–1140.

Outcome of the International Experts' Meeting on the Right to Water. 2009, July 7–8. UNESCO www.unesco.org. Accessed January 15, 2010.

Outler, Albert C., ed. 1964. *John Wesley*. New York: Oxford University Press.

Ovid. *Fasti.* Trans. by James G. Frazer. The Loeb Classical Library. Cambridge: Harvard University Press, 1951.

Pacific Institute Topics: Bottled Water and Energy. 2007. www.pacinst.org. Accessed February 4, 2010.

Palaniappan, Meena, Lee, Emily, and Samulon, Andrea. 2006. "Environmental Justice and Water." In *The World's Water 2006–2007*, 133–134. Ed. by Peter H. Gleick. Washington, D.C.: Island Press.

Palaniappan, Meena and Gleick, Peter H. 2009. "Peak Water." In *The World's Water 2008–2009*, 1–6. Ed. by Peter H. Gleick. Washington, D.C.: Island Press.

Palaniappan, Meena, et al. 2010. *Clearing the Waters*. Ed. by Nancy Ross. United Nations Environment Programme and the Pacific Institute. www.pacinst.org. Accessed November 22, 2010.

Patch, Howard R. 1980. *The Other World*. New York: Octagon Books.

Peacocke, A. R. 1979. *Creation and the World of Science*. Oxford: Clarendon Press.

Pelcyger, Robert S. 1977. "The Winters Doctrine and the Greening of the Reservations." *Journal of Contemporary Law* 4: 19–37.

Perry, Michael J. 2005. "The Morality of Human Rights." *Emory Law Journal* 54: 97–150.

Plutarch. *Moralia.* Trans. by Frank Cole Babbit. The Loeb Classical Library. Cambridge: Harvard University Press, 1962.

Postel, Sandra L. 1997. *Last Oasis*. New York: W. W. Norton.

_____. 2007. "China's Unquenchable Thirst." *World Watch* 20: 20–21.

Postel, Sandra L. and Richter, Brian. 2003. *Rivers for Life*. Washington, D.C.: Island Press.

Postel, Sandra L. and Wolf, Aaron T. 2001. "Dehydrating Conflict." *Foreign Policy* September-October: 60–67.

PUD No. 1 of Jefferson County v. Washington Department of Ecology, 114 U.S. 1900 (1994).

Pukui, Mary K. 1972. *Nana Ke Kumu (Look to the Source)*. Honolulu: Queen Liliuokalani Children's Center.

Rahula, Walpola. 1974. *What the Buddha Taught*. New York: Grove Press.

Raikes, R. L. 1965. "The Mohenjo-daro Floods." *Antiquity* 39: 196–203.

Ranquist, Harold A. 1975. "The *Winters* Doctrine and How It Grew." *Brigham Young University Law Review* 1975: 639–724.

Ransel, Katherine. P. 1995. "The Sleeping Giant Awakens. *PUD No. 1 of Jefferson County v. Washington Department of Ecology*." *Environmental Law* 25: 255–283.

Research Foundation For Science, Technology & Ecology. 2005. *Financing Water Crises*. www.navdanya.org. Accessed May 31, 2009.

Riley, Hugh M. 1974. *Christian Initiation*. Washington, D.C.: The Catholic University of America Press.

Rodríguez, Sylvia. 2006. *Acequia*. Santa Fe, NM: School for Advanced Research Press.

Rogers, Elizabeth F. 1976. *Peter Lombard and the Sacramental System*. Merrick, NY: Richwood.

Rolston, Holmes III. 1999. *Genes, Genesis and God*. Cambridge: Cambridge University Press.

Saleh, Walid A. 2010. "The Arabian Context of Muhammad's Life." In *The Cambridge Companion to Muhammad*, 21–38. Ed. by Jonathan E. Brockopp. New York: Cambridge University Press.

Salman, Salman A. 2007. "The Helsinki Rules, the UN Watercourses Convention and the Berlin Rules: Perspectives on International Water Law." *Water Resources Development* 23: 625–640.

Saso, Michael. 1990. *Blue Dragon, White Tiger*. Washington, D.C.: The Taoist Center.

Sax, Joseph L. 1970. "The Public Trust Doctrine in Natural Resource Law." *Michigan Law Review* 68: 471–566.

Scanlan, Melissa K. 2006. "Protecting the Public Trust and Human Rights: The Great Lakes." *Michigan State Law Review* 2006 Special: 1333–1346.

Scarborough, Vernon L. 2003. *The Flow of Power*. Santa Fe, NM: A School of American Research Resident Scholar Book.

Schilling, Robert. 1989. "Roman Religion to 100 BCE." In *Religions of Antiquity*, 193–217. Ed. by Robert M. Seltzer. New York: Macmillan.

Scott, Anthony. 2008. *The Evolution of Resource Property Rights*. Oxford: Oxford University Press.

Seward, Jack. 1968. *Hara-Kiri*. Rutland, VT: Charles E. Tuttle.

Shiva, Vandana. 2002. *Water Wars*. Cambridge, MA: South End Press.

_____. 2005. *Earth Democracy*. Cambridge, MA: South End Press.

Silk, Nicole, McDonald, Jack, and Wigington, Robert. 2000. "Turning Instream Flow Water Rights Upside Down." *Rivers* 7: 298–313.

Shuman, Emily K. 2010. "Global Climate Change and Infectious Diseases." *The New England Journal of Medicine* 362: 1061–1063.

Simmons, Marc. 1972. "Spanish Irrigation Practices in New Mexico." *New Mexico Historical Review* 47: 135–150.

Smith, Jane, and Haddad, Yvonne. 1981. *The Islamic Understanding of Death and Resurrection*. Albany: SUNY Press.

Spae, Joseph. 1972. *Shinto Man*. Tokyo: Oriens Institute for Religious Research.

Spinks, Bryan D. 2006. *Early and Medieval Rituals and Theologies of Baptism*. Burlington, VT: Ashgate.

_____. 2006a. *Reformation and Modern Rituals and Theologies of Baptism*. Burlington, VT: Ashgate.

Staten, Annie and Roach, Susan. 1999. "'Take Me to the Water': African American River Baptism." Louisiana Division of the Arts. www.louisianafolklife.org. Accessed August 30, 2010.

Stephan, Raya Marina. 2007. "L' heritage commune: le Mejellé, le droit musulman codifié." Unpublished manuscript.

_____. 2011, March 4. Email to the author.

Stewart, Benjamin M. 2011, February 8. "Water in Worship." *The Christian Century* 128: 22–25.

Sykes, Stephen W. 1990. "Baptisme doth represente unto us oure profession." In *Cranmer*, 122–143. Ed. by Margot Johnson. Durham: Turnstone Ventures.

"Taking water to the Jordan." World Council of Churches. www.oikoumene.org. Accessed July 22, 2010.

Tappert, Theodore G. *The Book of Concord*. Philadelphia: Fortress Press, 1959.

"The Teaching of the Twelve Apostles, Commonly Called the Didache." In *Early Christian Fathers*, 171–179. Ed. by Cyril C. Richardson. The Library of Christian Classics. Philadelphia: The Westminster Press, 1953.

Teclaff, Ludwik A. 1996. "Evolution of the River Basin Concept in National and International Water Law." *Natural Resources Journal* 36: 359–391.

Temple, William. 1953. *Nature, Man and God*. London: Macmillan.

Tertullian. "On Baptism." In *The Ante-Nicene Fathers*, Vol. 3, 669–679. Trans. by S. Thelwell. New York: Charles Scribner's Sons. 1903.

Thompson, David. 2010, October 17. "Addicted to Water." *Williamsport Sun-Gazette*: A1, A6.

_____. 2010, October 18. "Limiting Fracking Contamination." *Williamsport Sun-Gazette*: A1, A6.

Transboundary Freshwater Dispute Database. Oregon State University. www.transboundarywaters.orst.edu. Accessed October 12, 2007.

Tromp, Nicholas J. 1969. *Primitive Conceptions of Death and the Nether World in the Old Testament*. Rome: Pontifical Biblical Institute.

Tucker, Karen B. Westerfield. 2006. "John Wesley and the Methodists." In the *Oxford Guide to the Book of Common Prayer*, 209–213. Ed. by Charles Hefling and Cynthia Shattuck. New York: Oxford University Press.

Tuggle, David H. 1979. "Hawaii," In *The Prehistory of Polynesia*, 167–199. Ed. by Jessie D. Jennings. Cambridge: Harvard University Press.

Tyler, Daniel. 1991. "Underground Water in Hispanic New Mexico." *New Mexico Historical Review* 66: 287–301.

_____. 1995. "The Spanish Colonial Legacy and the Role of Hispanic Custom in Defining New Mexico Land and Water Rights." *Colonial Latin American Historical Review* 4: 149–165.

United Nations Declaration on the Rights of Indigenous Peoples. 2008. www.un.org. Accessed May 9, 2010.

"UN Human Rights Council Acknowledges Formal Human Right to Water." www.pacinst.org. Accessed November 12, 2010.

"UN united to make the right to water and sanitation legally binding." www.ohchr.org. Accessed November 19, 2010.

United States v. District Court for Eagle County, 401 U.S. 520 (1971).

Universal Declaration of Human Rights. 1948. www.un.org. Accessed July 8, 2007.

UNESCO Water Portal Newsletter No. 159. 2006, October 13.

_____. No. 180. 2007, March 16.

_____. No. 183. 2007, April 6.

_____. No. 184. 2007, April 13.

_____. No. 185. 2007, April 20.

_____. No. 188. 2007, June 18.

_____. No. 189. 2007, July 2.

_____. No. 205. 2008, July 10.

_____. No. 206. 2008, September 9.

_____. No. 212. 2009, January 28.

_____. No. 215. 2009, May 5.

_____. No. 241. 2010, November 17.

_____. No. 244. 2011, January 28.

_____. No. 249. 2011, April 29.

Urofsky, Melvin I. and Finkelman, Paul. 2008. *Documents of American Constitutional and Legal History*. New York: Oxford University Press.

Varody, Robert, et al. 2008. "Strengthening Global Water Initiatives." *Environment* 50: 19–31.

Vock, Daniel C. 2008, July 30. "Great Lakes states protect their water." www.stateline.org. Accessed June 2, 2009.

Waley, Arthur. 1958. *The Way and its Power*. New York: Grove Press.

Webb, Walter Prescott. 1931. *The Great Plains*. Boston: Ginn.

Wesley, John. "The New Birth." In *The Works of John Wesley*, Vol. 2. *Sermons*, 187–201. Ed. by Albert C. Outler. Nashville: Abingdon Press, 1985.

Westermann, Claus. 1994. *Genesis 1–11*. Trans. by John Scullion. Minneapolis: Fortress Press.

White, James F. 1992. *Documents of Christian Worship*. Louisville: Westminster John Knox Press.

_____. 2000. *Introduction to Christian Worship*. Nashville: Abingdon Press.

White, Lynn, Jr. 1967. "The Historical Roots of Our Ecological Crisis." *Science* 155: 1203–1207.

Wilbanks, Pete F. 2000. "Marah." In *Eerdmans Dictionary of the Bible*, 855. Ed. by David Noel Freedman. Grand Rapids: William B. Eerdmans.

Wilkinson, Charles F. 1988–1989. "The Headwaters of the Public Trust." *Environmental Law* 19: 425–472.

Wilson, J. V. Kinnier. "The Epic of Creation." In *Documents from Old Testament Times*, 3–16. Ed. by D. Winton Thomas. New York: Harper & Brothers.

Winters v. United States, 207 U.S. 564 (1908).

World Health Organization. 2010. "How much water is needed in emergencies." www.wedc.lboro.ac.uk. Accessed July 23, 2010.

Worldwatch Report. 2007. "Oceans in Peril." www.worldwatch.org. Accessed September 21, 2007.

Worldwatch Institute. 2010. "Glacial Melt and Ocean Warming Drive Sea Level Upward." www.worldwatch.org. Accessed July 23, 2010.

Worster, Donald. 1985. *Rivers of Empire*. New York: Pantheon Books.

Yabur, Pedro de Jesús Pallares. 2006. "The Human Right to Water and the Great Lakes Basin." *Michigan State Law Review* 2006 Special: 1323–1331.

Yang, C. K. 1961. *Religion in Chinese Society*. Berkeley: University of California Press.

Zaleski, Carol and Zaleski, Philip. 2000. *The Book of Heaven*. New York: Oxford University Press.

Zaragoza Charter. 2008. www.expozaragoza2008.es. Accessed October 13, 2008.